MEN'S WORK

MORE PRAISE FOR *MEN'S WORK*

"Paul Kivel's brave and thoughtful book goes back—way back—deep into the structure of men's lives to explore the centrality of violence in men's lives. Drawing on his personal experiences, careful analysis, and years of therapeutic experience, Kivel offers insights and a step-by-step guide to challenge and begin to overcome violence. In doing so, he offers men hope."

MICHAEL S. KIMMEL, professor of sociology, SUNY/Stony Brook

"Violence against women can only end if men who rape, batter, and kill women change their attitudes and behaviors—and challenge patriarchal assumptions. This book will help men confront the political, social, and personal forces that generate hatred and anger at women."

LESLIE WOLFE, executive director, Center for Women Policy Studies

Letters to author Paul Kivel from men in prison on the effectiveness of the Men's Work *program in helping stop the violence*

"No one took time to help me learn to interact with people and to show me how our society sets men up to be violent. They taught me reading, writing, and arithmetic, but not how to interact with people without being violent. . . . I look forward to helping myself and other men break the violent patterns in our lives. We are starting to develop bonds with each other as we start trusting and accepting each other for who we are."

INMATE, correctional institution, Bowling Green, Florida

"The part that I found to be most helpful was the 'Act Like a Man' box. Also, the in-depth questions . . . really made me think about myself and my past, helped me to see who I am and why I behave the way I do."

INMATE, correctional institution, Bowling Green, Florida

"I have been involved in a project at the prison. When first introduced to it, I protested because none of my crimes had any violence in them. . . . I found your book so helpful, so powerful and empowering. . . . The exercises brought me to a whole new level of understanding and allowed me to face myself and my world of violence in a way that it has never been explored."

INMATE, federal prison, Alberta, Canada

"I am a recovering alcoholic and drug addict. . . . Nothing in recovery has touched me like *Men's Work*. I've been able to release feelings of inadequacy, my need to control, sexual inhibitions that interfered with far more of my life than I ever thought, and anger and resentments that enabled me to carry on the violence and hurt many lives."

INMATE, correctional institution, Bowling Green, Florida

"I would recommend *Men's Work* to anyone [who needs to deal] with anger."

INMATE, correctional institution, Bowling Green, Florida

MEN'S WORK

**How to Stop
the Violence
That Tears
Our Lives
Apart**

PAUL KIVEL

HAZELDEN

Hazelden
Center City, Minnesota 55012-0176

1-800-328-0094 (Toll Free U.S., Canada, and the Virgin Islands)
1-651-257-1331 (Fax)
www.hazelden.org

ISBN: 978-56838-233-3

Library of Congress Catalog Card Number 93-132962

14 15 16   11 10

Book design by Will H. Powers
Typesetting by Stanton Publication Services, Inc.
Cover Design by David Spohn

Editor's Note:
The following publishers have generously given permission to use extended quotations from copyrighted works: From the *Oakland Men's
Project* © 1987, 1990, 1991, all rights reserved. From *Everyday Racism*,
by Philomena Essed. Copyright 1990. Published by Hunter House, Inc.,
2200 Central Avenue, Suite 202, Alameda, CA 94501. From *Getting
Free: You Can End Abuse and Take Back Your Life,* copyright © 1982 by
Ginny NiCarthy, Seal Press. 3131 Western Avenue #410, Seattle, WA
98121. Reprinted with permission. From *The Second Sex*, by Simone
de Beauvoir, Bantam edition, 1961. Reprinted with permission of Alfred
A. Knopf, Inc. From *A Woman's Place,* by Marita Golden. Reprinted
with permission of Dell Publishing Group. From *nappy endings*, by
ntozake shange, copyright © 1972, 1974, 1975, 1976, 1977, 1978 by
ntozake shange. Reprinted with permission of St. Martin's Press, Inc.,
New York, N.Y. From an Alice Walker interview in *Women of Power,* issue 12, winter 1989, page 29. Reprinted with permission of Alice Walker.

To Micki, the love of my life.

To my children, Ariel, Shandra, and Ryan.
May their generation share
a more peaceful world.

Contents

PART IV
Men's Work: To Stop Male Violence

PART V
The Next Generation

List of Exercises

Preface

I felt that I could only really take this position and express and share the way I feel about [the horse] as a fellow being if I didn't eat meat already. I kept asking myself how can I dare to presume to say this if I am not already at the point where I want to take people. I finally answered by saying to myself that I have the responsibility to share the vision even if I am not already in the vision, even if I haven't already gotten where I want us all to be. There's value in sharing the process.

. . . You want to encourage people by appearing as if you have it all together, but I frankly feel it's better to share that you don't because that's the truth and that's the reality of people. Nobody has it all together.

ALICE WALKER *

This is a book about men breaking a cycle of violence that endangers all of us. It was not an easy book to write because breaking that cycle is a painful process.

When confronted with the impact of male violence on women's lives I originally wanted to say, "It wasn't me," "I respect women," "I wouldn't hurt anyone." When confronted with the effects of racism on people of color I wanted to say, "My family didn't own slaves," "I have it hard too," "I don't see color." Yet as I learned more about male violence it became all too clear that I participated in perpetuating the system of violence that engulfs and imprisons us. Sometimes it was through my actions; other times it was through my denial or complacency.

---

* "In the Midst of All Being," an interview with Alice Walker, by Ellen Bring, in *Women of Power*, issue 12, winter 1989.

I could no longer claim innocence or feign ignorance. Instead, I wanted to believe that I had quickly moved beyond those kinds of behaviors and was now "correct." During the first years of doing this work I wanted to believe I had stepped over some invisible line and was no longer abusive or controlling. Other men might be sexist, but I was liberated. Other white people might be racist, but I was now color-blind.

After several years of doing community prevention and education work, it was hard to admit that I had more to learn. The persistence of my old patterns of behavior discouraged me. I was disappointed to realize that there is not some magic point beyond which we are free of violence, controlling behavior, and abusive attitudes and actions.

> They [white people] are often *more concerned about maintaining a positive or non-racial self-image than about the injustice of racism itself** [emphasis in original]

If my struggle had simply been about my self-image, or about the costs to me personally of my attitudes and actions, I would not have written this book. I could have learned to control my anger, and say the right things to women and others around me, and felt satisfied with what I had achieved. Eventually, I could have pretended I had never really been like other men and anyway, now I was different. But that would have left me with yet another image, just as false and isolating as the others. I did not want to be a "good" warrior or hero. I wanted to challenge the existence of those male roles altogether.

I decided to write this book to expose on a deeper level the terribly destructive training men have received. We've been trained to be soldiers—in our families, in our neighborhoods, on the job, and overseas. I also wanted to share a vision of how we can begin to live without violence.

---

* Philomena Essed, *Everyday Racism: Reports from Women of Two Cultures* (Alameda, Calif.: Hunter House, 1990).

But could I write about alternatives to homework wars when I was still engaged in one with my son? Could I write about treating women with respect when I still evaluated women's bodies? Could I write about fighting against racism when I still treated black men with more suspicion than white men?

I realized I could only write honestly about our lives as men and about male violence if I could acknowledge where I was and where I had come from. It was not easy to admit that I wasn't nonsexist, nonracist, enlightened, caring, peaceful, and a perfect parent. I had a lifelong image of myself, carefully maintained, that I was afraid of destroying. I really thought that was why people liked me, or at least respected me. But the evidence was all too clear: I am not perfect and this book is not about my self-image. This is about our struggle for justice, respect, interdependence, and alternatives to violence.

There are many women and men throughout our society engaged in the struggle to end male violence. I wrote this book to invite you to join us. Together we can share the joy of our common endeavor to bring more human dignity, mutual cooperation, and peace into the world.

Acknowledgments

This book grows out of the struggles, creativity, and resistance of multitudes of people around the country who have been on the front lines of the struggle to end violence of all kinds. Many of the ideas in this book have been influenced by the work of people who regularly challenge traditional ways of thinking about the causes of violence—and seek new remedies for its cure. The authors listed in the bibliography reflect some of these sources and some of the movements these authors participated in.

This book grows directly out of the work of women during the last twenty years to recover from and resist male violence. These women built a rape prevention movement, domestic violence movement, child assault prevention movement, and the movement to end violence in pornography and the media. These movements have influenced and inspired my writing. Of particular importance and clarity has been work and writing by lesbian and bisexual women, women of color, Jewish women, and working class women. I owe a tremendous debt of gratitude to these women for their courage, insight, and ability to truly make the personal political.

I want to acknowledge and thank the friends, co-workers, and family who directly contributed to making this book possible. Over the last twenty years I have been privileged to work with a group of men who have embodied strength, clarity, and compassion, and who have developed the models upon which this book is based: Robert Allan, Chris Anderegg, Martin Cano, Allan Creighton, Michael Foster, David Landes, Victor Lewis, Heru-Nefera, Kiran Rana, Harrison Simms, and Hugh Vasquez. I want to particularly thank Allan Creighton, whose friendship, personal support, and editing skills helped make this book a reality.

Others I want to thank for their contributions to the Oakland Men's Project or for their support and challenge to me personally are Margo Adair, Bob Boardman, Jim Coates, Charlotte Cook, Hari Dillon, Steve Falk, Barbara Fisher, Laura Head, Beth Kivel, David Lee, David Lee, Susie Lee, M. Nell Myhand, Daphne Muse, David Rompf, and Bill Rosenthal.

My editor at Hazelden, Bill Chickering, has been as good as they come, from his initial excitement and confidence in the book, through the final stages of production. The rest of the staff at Hazelden has been equally supportive. I also want to thank Steve Lehman who has guided the revision process into this fine new edition.

I want to thank my parents Betty Jean Kivel (1923–1997) and A. Victor Kivel (1919–1982) for their love and encouragement. My mother, especially, supported the Oakland Men's Project from its very earliest days.

Finally, and most importantly, I want to thank my family: My children Ariel, Shandra, and Ryan for the inspiration, challenge and hope their lives provide me. My partner, Micki, for her love, her faith in my writing, her practical support, and the joys we have shared over the years.

Introduction to the Updated Edition

Since the first publication of *Men's Work* we have witnessed the William Kennedy Smith trial, the Clarence Thomas hearing, the Mike Tyson trial, the Bob Packwood affair, and the O.J. Simpson trial. We have had recent allegations of incest by the daughter of ex-President of Nicaragua, Daniel Ortega, and documentation of the sexual assaults and harassment of young women by Shlomo Carlebach, a leading modern Jewish theologian. There have been many stories of the sexual assault by clergy on young men within the Catholic Church, and by new age spiritual gurus and fundamentalist preachers. We are still regularly provided with stories of college and professional sports figures who have beaten their wives or sexually assaulted women. Against these dramatic stories there is a daily background of local accounts of men who have raped, beaten, molested or killed women they know. We are even getting reports of twelve- and thirteen-year-olds beating or killing their ex-girlfriends, such as happened so tragically in Jonesboro, Arkansas earlier this year.

Despite this constant barrage of evidence about the devastating and often deadly effects of male violence, most of us still greet each new instance as a surprise, perhaps saying to ourselves, "I can't believe that so-and-so could have done it." We continue to look at each individual case as a unique circumstance. Many of us still question the woman's motives and are prone to excuse the man because somehow we think he might be the target of other people's anger or jealousy and it would be an injustice to single him out for punishment when others get away with the same thing.

It remains hard for us to grasp the bigger picture, hard for us to accept the reality of male violence. We want to say, "I know that male violence happens, maybe even happens a lot, but not him, not here, not among my community, not in my family, not by my neighbor, or coworker, or colleague, or relative, or friend. Recently I had a sobering experience of that reaction in myself.

After I had written *Men's Work*, after I had worked with incest offenders and batterers and had even said that I am never surprised to learn that any man is a batterer or child molester, my sister revealed to my mother and me that my father had molested her many times when she was between eight and ten years old.

I had conflicting feelings. I believed her. And, at the same time, I wanted to believe that there was some mistake, or that the abuse wasn't as serious as she described it, or that there were, somehow in a way I couldn't even imagine, attenuating circumstances. I hoped there was some way that I could deny the abuse because it contradicted everything I had believed about our family life and my childhood. Of course incest was common. Of course ordinary men did it. Of course you never knew. But my own father?

I quickly realized that I couldn't deny it, that it was perfectly and unfortunately believable, and in fact, was quite consistent with everything I knew about my father, and what I knew about my sister and her life struggles. When my sister told some of our relatives they had the same responses but even more strongly than I had. My father had been successful, educated, Jewish, likable, and a contributor to the community. How could he possibly have molested his daughter?

As I supported my sister and dealt with my own anger, pain, and sadness over my father's abuse I realized again how fundamental male violence is as a force which keeps systems of exploitation and violence in place. As I confronted the denial within myself and among my relatives I realized again how thick are the layers of denial which keep us from confronting and stopping the violence.

I wrote *Men's Work* to address the pervasive effects of male training on our lives as men and the terrible impact that training has on the women, children, and other men around us. I hope the book contributes to making us less surprised when we hear stories of male violence. We will still have to investigate each individual situation and try to determine what happened and what we should do about it. But if we are less surprised we will notice the abuse more often; we will listen to the survivors more seriously; and we will collude less with the men who perpetrate attacks on those around them. We will begin to end the silence which keeps the violence unchallenged.

My larger goal in writing this book was to aid in developing policies, intervention strategies, and community education and prevention programs which provide safety and equality for women, and different models of what it means to be a man.

I have received many letters and comments from men saying that they have been able to use this book and the exercises in it to create better lives for themselves and for those around them. I hope it will continue to be a tool for change. But a tool is only useful for those who pick it up to build something. I invite you to pick up this tool and use it to build a better, safer, and more just community.

Oakland, California
April 1998

Original Introduction

Why are men violent and what can we do about it? As we face the daily and deadly effects of men's violence, the need to find an answer to this question becomes increasingly urgent. The question leads us to others, equally urgent. What kinds of violence are we talking about? Which men? Can we do anything about men's violence?

This book is about men's lives and how the fabric of our lives is interwoven with violence. The very threads of our lives seem dyed the color "violence"; its pervasive influence could not be more pronounced, or harder to unravel. Some parts of the coloring are clearly visible, as in "He beat up his wife," or "He raped her," or "They fought it out in the bar."

Other parts are less pronounced, as in "He's been drinking like that for years," or "My father never talked with anyone, even my mother," or "He refused to see a doctor for the longest time. By the time he did it was too late."

Some shades of the violence are so subtle that we barely know they exist. These shades come out in the way we walk, the way we talk to our children, and the way we relate to our bodies, to women, to other men, to our souls, and to the earth itself.

I have tried to capture the whole pattern of the fabric itself. When we look at the whole fabric, we see how to create new weavings free of physical and sexual assault, free of the intimations of violence—the anger, stress, pain, and frustration that shorten our lives, destroy intimacy, alienate us from our bodies, deaden our feelings, our responsiveness, and our ability to act creatively.

In order to radically rethink the role of violence in our lives, I felt I had to start with my own life as a man. From there, I took a reflective look at the lives of men I've talked with over the last twenty years. I have examined our sexuality and our spirituality. I have noticed our relations with women and our relations with other men. I have reflected on our roles as sons, growing up with fathers, being fathers and raising sons. I have looked at the ways racial, economic, ethnic, religious, and other differences have influenced us. I have had to describe how even these differences are situated in a larger social context of the power relationships we live and work within each day.

When I began this work in 1979, there was a rape crisis movement, an antipornography movement, and a battered women's movement. The male activists supporting these movements fluctuated between believing that each kind of violence was a separate pathological category involving distinct kinds of men (rapists, batterers, incest offenders), and believing that all men contributed to the problem. For example, on the issue of rape we said that although not all men were rapists, all men were complicit with rape culture because we did not challenge the sexual harassment, the jokes, or the pornography that devalued women and set them up to be victims of rape.

In theory we were supportive. In our lives, however, we were ambivalent. Sometimes we said we were completely different from the sleazy strangers in overcoats who lurked in the dark alleys. *This is the type of man who rapes,* we thought. At other times we blurred all distinctions and lumped men together as bad and oppressive. In either case, we distanced ourselves from men so we could feel less guilty about ourselves and more self-righteous and angry about them.

In 1979 I thought I knew all about men and violence. But as I worked with incest offenders and batterers, as well as hundreds of men in workshops, it became harder for me to tell the men apart. The batterers and sexual offenders were not very different from the "ordinary" men we encountered in public workshops. Not only that, the ordinary men in our workshops turned out to be much more violent than I would have ever assumed. In other words, the offenders were extraordinarily ordinary by any standard I could devise, and the ordinary men were extraordinarily violent.

As I worked with them, I grew to like almost all of these men. I also found it harder to separate myself from them. We seemed to have the same training, the same pressures, the same hopes, expectations, and disappointments. I remained horrified by what some of these men did to other people; I could not deny the destructiveness of their actions. But neither could I deny the humanness of the men and my connections to them.

The complexities of our personal histories, male socialization, cultural backgrounds, and present relationship to violence ended the possibility of finding any simple answer to why men are violent. But I did begin to see ways of understanding male violence that promised to help create a safer world.

The forum I worked in was a men's collective, the Oakland Men's Project. Our slogan was "Men's Work: To Stop Male Violence." That work has never been easy. The Project began with a commitment to challenge violence against women, but we were constantly forced to adapt our workshops to the needs of different populations, age groups, or organizations. We continually had to confront our own prejudices, our own histories, and our relationship to each other.

As we understood more deeply what male violence is about, we moved toward a bigger challenge. We not only aspired toward lives free from violence, we also wanted to create lives that were healthy, intimate with others, and models for our children. We aspired to help build stronger communities and to nurture the natural environment.

This book is larger than my life. It reflects the work, the thinking, the experience, the sharing, and the *vision* of the wonderful men I have worked with at the Oakland Men's Project since 1979. It also reflects the larger struggle of many men throughout the country to redefine our roles and lives, reject violence, and create new possibilities for ourselves and our children. It reflects, finally, the attempt of all of us who have been violent to weave a new cloth of maleness. This cloth is strong, bright, and many-colored. It is woven from different colors and patterns, but the colors are not blurred. It complements the patterns that the women, children, and other men in our lives are working to weave.

This book addresses many aspects of violence. It certainly addresses men who are doing the work of trying to be less angry and violent. More broadly, this book is based on the assumption that we all have a role to play in stopping men's violence. Women are not responsible for male violence, but there are many things that women, as teachers, co-workers, managers, government officials, friends, lovers, and mothers, can do that make a difference.

This book looks at different ways to challenge male violence. I have assumed that because violence is so built into our lives, we are constantly faced with the opportunity to confront it, subvert it, heal from it, and take whatever steps possible to stop it.

Our challenge is to reweave our lives as men. Many women have decided already that the violence has to stop, and they are weaving strong, new fabrics with beautiful patterns that will not be weakened by violence. It is up to us, as men, to reweave the fabric of our lives into something strong, vibrant, and nurturing, unflawed by the presence of violence. I offer this book as one thread in that process.

PART I

Growing Up Male

Men don't suddenly appear in life armed and dangerous. It takes years and years of training to turn boys into violent men. Starting with my personal experiences of raising a son and being a son, this part looks at the ways boys are trained to be men. That training includes how we are taught to relate to other men, what we are taught about women, and how we are taught to relate to our own cultural and ethnic traditions.

ONE

Men Relating to Men

Homework Wars

It's Sunday night and my son, Ariel, is supposed to be finishing his week's homework assignment, due tomorrow. He sits down at the table, looks at the last page and says, "I can't do this."

"Why not?" I ask in disbelief.

"I don't have an encyclopedia."

"But we went through this last week. You are supposed to check your homework ahead of time to see if you need an encyclopedia. I've told you before that's not an acceptable excuse." I can feel my anger rise.

"I looked at it. It's a crossword puzzle on domestic cats. I didn't think I needed an encyclopedia."

I know I'm stuck. There is no way he can do the assignment. Once again he has managed to postpone some of his work so that when the final hour comes he can't finish it.

"Can I watch television now?" he asks in all innocence.

"No, you can't. I told you that you couldn't watch television until your homework was done; I said that forgetting to bring home the right books isn't an excuse."

"But Dad . . ."

"That's it. You can just sit right there and figure out a way to do your assignment."

I leave and he starts to cry. We both feel terrible. We are again on opposing sides in the weekly homework wars.

I thought I was doing all the right things. I care about Ariel and want him to do well. As his father, my role is to provide the firm

3

but caring discipline he "needs" to confront the harsh realities of life. But somehow it doesn't work. I feel stuck in a role that separates me from him.

As test scores have plummeted throughout our school systems, one response has been to give children piles of homework to improve their grades. Ariel's school sends home a packet soliciting parent support for homework. It is our loving obligation to their educational future.

So there I am, signed up for nine months' duty as homework cop. I hate the job. I would just as soon say to my son's teacher, "This is ridiculous. You have him for six straight hours, five days a week. If you can't teach him in that time, turn in your license." And I would just as soon say to my son, "Homework is between you and the teacher. I don't want any part of it. Just forget it. Go out and play if you want." Our time in the evenings is too short and precious to be always fighting over pages of math or spelling lists.

Yet I often try to convince myself that the homework battles are worth the effort. The internal dialogue goes something like this:

- Homework is part of going to school; he just has to do it.
- I did my homework, even though I didn't like it, and it didn't kill me.
- He's going to have to learn discipline sometime; it might as well be now.
- If I let him off the hook, I'm neglecting my responsibility to him.
- There's probably some value in the homework even if it seems repetitive and boring to both of us.

None of these lines convince me. Then, one weekend, we fought the final round. Once again he hadn't finished on Sunday. He brought the work back home on Monday. The teacher had given the class one more day. This was my first inkling that there were other homework wars occurring in our peaceful neighborhood. Monday night Ariel waited until he was too tired and the words were too hard; besides, the dictionary he had didn't have all the words. Once again he couldn't finish.

"All right," I said in disgust, "Just go to bed. It's between you and the teacher."

He went to bed angry and in tears, hoping to wake up early to do some of his homework in the morning. He woke up late and refused to get dressed or come down for breakfast.

"I'm not going to school," he announced.

"You don't have a choice," I responded.

After a few minutes of yelling at each other he stormed off to his room, got back into bed, and picked up a book to read. We do let him stay home occasionally if he needs to rest or recuperate, but staying home because he hadn't finished his homework? That could end his school career right there. *Bad precedent,* I said to myself.

We fought for another forty-five minutes before he finally got dressed. I then ordered him out the door, threatening all kinds of cruel fates, and watched him tearfully walk off to meet the wrath of his teacher. So much for my stepping out of the process.

I know my son's teacher is overworked, underpaid, and has thirty-three eight- to twelve-year-old children, all nominally labeled fourth and fifth graders. I know my son wants to do well and wants to have fun. He loves to read and learn, but doesn't structure his own time well. He wants my participation and support.

I also know that I am a working parent of three children. I don't have the infinite patience, all-encompassing understanding, fresh energy, and creative imagination to deal with homework wars every evening. I have talked with my partner and with other parents. These talks helped me realize that ours is not a unique situation, mine not a unique frustration. They helped me see that my son's teacher is no different from others, nor is her homework harder. My child is no more recalcitrant, rebellious, or fun-loving than other children. Other parents face the same problems I do, such as the isolation, lack of societal support for childraising, and pressures from school systems.

Finally, and perhaps most importantly, as a man I had learned that I was supposed to figure all this out by myself. Yet I realized that my relationship with Ariel wasn't working because I had all the power and all the responsibility. I resented my responsibility and Ariel resented my power. It finally occurred to me to sit down and talk about it with him.

I told him I didn't like playing the enforcer when it came to his completing his homework assignments; I didn't like yelling. But I was concerned and wanted to know what kind of support he needed from me.

"What I need from you is to back off some, stop yelling at me every day about my assignments."

"What can I do? Stay out of it completely?"

"No, don't stay out of it, just lighten up some."

"What else would help?"

"Ask me when I'm going to do my homework instead of telling me to do it now. Then I can plan out the right time."

"What if you save it till too late and you're too tired?"

"I just won't save it all for late."

(I found this hard to believe, but I bit my tongue). "Okay, it sounds good to me."

"Yeah, I need you to answer questions about the assignments and things."

"Sure."

This conversation was a tremendous relief—to both of us. It didn't completely end the arguments, but it confirmed that we were both on his side. It also shifted the responsibility from me to him for planning his homework schedule. The next day after school he told me the schedule he had planned. And he followed it.

He still forgets his books at times, or loses assignments. But he doesn't feel like a billiard ball bouncing between the wrath of school and home. He feels in charge of his homework and I feel like his ally.

Society's dictates say that as a father, I should make Ariel do what's best for him without giving him a say in the matter. This, I'm told, will help him develop the discipline he needs to succeed in the world. I know he must learn to live in the world with the expectations that school, work, and other systems have of him. He has to learn the consequences of his actions. But there's no need for me to force him to learn—and it doesn't seem to work anyway. My support will enable him to make choices and evaluate the consequences of those choices early in life, when the stakes aren't high.

I'm trying to let go of the sense of desperation I carry into this relationship—the feeling that if I don't teach him now, immediately, he will grow up to be a failure. I know he needs to make mistakes and learn from them. I am practicing letting go of the need to force him to learn, and letting go of being society's enforcer of homework and other expectations or roles thrust on him. With my support he can make his own choices.

I know Ariel and I are on the same side. But it's hard to let go of the responsibility I was taught that fathers should bear. I want my involvement to be less top-down and more side-by-side. And though it's still not easy for me to trust him, I can see that the more trust I show him and the more responsibility I give him, the more successful he is. What a relief! We also have a lot more fun in the evenings as we talk, watch television, or play basketball together after he has finished his homework.

Street Wars

I can change the way I behave in homework wars because I'm one of the primary participants. But there are also wars out on the streets and at school where my role is not primary. Ariel is a solid, strong eight-year-old with a lot of energy. He attracts other guys who like sports and who challenge each other physically. My partner and I have tried to explain to him how traditional training makes boys aggressive. We want him to be sensitive to the personal rights and feelings of those around him. He understands all that. But when push comes to shove, he shoves back, and sometimes he shoves first.

Among the children in our neighborhood, there is a broad range of family backgrounds. There are usually some children in my son's class who are a couple of years older than he is. They're bigger, angry, and have a lot to prove to themselves and others. Robert is one such kid. He comes to school overflowing with violent talk and threatens children to make them do what he wants—a classic bully. Ariel has a fair amount of pride; one day he got tired of the bullying and socked Robert in the stomach. At home later that day, Ariel started a conversation with me.

"Robert said he's going to kill me tomorrow at school."

"He said what?"

"He's going to get some kids and kill me."

"Why would he say that? What happened?"

"He's always bossing everyone around, so today I hit him. He chased me after that, but the bell rang, so he said he would get me later. I can't go to school tomorrow."

"Sounds like you're scared."

"Yeah, he's eleven and I'm only eight. He'll clobber me, and he has big friends."

"Well, you have to go to school, but maybe we can figure something out. What do you think we could do?"

"I don't know."

"Could you get some help at school?"

"I don't know. The playground teacher never sees what happens and my regular teacher won't deal with stuff on the playground. She just says to take it to the playground teacher."

"What about the principal?"

"What can she do? Why don't you come to school with me?"

"I can't stay with you all day. Could you talk to Robert?"

"What good would that do? He'd just hit me."

"What if you talked with him with an adult there?"

"That might work, but what about when they left?"

"What if it was the principal who was there?"

"That might work. But I can't just go into the principal's office and do that. Why don't you come with me?"

"I suppose I could go in in the morning to be with you when you talk with the principal."

All the time I was talking with Ariel there was an angry voice in the back of my mind saying, "Who does this kid think he is, bullying my son? Maybe I should just stop by the school and let him know what he's up against." This voice rose up, remembering all the times I was pushed around as a kid. It was still angry and ready to strike back.

But another voice answered that one: "Ariel is big enough to take care of himself. He's just going to have to learn how to handle this situation and fight it out for himself. Just give him a pep talk, remind him he knows aikido, and send him back out there ready for anything. If he doesn't learn now, he might always be pushed around."

These two loud, insistent voices come directly out of my training to be a man, reinforced by experiences growing up with the guys in my neighborhood. It is very hard to quiet those voices so that I can listen to what my son is saying about his needs. I want to support him, but the voices of my training are often too insistent to allow me to listen to him.

The next morning we went to the principal's office, and Ariel told her about Robert's threatening him and being a bully. She suggested he tell Robert directly, and he felt okay about doing that. First Robert came in alone and the principal talked with him in my presence. Then Ariel was invited back and was able to tell Robert what he didn't like about his actions on the playground. Then he asked him to leave him alone. Robert agreed. They shook hands and went back to class. That was pretty much the end of it. Robert knew my son had support and that the principal was paying attention. Ariel had decided what he wanted to do and was able to talk directly to Robert in ways that made him feel more powerful, more supported. He did not have to fall back on fighting to protect himself or depend on me to rescue him.

Ariel also had problems with William, another classmate. One day we had this conversation:

"I don't like what William does."

"What does he do?"

"He gives out candy and even money sometimes."

"He just gives it out?"

"Well no, just if you're in his club."

"What does that mean?"

"If you are in his club and say he's the boss and do what he says, then he gives you candy and money."

"And you don't like that?"

"He's always asking me to do stuff I don't want to, and then if I don't do it I don't get the candy."

"And you want the candy."

"Yeah, sure, but I don't like to be bossed around. He's real bossy."

We talked a while longer. I let Ariel describe what was happening and what his feelings and thoughts were about William and the other children.

I didn't think much more about it until one day after school a couple of weeks later. Ariel came in:

"I'm in trouble now."

"What's up?"

"William's really mad at me. He clobbered me in the stomach today and said he'd do it again tomorrow."

"Why did he do that?"

"I told him I wasn't going to be in his club anymore."

"Oh yeah, and that made him angry?"

"You bet."

"It must have taken courage to tell him you wouldn't be in his club. You sound scared to me."

"Yeah, he's a lot bigger than me. I don't know if it was worth it."

Ariel and I talked over what he could do the next day. We finally agreed I would go with him to the principal's office and he would talk to William with her there.

The next morning we went off to his school. The principal talked with my son, then phoned William's teacher. The principal then turned to me and said that Ariel was also one of the rougher boys and had been pushing other children around.

Uh-oh, I thought to myself. *This is embarrassing. My son the innocent victim is also one of the bullies.*

The principal gave Ariel a talk about his behavior while we

waited for William. William came in and greeted my son. The principal explained to him why we were there, and then Ariel and he talked. They reached an agreement about not fighting and the principal gave another talk to both of them about their responsibility to the other children.

The next day after school my son told me that William gave him a tape to borrow. I looked perplexed until he explained, "We're friends now."

A week later, my partner dropped Ariel off at school. She said he headed straight to William and struck up the following conversation:

"Hi, William. What's up?"

"Nothing much. It's hard work just hanging out here trying to look cool."

Ariel nodded seriously, "Yeah, it's hard work looking tough." And he settled in next to William to take his stand.

Is It War?

Ariel isn't a bully usually, but he hasn't been just an innocent bystander either. He is beginning to see the consequences of his actions and is learning about the ins and outs of male bonding. He is finding a way to survive and make his way in a complicated, constantly changing social environment.

Ariel is seeing how peer pressure can be a strong influence in pushing men to be aggressive. We are trained to present ourselves as tough so no one will mess with us. But that's not who we really are. When given a chance, in a one-to-one situation, we can sometimes relax and be the less aggressive person we really are. Ariel is beginning to negotiate the difficult terrain of male/male relationships, full of camaraderie, full of danger.

When you are in a war zone, nothing helps more than having powerful allies on your side. As my children go off each day to fight their way through life, I hope they feel secure that I'm on their side, not to protect them from the world, but to help them develop the skills to deal with their battles safely and effectively.

Homework wars and street wars. Is it really a battleground out there? As adults we tend to forget how unsafe it was for us as children. For so many of us, those were devastating times, when we had little power to protect ourselves from older brothers and sisters, from our parents' anger and abuse, from the other children on the block, and from teachers and other adults in authority. Power counts for everything in our society. Those without it are very vulnerable to violence from others.

As adults and parents we can try to protect our children from some of that violence, but most of it is beyond our control. There are several responses we can bring to the dangers. Traditionally, we have protected girls from danger by keeping them inside, in our sight, and chaperoned constantly. We taught the boys how to fight, stand up for themselves, stay in control, and have no feelings that would make them vulnerable. This strategy set up both girls and boys as targets of violence. Girls grew up with the unrealistic expectation that they were safe if they stayed in our sight and followed the rules. But they experienced violence anyway because we could not always protect them and we did not give them skills to protect themselves. Boys were led to believe that they were tough enough to take care of themselves and shouldn't ask for help.

Working through each situation with my children is the hardest part of parenting for me. It is easy to overreact to my own pain and to exaggerate their danger. It is also easy to pretend not to notice the dangers to my children—and therefore not prepare them adequately. I am often torn between wanting to protect them and throwing up my hands, saying there is nothing I can do and they will have to learn how to deal with it themselves.

A more useful approach is to give my sons and daughter the physical and practical skills, emotional confidence, and information to deal with conflicts. With these tools, and with parental support, they can learn to handle most situations themselves, asking for help from me or their mother when they need it.

It is not easy for me to nurture my children when I have so little control over what befalls them. It takes patience for me to help them without my own agenda getting in the way. I have to be able to see the complexities and personalities involved in each of their problems and help them choose responsibly without making their choices for them. Developing these skills will make a big difference in my children's ability to respond to difficult circumstances.

Though it isn't always a battleground for our children, it would be foolish to deny the dangers of physical and sexual abuse, drugs, guns, and street wars, not to mention the battleground of academic and athletic competition. Our children can experience plenty of hurt and abuse in this society. If I can make the world a little safer for them, and if I can help them grow a little stronger and more confident, I will have increased their chances of living safer and stronger adult lives.

As a boy I was raised for battle. I was taught to be a soldier in the street wars, homework wars, and overseas wars that I knew I would be called on to fight. As boys, we're taught to be ready to fight to protect ourselves, our families, our country. It doesn't matter that most of us don't really want to.

When I think about how to raise my sons so that they will not become soldiers, I think about how I was trained. I learned how to be a man from many different sources. The most powerful model of manhood for me, and for most men, was my father.

The Father That I Knew

I spent the first seventeen years of my life trying to be like my father. The next ten I spent in a complete panic that I had succeeded. Finally, I realized I was different from him and could take what I wanted from the model he had furnished me. This realization was painful because it confirmed the distance between us.

My father and I knew each other all my life. At least that's what I'm told. There are a few early photographs documenting some kind of relationship. But every day? Did we really see each other every day? How could we have, if that seventeen years has created the distance I feel between us now? I hardly remember weekdays with him. He was gone to a busy world before I awoke.

I know he hated getting up to be at work by seven, but the stock market opened in New York at ten and we lived in Los Angeles. That was why he got to sleep in late on Sundays. So late, until at some magical hour, my mother would signal my sister and me. Then we could rush in to bounce on their big bed, wrestle with my dad, and feel the physical contact we had missed all week.

My mother says that he used to take care of my sister and me on Saturdays so she could have some time away from us. He never mentioned this time together, even when I became a father and took care of my son. My mother still tells me many things about my father. She even tells me he loved me and was proud of me. I believe her; I really do. But I also trust the unspoken communication from my father that he believed I would never have the right values, the right skills and experience to make it in a world he clearly saw as hostile. And I trust my intuitive feeling that he never really felt confident in his own ability to make it. He had all the outward signs of success in his life, but he never let go of the inner doubts that made him angry, mistrustful, and fearful of others.

In sixth grade we had to write about the person we respected most in the world. I chose my father. He represented the ultimate in male success. He had a wife, children, and a good job. He was smart, good at sports, solid to the core, successful, and never made mistakes. In junior high school I wrote, "In ten years I will be working for a large corporation as a department manager and be on my way up to the top of the organization. . . . I will have achieved three of my goals: influence, respect, and money. . . ." My place in life seemed so clear. If I did things seriously and carefully I would succeed, just like my father. I even combed my hair the way he did. I kept testing myself by competing with him in conversation, at ping pong, at tennis, and in school honors. We did things side by side, and I practiced being like him. I became quieter, like him. I became cynical and sarcastic, like him. Like him, I became careful.

He and I grew up in similar families, each of us the oldest child of a hard-working father who remained distant from us. But he went to the University of Southern California business school and then was drafted into the army during World War II. I went to a radical, liberal arts college and then spent three years on a communal boat sailing around the world. Had that made the difference? Later on it became important for me to find out.

A few years ago my father was dying. He had been sick for months. Finally, the doctors would take no more heroic measures to save his life. I felt horrible, yet relieved. He was alive and alert, yet so withdrawn from the world that I did not know what was best for him, or my mother, or any of us. I felt guilty for wishing that the terminal, yet interminable, process would be over.

His body wasn't working anymore. He had watched its decay. His sharp, clear questions to the doctors revealed his grasp of medical complexities. Yet I wondered if he really understood that he was dying. He refused to talk about it. Nor would he talk about him and me, us.

He had few words for anyone during his illness. But one week, when the doctors told him his heart was working at only 25 percent capacity, he suddenly wanted to tell me a great deal about what he thought I should know. With sadness, self-pity, and anger, through the first tears I had ever seen him shed, he not only explained to me what he thought was important financially, he also made a final attempt to get me to value the things he had—security, stability, family, and civic responsibility. His major role as a man had been to provide for his family. On his deathbed he was trying to get me to shoulder that role while conveying his anger and despair that he would be unable to do it himself. In his eyes he had failed on two counts.

I had romanticized his death and thought, *Aha, there will yet be a final scene when he confesses his love for me. Then we will cry in each other's arms and forgive each other.* Instead, after spending hours unloading all the family business onto my shoulders and criticizing me, he lay back on his bed. My mother said, "Why don't you tell Paul you love him and appreciate what he's doing?" My father simply said, "No, he doesn't need that ego-boosting stuff." My father was dying as he had lived, with my mother interpreting him to the world. So much for nicely packaged happy endings.

Shortly after this I had to go into the hospital for some emergency surgery. Before my operation I had to confront the possibility of my own death, as well as my father's. As I lay in a hospital bed across the city from him, I remembered afternoons working together with him on my stamp collection, side by side yet so silent, so distant, like parallel lines. And yet, for a moment, those lines did touch. My father's dying became a gift to me. It provided the final impetus to let go of the need for his understanding and acceptance. If I couldn't get it from him, I would have to give it to myself.

As I recovered from my operation, my desperate longing for his approval turned to defiance, and then to determination. For the next several weeks I repeated to myself every day, "I approve of myself. I accept myself." After a great struggle I reached a point where I could say, "I do accept myself. I am not my father." As I recovered from the operation and he became sicker, I knew I would survive and grow. Crying, laughing, writing, talking, with the support of my family and friends, I could reach out and embrace the world even as my father withdrew from it.

It has been several years since my father died. Every year my mother asks, "Are you still angry at your father?" For the last three to four years I have said, "No, not primarily." She continues to ask, and each time I have to take her question seriously and see where my anger lies, and how much is left. There are times when my anger surfaces, when I remember something my father said that cut me down or tore me apart, or a time when he hurt someone else with what he said. Below my anger at him I feel hurt. I recognize his inability to speak his love out loud, and that makes me sad.

I've talked with many men about their fathers. From these talks I've come to realize that my father did the best he could given the traditions handed down to him. I wonder if his thoughts at the end of his life were like those of a dying man in Marita

Golden's book *A Woman's Place*. This man is unable to speak his thoughts, in this case to his wife.

> So I'll sit in this chair instead, and will my body into stillness, to dull the band of pain tightening around my head.
>
> I never wanted to speak to her as much as I do now. But I don't even know what I'd say to her if I could talk. Before, she was the one who asked for words. But I built this house, provided for her and our children, worked hard in my business to become a man in my and everyone else's eyes. This has been my language—all those things were my words—and sometimes it's like she never heard any of it.*

Sometimes I would like to know how much I'm like my father. My identity as a man different from him was a major preoccupation during my teenage years and early adult life. But occasionally I find myself making some physical gesture that reminds me of him, and I wonder if he felt as I do when making that gesture. Other times I feel his presence as a benevolent glow around me and my family. I have also become aware of some of the unhealthy ways I responded to some of his behavior. My father destroyed personal relationships, abandoned and pushed people away. To counter that I have tried to save every relationship regardless of the cost. I could never admit that a relationship was not working; I had to save all those friendships my father had abandoned.

Ultimately, my father abandoned himself. He spent his life achieving success. When he reached the age of fifty-six he had reached the limits of what he was allowed to do. He could go no further without breaking some of the rules that had defined his life as a man. Over the next seven years he experienced a series of health problems that he ignored or denied until death became inevitable. My father did not commit suicide. But given the choice

* Marita Golden, *A Woman's Place* (New York: Ballantine, 1988), 194.

between growing beyond his traditional roles or neglecting his body, staying who he was, and dying, he chose the latter.

He remained true to his training right to the end. He did not ask for help, he ignored his body, and he did not admit his fear or his anger. He remained alone.

After years of exploring our different responses to life, I have begun to understand and forgive my father. I can identify what we faced as men—the pressure to succeed and be in control in a confusing and unforgiving world, the pressure to have a stable income and support a family, the pressure to be acceptable and safe, and always the pressure to be approved of by our fathers. I wish my father and I could have talked about those pressures, rather than working in silence on my stamp collection. Now I talk with others and I will share my experience with my sons. In the process of losing my father, I gained a new sense of myself.

I think about my father occasionally, mourn his loss in my life once in awhile, find my own joys in raising children and carrying on my work. When a friend tells me about reconciling with his father, I rejoice with him. When another friend tells me about losing his father, I sympathize. I try to let the feelings I have about my father rise and fall, ebb and flow as they will. They are part of the background that adds texture and depth to the design of my life.

And now, as I kiss my son good night and notice how big he's grown and how much we have grown together, I think about my father. And I know that I am not the father that I knew.

Growing Up Male

The way our society turns boys into men like my father, and into men we know who are angry or even violent, is a complex process. Our fathers teach us, our mothers teach us, the media, sports, teachers, and peers teach us. Whoever teaches us, the messages are remarkably uniform. My son Ariel is receiving the same training I received. He learns from his friends Robert and William, from television, and from his teachers. I think a lot about what he may learn from me.

I learned much from my father. Even though he was not physically abusive, his training left its marks. Here is a scenario, as performed in a high-school class on growing up male, that many of our fathers used to train us to "be a man."*

A ten-year-old boy is in a chair at home watching television. His dad walks through the door holding a piece of paper.

DAD: Turn off that set.

SON: Aw Dad . . .

DAD: Turn it off. Now! This place is a mess; why isn't it cleaned up?

SON: I was going to do it after this show.

DAD: Excuses. You always have excuses. Have an excuse for this? What is this?

SON: My report card.

DAD: I know that. Right here, math, D.

SON: I did the best I could.

DAD: Sure you did. You're just stupid. You know what D stands for? It stands for Dummy.

SON: (starting to get up) That's not fair.

DAD: Sit down. I didn't say you could go anyplace.

SON: (looks down, near tears)

DAD: What's the matter, you gonna cry about it? Poor little momma's boy. You're just a wimp. (Pushes him off chair onto floor.) When are you going to grow up and act like a man around here? (Storms off.)

(The son picks himself off the floor. He's angry, confused, hurt, and turns to the audience). "He's always coming up here yelling, pushing me around, shouting at me to act like a man. I hate it! It's not fair! You're my friends, aren't you? What can I do?"

What follows is a typical group discussion after this role play. P = participants from the class. S = son, still in role.

---

* © Oakland Men's Project.

P: Why don't you talk with him?

S: I want to, I really do. But you saw what he's like. He's always yelling. I'm scared of him.

P: You should get better grades.

S: I'm trying. I'm studying every day. You know how math is—I guess it's like he says, "I'm not too smart."

P: Get someone to help you.

S: It's not just my grades. If it's not one thing it's another—my chores, the television, staying out too late.

P: Talk with your mom.

S: Maybe I should. She's scared of him too.

P: Run away.

P: He's only ten.

S: I've thought of that, but I don't have anywhere to go. My grandma doesn't live around here.

P: Talk to a counselor.

S: I don't know if I can trust them. I'm scared my dad would find out.

P: Talk to your aunt or uncle or someone who knows your dad and can talk with him.

P: Yeah, and try to do better at school.

S: I guess I should talk to someone. My dad's always shouting at me to act like a man, act like a man. I don't know what that means. What should I be doing?

At the Oakland Men's Project, where I worked for thirteen years, this role play is used in workshops to capture the essence of our training to be men. Most men are very familiar with the scene. We can all remember some adult yelling at us like that when we were younger. I have seen many, many men moved to tears during this role play. It triggers memories of their own experiences of pain, humiliation, abuse, lack of love and acceptance, and powerlessness.

"Grow up!" "Act like a man!" What do we, as boys, learn about what it means to "act like a man"? Think of some of the adult men in our lives when we were children and the messages they gave us.

Act Like a Man[*]

men . . .	*men are . . .*
yell at people	aggressive
have no emotions	responsible
get good grades	mean
stand up for themselves	bullies
don't cry	tough
don't make mistakes	angry
know about sex	successful
take care of people	strong
don't back down	in control
push people around	active
can take it	dominant over women

We draw a line around these expectations and call it the Act Like a Man box. As young boys we are supposed to learn how to fit in and live inside that box. It's a list of expectations of who we should be, how we should act, and what we should feel and say.

Every time we step out of the box—when we're not acting tough enough or strong enough—we get called names. When I walk down the halls of any junior or senior high school, I hear these words ringing off the lockers.

sissy	geek	baby	loser
gay	fag	nerd	pussy
wimp	mark	boy	queer
punk	mama's boy	girl	wuss

These words are little slaps, everyday reminders designed to keep us in the box. They are also fighting words. If someone calls a boy a "wimp" or a "fag," he is supposed to fight to prove that he is not. Almost every adult man will admit that as a kid, he had to fight at least once to prove he was in the box.

* © Oakland Men's Project.

Notice that many of the words we get called refer to being gay or feminine. This feeds into two things we're taught to fear: (1) that we are not manly enough and (2) that we might be gay. Homophobia, the fear of gays or of being taken for a gay, is an incredibly strong fear we learn as boys and carry with us throughout our lives. Much too often we try to alleviate our fears of being gay or effeminate by attacking others.

There is other training that keeps us in the box. Besides getting into fights, we are ostracized and teased, and girls don't seem to like us when we step out of the box. Many adults keep pushing us to be tough, and that process begins early. They seem convinced that if they "coddle" us, we will be weak and vulnerable. Somehow, withdrawal of affection is supposed to toughen us and prepare us for the "real" world.

Withdrawal of affection is emotional abuse. And that's bad enough. But it often does not stop there. One out of every six of us is sexually abused as a child. Often, the verbal, physical, and sexual abuse continues throughout our childhood.

Another part of our training is achieved through the positive portrayals of violence in our culture. Our movie and sports heroes use violence and are rewarded for it with power, status, money, and women. The costs of violence are rarely shown.

Nobody is born in the Act Like a Man box. It takes years and years of enforcement, name-calling, fights, threats, abuse, and fear to turn us into men who live in this box. By adolescence we believe that there are only two choices—we can be a man or a boy, a winner or a loser, a bully or a wimp, a champ or a chump.

Nobody wants to live in a box. It feels closed in; much of us is left out. It was a revelation to realize how I had been forced into the box. It was a relief to understand how it had been accomplished and to know it didn't have to be that way. Today, it inspires me to see adult men choose to live outside the box. I did not get this inspiration from my father. He lived in the box all his life. I try to live outside it and hope to give my children a different model of what it means to be male.

Of course, we have more than our fathers as models for what

men can be. My son also learns a great deal from his friends. Imagine another role play we use at the Oakland Men's Project.*

The lunch bell has just rung. Three thirteen-year-old boys in junior high school are talking. A new kid walks by.

BULLY: (grabs new kid's book) Where ya going?

NEW KID: Hey, give me back my book.

BULLY: You want your book? Look at this, you guys, he wants his book. What's it worth to you?

NEW KID: Just give it back. Why are you doing this? (Makes repeated attempts to get book back. Finally bully twists his arm behind his back.)

BULLY: C'mon, give me your lunch money.

NEW KID: I don't have any. Ouch!

BULLY: Hand it over. Now!

NEW KID: Here! Now give me back my book.

BULLY: That's not all, you don't buy lunch with that.

NEW KID: Will you give me back my book? Ouch!

BULLY: Now!

NEW KID: Okay, okay. Here.

BULLY: That's right. Here's your book. I'll see you back here tomorrow at the same time. And you'll have two dollars. Understand, chump? (Releases the new kid's arm and walks off.)

There are a thousand variations of this scene, but most of us, at some time in our childhood, have met a bully. We knew the pain, the humiliation, and the fear of abuse faced by the new kid in this role play. Almost all of us have also been a bully at some point in our lives. Although we don't like to admit it to ourselves or to others, there have been times when we pushed someone around or made someone do something he or she didn't want to do. We might have bullied younger brothers or sisters or little children on

---

* © Oakland Men's Project.

the block. We might have bullied our own children, a woman, or a co-worker with less power. Why did we do it?

Most likely, it was because we were angry. We were angry because we had been hurt by someone who had pushed us around. Being a bully was a chance to pass our hurt around. It was a chance to counter our feeling of powerlessness by wielding power over someone else. We pushed someone around because our needs were not getting met. What were those needs?

power	attention
group approval	love
respect	trust
friends	self-worth
recognition	safety
something to do	

Most of these are everyday needs we all have. Why don't we just ask for what we need? The reasons all relate to our training in how to be men.

- We're afraid to.
- We don't know how.
- We don't think we'd get it.
- We don't know what to ask for.
- We believe we have to earn it.
- We are embarrassed to admit we need anything.
- We're scared we will be put down for asking or will be rejected.

We learned to be bullies because that worked for us, at least temporarily. For most of us, being a bully was also the only power available. Parents, teachers, coaches, school administrators, and the police had power over us and often abused it. We were taught to take pain and anger and pass it on to someone more vulnerable, creating a cycle of violence. We were not taught the tremendous costs of being a bully. In addition to the emotional and physical suffering we inflicted on those we bullied, we lost friends, intimacy, family, trust, respect, self-esteem, as well as the love, attention, and support we originally needed. It cost some of us our lives. There is always going to be a bigger bully, older brother, or police officer around.

Perhaps the greatest tragedy in our training was that we literally lost our souls. We became so cut off from our feelings that we no longer connected with other people, with life, or with the natural world. We became protective and controlling, unable to participate in the giving and receiving of love, intimacy, and relationship.

Few of us, boys or men, want to live in the Act Like a Man box. It is a limiting, lonely, and dangerous place to live. Yet every time we try to get out of it, someone comes along and pushes us back in with a punch, or a name, or a put-down. We internalize the pressure and after a while, all but lock ourselves in the box, bearing the costs silently.

The Fear of Men

When my colleagues and I do a school workshop for the Oakland Men's Project I always look around at the young men. I note how much activity there is. Many are testing each other by name-calling, making sly comments, shoving, and punching on the arm. These thirteen- and fourteen-year-olds are already wary of each other and of the constant testing every day in class, in the halls, and on the field. When I walk down the halls I hear "wimp!" "fag!" "punk!"

I remember sitting in class at that age. Sometimes I would sit next to a friend. He and I would take turns hitting each other on the arm as hard as we could. I would put everything I had into making him wince with the force of my punch. Then I would steel myself for his blow, making sure he couldn't tell that it hurt. Day after day we tested each other this way.

That testing is still going on between boys. I notice it when the
bell rings. Class starts and everyone gets quiet. The subject of male
violence is a little scary for them. They aren't sure at first about
these adult men in their classroom, or how it will look to the other
guys if they speak during the workshop. It might look bad.

Much has been written about how men fear women, and most
of that writing blames women for men's insecurities. The fear I see
in the classroom, however, and the fear I identify within myself, is
not a fear of women (although I'm sure there is a small element of
that present), it is the fear of other men. And anyone who tells me
it was my mother, or breaking away from my mother, or the absence of my father, or my women teachers, or girlfriends does not
hear, see, and feel my pain and hurt at the hands of men, men I
knew and loved who violated my trust in them.

This fear grows out of forty years of being tested, judged, attacked, competed against, dominated, and challenged by other
men and boys. It is not an irrational fear. This fear in me was built
by getting beaten up after school by some older kid in the neighborhood who didn't like me, by being teased and called names because sometimes I cried after I got beaten up. This fear was built
by all the times my dad put me down because I wasn't good
enough in sports, at school, or whatever he decided was the standard that day. It is the fear that I wouldn't get a job, have a career,
find a safe place in the world. And some of it was the fear of what
I might do to someone else to take care of myself.

There is danger from other men. Women know this in the core
of their being. So do men, even if we deny it. There is different
danger for each of us, depending on our place in society and the
amount of power we have to protect that place. There is physical
danger from men we meet on the street and danger from men we
work for and with. There is danger from men who hold administrative power over us, from white men if we are men of color,
from men who have more money than we do, from any man who
has the power to affect our lives if we don't "act right."

The Love of Men

When I was a teenager I lived in a world inhabited entirely by men. All my friends were the other guys on the block or at school. I spent almost every minute with them. Every book I read, every television show or movie I watched, was by and about men. Everything I learned in history, social studies, math, or science was about men. At home I tried to be like my father—I discounted my mother and ignored my sister. Girls were distant, shining, sexual objects that I dreamed about but who did not figure into my daily experience.

I loved the guys I hung out with. Just being in their company was reassuring. They provided a cushion against the world. I also feared them and the loss of their approval. Because I loved them I would do almost anything for them. Because I feared them I would do almost anything they challenged me to. The love and the fear created incredible intimacy between us. We were best friends plus.

I didn't know what "homosexual" meant, but by age six I could use "fag" and "wimp" with the best of them, hundreds of times a day. Long before I knew about sexuality I had been taught that being gay was the worst possible fate for a guy. Later on I learned that the only way to avoid accusations of being gay was to be tougher than anyone else, stay in the Act Like a Man box, and have girlfriends or at least constantly talk about girls. The fear of being gay kept me towing the line through many agonizing trials. I tried to stay safely hidden in the box, only poking my head out to label other boys queer so attention would be off of me.

As a teenager, my world was completely male-dominated and male-focused. The only people I was intimate with were other guys. We had to constantly draw the line around that intimacy and prove to each other that we were attracted only to women. We all talked straight and constantly put down homosexuals. We all claimed absolute fascination with women as sexual objects. We veered away from sensitive actions and activities and anything else we thought might make us look unmanly or gay. We avoided crying, dancing, concern for women as people, and especially touching, hugging, or being affectionate with another guy.

Being gay was the unspoken and unseen fear. I never saw gay men. No one ever talked with me about homosexuality. I know now that some of those boys I was so close to were gay but lived in a closet of fear I knew nothing about.

I was taught to fear getting emotional support, affection, and nurturing from other men because of how it might look. The answer, I was told, was to find a woman who would meet all my needs for nurturing. As a result, my relationships with both men and women were limited, frustrating, and unnecessarily agonizing. These expectations contribute to violence toward women and gay men.

Many of us who are heterosexual believe we can get our emotional needs met only by women. Therefore, in relationships we dump all of our needs on women and expect them to take care of us. Since women work, often help take care of children, and have needs of their own, they inevitably fail to take care of us the way we expect them to. When this happens we become panic-stricken. For some of us, it seems life-threatening when a woman denies or takes away our emotional support. We might feel deceived, frustrated, disappointed, hurt, and vulnerable. For a man with unrealistic expectations of women, these are dangerous feelings to have. Almost immediately, we cover these emotions with anger, and some of us lash out at our partner to regain what we feel she has taken away. Out of our panic comes much of the emotional and physical violence that we direct at women. This violence often escalates if our partner leaves or threatens to leave, because then the loss would be permanent. This feeling of panic is often tied to our fear and inability to receive nurturing and support from other men. The woman we are with becomes our lifeline; we perceive her as our only source of emotional sustenance.

In many cases, this panic is tied to our fear of being gay or of being thought gay. This fear keeps men in the box, makes finding a woman to take care of our every need and certify our manliness most important. Most of us don't go gay bashing, looking for gay men to beat up. But all of us participate in the homophobia. Many of us pass on the jokes and comments that set up gay men as targets for violence, making it unsafe for all of us to step out of the box. Few of us intervene when we witness other men putting down gay men, telling jokes, or making inappropriate comments. Many of us buy the stereotypes and believe we can tell gay from straight by look, action, mannerisms, profession, address, or body shape.

Almost all of us in heterosexual relationships expect our partner to nurture us, our children, and our environment, and we are afraid to turn to men for support. That fear keeps us at a distance from other men, including our fathers, brothers, and sons.

By keeping our distance and ridiculing men who seek support from other men we indirectly become participants in the violence against gay men. The immediate effect is to place those who are gay in physical danger, and we place unnecessary limits on our own lives. Some of these limits include the following:

- We fear other men who want to prove they're tough, winners, and not wimps. And they fear us in return.
- We fear giving or receiving any affection from other men.
- We go without the intimacy, nurturing, and support we might get from other men.
- We fear acting in any way that will look gay.
- We don't admit to feeling weak, inadequate, incapable, or vulnerable because we think that is what being gay is about.
- We put tremendous pressure on our relationships with women to make up for the lack of male nurturing in our lives.
- We have few models of how we can be different because many of the gay and straight men who have

stepped out of the box and stood up for women's rights, nonviolence, and alternative male roles have been censored from our history and literature.
- Perhaps the most painful cost of all is that we feel compelled to pass on to our sons the training to fear men, to fear being gay, and to stay in the box.

It's not easy to break down these patterns, but there is a lot we can begin to do. When we examine our fear of gay men we begin to discover parts of our self we fear or were never allowed to express. When we stand up for gay men and interrupt gay bashing, we are standing up not only for their rights but for ourselves and our ability to step out of the Act Like a Man box. When we acknowledge and nurture our relationships with male friends, we are building trust and safety in the world for ourselves, for our male friends, and also for the women in our lives. When we allow our sons to play with nonviolent toys, participate in nontraditional activities, and show their feelings, we are breaking the cycle of violence that would otherwise get passed from one generation to another.

I still hesitate when reaching out to another man. Will he take advantage of my vulnerability? Will he think I'm coming on to him? Will he think I'm weird? Will he respond? Will he reject me? Will I look silly hanging out there? Too often the other man will pretend not to notice. Or he will be too busy to get together. Or he will just want to hang out at the ballpark and never really talk. Or we'll talk about the weather, baseball, politics, or our children, but never about ourselves. There is genuine affection in many of our relationships with other men. I don't want to diminish that. But our fears often keep us apart. We desire more from each other but can't break through the traditional forms of male bonding.

What we need is a different kind of male bonding—not one based on team or war experiences, not one based on blaming or harassing women, guys, or ethnic and racial groups. I am describing an intimacy built on honest sharing, mutuality, respect for others, and emotional risk-taking. This kind of man-to-man relationship is caring, close, fun, and enduring—the kind we often envy women for, the kind that we each long for ourselves.

Generally it is only when I have the courage to share my thoughts and feelings that another man will open up as well. I have to be patient and call back even if he doesn't respond. I have to understand how difficult it may be for him to trust me. It is often easy for me to be angry at him and blame him for things not happening in our relationship. It helps me when I realize that he was trained just as I was. He has learned too well the cost of being open with another man. I can challenge his behavior better if I set the anger and blame aside and focus on the person inside who may want to be closer, even though he doesn't know how.

We want and need to love other men. Even using the word love in thinking about a male-to-male relationship is scary. But not acting on our love for other men keeps us sitting around waiting for another man to initiate a friendship. Think about one man in your life who you want to be closer to. What are you waiting for?

EXERCISE 1 *
Men Relating to Men

We do an exercise at the Oakland Men's Project that shows us the cost of our training all too clearly. We ask the men in the group to stand silently for each statement that applies.

Stand up if you've ever
- worried you were not tough enough.
- exercised to make yourself tougher.
- been disrespected by an adult.
- been called a wimp, queer, or fag.
- been told to act like a man.
- been hit by an older man.
- been forced to fight.

* Created by Allan Creighton.

- been in a fight because you felt you had to prove you were a man.
- been deliberately physically injured by another person.
- been injured on a job.
- been physically injured and have hidden the pain.
- been sexually abused or touched in a way you didn't like by another person.
- stopped yourself from showing affection, hugging, or touching another man because of how it might look.
- been in the military or are a veteran.
- got so mad that while driving, you drove fast or lost control of the car.
- drunk or taken drugs to cover your feelings or hide pain.
- felt like blowing yourself away.
- hurt another person physically or sexually.

EXERCISE 2
The Pain of "Acting Like a Man"

1. What feelings or thoughts did you have while going through the list above?
2. Which of the experiences just listed have been most painful?
3. Identify three qualities from the Act Like a Man box on page 21 that you are still trying to unlearn. What is hard about unlearning them?
4. What were some of the names that were used in your youth to keep guys in the box? Are there any that you use now on other people?
5. Do you have any "fighting" words that make you feel attacked and make you want to defend yourself? Why are they so powerful for you?

6. Write down or describe to a friend one of the most recent times you were a bully.
7. Thinking of the time you were a bully, answer the following questions:
   A. What did you really need in that situation?
   B. Why didn't you ask for what you needed?
   C. What did you gain in the short term?
   D. What did it cost you in the long term?
   E. Are there any connections between what you needed and what bullying cost you in the long term?
   F. How do you think the person you bullied felt?
8. Write down or describe one time when you were bullied by someone. Then answer the following questions:
   A. How did you feel when it happened? If you were angry, what feelings might have been beneath your anger?
   B. What did you need from people around you, besides revenge?
   C. What do you carry with you from that experience?
   D. List five reasons why bullying people to get what you want doesn't work well.

EXERCISE 3
Changing Your Relationships with Men

Questions to ask yourself:
1. How might your relationships with other men be different if you had not been trained to avoid closeness with men and get all of your needs met by one "special" woman?
2. How might your relationships with women be different if you had not been trained to see them as

your only source of love, affection, and emotional support?

3. If you are straight, in what ways do you act or talk to show people you are not gay?

4. How has the fear of appearing gay kept you in the Act Like a Man box? What activities or feelings have you avoided because of that fear?

5. Have you ever not hugged or touched another man because of your fear of how it might look?

6. How would your life be different if you had one or more close male friends you could get support from—men you could tell everything to?

7. What emotional needs do you expect women to take care of for you because you have assumed men can't do it?

8. What have you done with the pain, sadness, frustration, anger, or other feelings that come from having to live in an environment where you cannot love other men but need to fear them? How have you taken those feelings out on gay men? On women? On yourself?

9. When was the last time you said something that put down gay men?

10. When was the last time you intervened when you overheard a comment or joke about gay men?

11. Name one woman who you were angry at or abusive to because she did not take care of you well enough.

12. Name one man who you loved in your life.

13. Name one man who you wanted to be closer to but didn't know how. What will you do to prevent this from happening again?

14. Name one man in your life right now who you want to be closer to. Describe how you are going to go about it.

TWO

Men Relating to Women

Gender Roles

This is fourth grade now. The girls sit on the bench, trading stickers; the boys are out on the field playing ball, getting into fights, and bullying other children. Ariel doesn't like either set of activities, feels he doesn't belong, yet doesn't want to be excluded from either group. He's joined the guys in pushing the girls around and being more aggressive, but he's not happy about it.

Figuring out why the boys and girls separate and how to deal with that is infinitely more difficult for him. I grew up accepting that boy/girl division. I'm proud he recognizes the problem and doesn't like the system of gender segregation. I sure didn't have his understanding when I was a child.

Recently, Ariel came home from school with Robert in tow. "Hi, Dad, we're going to play upstairs."

I have had a report from one girl's father that he and Robert are bullying girls. Later I ask Ariel about it:

"Oh yeah, Robert does choke girls."

"It sounds like you are there helping him."

"I don't help him."

"Tina says that you're not her friend, that you're on Robert's side. What about the barrettes she says you've been breaking?"

After several minutes of conversation in which he finally admitted he had been breaking barrettes, he said, "But that's all over now. I have a pact with my friend, Ali."

"What do you mean?"

"Ali and I talked about it and agreed not to do any bullying ever again."

"That sounds good. So you support each other in acting right to other children?"

"Yeah, and we're friends."

"Sounds like you're beginning to see the difference between friends like Robert who support the negative things, and friends like Ali who support the good things in you."

"Robert and I do real well when we are just by ourselves with no one else around. But when there are other children around he is always getting me into trouble."

"Let me know how this pact with Ali works out."

"Okay."

The Love of Women

As I grew up I learned not only what men were supposed to be like, but also what women and sex were supposed to be like. I had no idea I was being trained so thoroughly. This training and my relationships to other guys were the sea I lived on. Finding a woman to take care of me was the ship on the horizon. Marriage was the port of safety I could dock at. It was all part of the natural order of things.

One of the first times I noticed how thoroughly I'd been trained about sex and women was in my late twenties while thinking about orgasms I had experienced. I realized some were short and sweet, others were long and leisurely. Some tingled all over; others were intensely centered in my penis. Still others seemed to have wave after wave of pleasure.

Men experience different kinds of orgasms? I never would have guessed it. I was brought up believing that men came. It was more complicated for women, I subsequently learned, involving foreplay, erogenous zones, and tenderness. But men just came. In fact, we came all the time, whenever we could, sometimes even when it was embarrassing.

When I was younger I didn't know what orgasms were. Men

had sex. I grew up knowing that part of being a successful man meant having beautiful women around you, available for sex. The more sex you had, the more of a man you were. I expected to be a real man, and I expected there to be lots of women to get sex from. After all, that's what I had learned they were there for.

> For him she is sex—absolute sex, no less. She is defined and differentiated with reference to man and not he with reference to her; she is the incidental, the inessential as opposed to the essential. He is the Subject, he is the Absolute—she is the Other.*

I first became aware that women have a point of view, a perspective on relationships different from that of men, from reading Simone de Beauvoir's book *The Second Sex*. I didn't immediately become a feminist, and it was years later before the women's movement challenged me to change my assumptions and attitudes toward women. But I was struck by her understanding of woman perceived as the Other by men.

Since I had always experienced women as Other, I knew immediately what she meant. But it was startling to hear the Other speak in a forceful, coherent, dynamic voice. I was surprised to find out that the Other was a subject like me, a person with insights and critical understandings. I reflected a lot on de Beauvoir's words, but only as an intellectual exercise. I didn't connect her ideas to my daily life.

One other passage from her book stayed with me.

> The women of today are in a fair way to dethrone the myth of femininity; they are beginning to affirm their independence in concrete ways; but they do not easily succeed in living completely the life of a human being. Reared by women within a feminine world, their normal destiny is marriage, which still means practically subordination to man; for masculine prestige is far from extinct, resting still upon solid economic and social foundations.†

* Simone de Beauvoir, *The Second Sex* (New York: Bantam Books, 1952), xvi.
† de Beauvoir, *The Second Sex*, xxix.

I've been aware of marriage from the time, as a child, that I learned my parents were married. I soon noticed that all the other children in the neighborhood lived in the same circumstances. From television, I was aware of certain families focused around a married couple. These were families like those in "Ozzie and Harriet," "My Three Sons," and "Dennis the Menace."

What I knew was what I saw. Married men had steady jobs so they could support their wives and children. They cared about children, although they were usually at work or busy. The women were always there, taking care of the children and the husband, providing emotional support, services, and discipline, with only a loving smile from Dad in return.

The families appeared very stable in spite of the minor weekly crises. The man acted as the stabilizing force by calmly and rationally solving family problems with a few bits of sage advice in the last five minutes of each show. Since the children and the wife tended to be too emotional, too dramatic, too out of control, the situation always called for the man to step in and reestablish what appeared to be a natural, reasonable calm.

I grew up with a vision of the perfect nuclear family. And I expected that would happen to me. Of course, the woman I would marry would be younger and sexier than my mother, but that would be the main difference. I learned about girls even earlier than I learned about marriage. I had a young sister and I could see differences from me in the way she dressed, what she was interested in, and the activities she was encouraged to pursue. But since she was part of my family and always there, she was less visible in a way than the girls at school. They were truly different.

The guys played cops and robbers or cowboys and Indians every recess when we weren't playing handball. The girls played quieter games like hopscotch and foursquare. By kindergarten we had separated ourselves into same-sex groups. By second grade we were teasing and taunting each other. The boys generally chased the girls. Their difference was fascinating to us. We were not allowed to see girls' bodies, so we were curious about what was under their skirts. We dared each other to peek.

Girls also seemed easy targets. When we were bored we chased them just to see them scream and run away. They were sooooo emotional and dumb! That was exciting. Their presence in school seemed almost decorative. We saw and heard from no women role models except teachers, and they were clearly subordinate to the male principals and deans. We didn't hear about girls' experiences; all we heard from others and from television indicated that girls didn't really count. The stereotypes of empty-headedness and domesticity seemed sufficient.

By fourth grade, the guys felt totally in control of this male/ female difference. We knew exactly what boys could do and what girls could do. We were quick to point out when someone went outside his or her role. We also knew what we could become, what the limits were on our growth, creativity, and achievement. As boys we could be anything we wanted, and we could see men who had done it before us—presidents, space explorers, athletes, and businessmen.

Girls hadn't done anything, according to what we read and saw, and therefore couldn't do anything. Girls couldn't because they did not have what it took. They weren't smart enough, active enough, or ambitious enough. They were devoid of all that.

As compensation for this emptiness, girls were "good." They were kind and gentle and polite. They were good at taking care of people, especially when they didn't get too emotional. Girls were also self-sacrificing, which was an important reason why every boy should eventually have one.

If girls were good, then boys were bad. We didn't always act bad, but we did act up. We were too noisy, too rambunctious. We used cuss words and we got dirty. For example, in the third grade it was great fun to play handball and cuss outrageously at each other. We felt powerful, defiant, and a little furtive, since we knew it was wrong.

Since girls weren't supposed to do rough stuff themselves, we were told they admired us for doing it. We saw this on television all the time, especially in Westerns. The hero had to fight someone to save the woman. She would then look up to him with admiration, respect, and a beaming smile of eternal gratitude. It was obvious that the hero did not want to fight or kill anyone, but when the town or the women had to be protected, he saw his duty and did what a "man had to do." Girls, we were led to believe, did not have this kind of fortitude and realistic outlook. They, therefore, did not have what it took to succeed in the real world.

This understanding was difficult to hold on to when girls did succeed. There was Mary in the fifth grade. She was a great math student, always did her homework, and received top marks on her tests. Guys talked about her success and explained it this way: she worked very hard, was studious, careful, and memorized all the problems in the book. Guys, of course, didn't have to work so hard because we believed we were naturally smart. Girls were not supposed to be smart in something like math. They simply seemed to be diversions to keep us amused.

Then I entered junior high school. Girls suddenly became important because they had something we were fascinated by—sex. I knew nothing about sex except that girls had it and held it tight. Real men were supposed to know how to maneuver it from them with the right lines and techniques. I quickly learned three important things about sex and girls: First, that eventually I would find the right girl, get married, and have all the sex I wanted. Second, that in the meantime, I could try to get sex from girls as long as I followed certain rules. This wasn't what I was supposed to do, but being a boy, I would "naturally" want to do it. Third, besides sex, there was nothing much else of interest about girls.

These three lessons influenced all of my relationships with women. I knew that girls were fascinating, powerful, and mysterious. At the same time, because I believed that I would have women and sex if I fulfilled my responsibilities as a man, I was set up to get angry with women when I didn't get what I believed I would get.

In junior high I knew it was time to get serious about looking for my one and only, the one woman in all the world who was the perfect match for me. She and only she could be my wife. Of course, I knew I probably wouldn't find her until I got older. I also knew that I should begin to define who I was looking for so that I could reject all other women and not overlook her if we met early on.

I spent long hours imagining who she would be. I imagined what she would look like. That was the only thing that mattered. Every girl, after all, would be a mother, caregiver, and homemaker. Since I didn't expect my wife to be smart or talented, creative or independent, only the outside mattered. I knew that I would find her eventually, that we would recognize each other instantly, get married and have lots of wonderful sex, whatever that was. I dreamed of a blond, blue-eyed *Playboy* beauty, the kind that came with cars and stereo sets. I spent lots of time looking for her.

By high school, I felt I had to test other girls to see if I could get some sex from them, to see if they were my one and only. My one and only would be a virgin when I married her. Anyone giving me some action before that time was automatically eliminated. I could hope that a girl would put out because I was horny, and hope that she would not because that would destroy her reputation for me.

Girls were "bad" for fooling around, and my wife was "good" for waiting for me. Girls would try to hook me because I was eligible for marriage. I was told they could do this by using sex, falsely accusing me of paternity, giving me a venereal disease, or enrapturing me and tricking me into falling in love before I found the right woman. I owed it to my bright future, and to my future wife, to protect myself.

While I was learning to reduce women to sexual objects I was developing a particular male "skill." During high school I perfected it. I must have developed it gradually over the years, because I don't remember a single person ever talking about it. At a moment's notice I could whip my head around, pinpoint a girl alone or in a crowd, and size up her body. I learned to do this accurately in all kinds of trying circumstances—hanging upside down, in large crowds, while driving, when walking with other girls, or during an animated discussion. It became an intuitive reflex that momentarily interrupted my concentration many times a day.

Part of this process was simply noting the women among the people around me. Another part involved making a split-second judgment about whether any particular woman was pretty, sexy, or attractive in some way. Most of the time it was an intellectual exercise that had no connection to what I was doing. I wasn't cruising for girls or aggressively pursuing relationships. I seldom even talked with women I didn't know. But I was practicing what I had been taught, to take any woman and reduce her to a sexual object with my gaze. In this way she became a target for possible sexual conquest.

My immediate focus was on sex and women's bodies. My long-term interest, however, was in marriage, settling down, and ending this constant pursuit. For the next fifteen years I sized up every woman I dated or was friends with to see if she was a possibility. Naturally, none measured up. Mine were exacting standards, and fairy princesses weren't as available as I had believed. So I separated all the women I knew from the one woman with whom I would live happily ever after. In many ways, I withheld major parts of myself from them, waiting for the mate I could confide in, trust, get emotional support from, and settle in with.

Instead, what they got was my Dating Self. This was the self that worried about appearance and presentation more than intimacy. This was the self that projected romance and thoughtfulness, the self that performed and acted the role of the suitor, though it always felt like a poor fit with who I really was.

In my late twenties I became more and more anxious to meet my soul mate, because then all the struggle would be over. My wife and I would "understand each other." I had never seen much struggle, argument, or fighting in marriages, and I assumed ours would have none. After all, we would be perfectly matched, because I would have found the "right" woman for me.

I thought that my expectations of women reflected who women were and what they wanted. I know that these expectations are common for men. Though our particular experiences with women are different, we are taught many common expectations about who women are. We then project these expectations on women in our everyday interactions. I had no idea that women were anything but the stereotype I had projected onto them.

One exercise we do at the Oakland Men's Project when we work with a male/female group is to ask the women to share one thing they never want to hear from a man again. We ask for one phrase, one word, one expectation that they don't want to deal with. Here are the most common ones. Usually there is much agreement among the women about them.

- You're just like your mother.
- It must be that time of month.
- Girl, honey, sweetheart, little lady.
- What's for dinner?
- Where are my socks, shirt, etc.?
- Bitch.
- You're too emotional.
- Let me take care of that for you.
- I'm not angry.
- That's your problem.
- You're always nagging.
- You did that like a man.
- Must be a woman driver.
- Why is this place a mess?
- The baby needs changing.
- Nothing's bothering me.
- Can't you keep those children quiet?
- Shut up.
- You'd better not make me angry.

Behind these phrases are core expectations men are trained to have about women.

Act Like a Lady[*]

Men expect women to . . .

be polite	be sexy
be nurturing	take care of the house
be emotional	take care of the children
be submissive	be superwoman
be dependent	put their own needs aside
not be too smart	be clean
be pretty	be available to men

We call these expectations the Act Like a Lady box. It is enforced in the same ways the Act Like a Man box is, through names—like tomboy, bitch, whore, dyke, lesbo, feminist, women's libber, ball-breaker, and cunt. It is also enforced through hitting and sexual assault. Men are constantly angry at women because they are always failing to live up to our expectations.

My expectations about women, marriage, and sex had a major impact on my life. I was constantly frustrated and angry at the women I knew because they failed to meet my standards. It was only slowly, through painful encounters with women, that I realized almost everything I had learned was wrong and harmful, and made loving and intimacy impossible to achieve. My training unraveled most quickly in bed, where I was trying to achieve the orgasms I thought would certify me as a real man.

After a few brief sexual encounters, I was assured that my equipment worked and everything was in order. I was assured that a woman saw me as sexual and manly. These reassurances lessened my anxiety, and I became more aware that the sensations that went along with sexual contact were terrifyingly strong. And they felt so good.

Ah, so that was an orgasm, I said to myself. I can do that by myself. And I did, a lot. I remember masturbating as a child, but when I became a teenager, sexuality became so focused on girls

[*] © Oakland Men's Project.

that I no longer associated it with myself. I had become convinced that only they could give sex to me or withhold it from me.

I was ecstatic when I rediscovered I could enjoy an orgasm any time I wanted. Mornings, evenings, in the shower, in bed, or alone in the woods. These orgasms were sweet to be sure, but short and quick.

I was beginning to learn something that became very important later on when I developed a long-term, intimate relationship with a woman—I could take care of my own sexual pleasure. It wasn't something that women had to give. I wasn't dependent on them. Therefore, there was no reason to get angry at them for not putting out.

It took a long time to learn this. I still had lots of expectations about what women should do for me when we were together. I had been taught that women's primary function was to take care of men and children. Men deserved this from women because we were better; we did the important things in the world. As long as I did my part, they should do theirs. I believed that if I initiated dates, paid for our time together, arranged transportation, and protected them on the streets, then they should show their appreciation by taking care of me emotionally, putting their own concerns and interests aside, and taking care of my sexual needs.

When women did not respond to me the way I expected them to, I felt angry, frustrated, and resentful. But I was beginning to separate my needs for sexual release from my expectations that women should take care of me.

I realize now how much of my sexual life occurred in my head, a constant, silent monologue that my partners never heard. The conversation moved from head to penis and back. The rest of my body played virtually no role in my sexual life. Back then, I could not imagine talking with women about my concerns. Nor was I able to listen to what they were thinking or feeling.

This conversation was not really with myself. It was with the voices of all the male training I had received, including the voice that told me what women "really" liked, wanted, and expected. I had accumulated a miscellaneous but generally consistent rule book about how to be a man. But when I tried to follow it, I didn't get what I wanted. The more successful I was at sleeping with women, the more often I would wake up and wonder why I had bothered. I was discovering that I wanted more intimacy with women, but sex often made intimacy harder to achieve. Since I was focused on their bodies, I didn't get to know them as people with feelings and thoughts. Since I wanted them to be impressed with me, I withheld much of myself from them. I made it impossible to develop the loving, supportive intimacy and affection that I needed and wanted.

Yet I played the game, followed the rules as best I could. One primary rule was that men never spoke about their confusion. If I so much as hinted that everything wasn't all right, I thought men would disrespect me and women would not go out with me. I wanted to be liked, respected, and popular. This was the only way I knew how to do it.

I didn't hit women, but I used my verbal, emotional, and intellectual tools to control relationships and pressure women for sex when I wanted it. The following were some of my lines:

- Don't you like me?
- Have another drink.
- It's still early.
- Let's get to know each other better.
- You look tense. Let me give you a massage or rub your shoulders.
- Relax, you'll enjoy it.
- Show me you love me.
- You know, there are lots of other women out there.
- The other guys are only interested in sex, but I like you as a person.
- I spent a lot of money on you.
- It's time.
- You got me all excited.
- You can't leave me like this.
- You are special; you're different from other women.
- Let me show you I care.

- You don't know how good it can be.
- Let's just sleep together, no sex.
- You're responsible for this.
- I need you.
- Don't you like me?
- I'm not leaving.

I grew up believing there were two categories of sexual assault—violent and nonviolent. I thought rape was not inherently violent unless accompanied by a weapon such as a fist, a gun, or a knife. Nonviolent rape was, I believed, unfortunate, but not serious. In any case, I believed rape happened only to women who were asking for it from sleazy men. There seemed to me no connection between sexual assault and dating sex. Now that women have spoken up, we know how devastating and violent all rape is. We also know that most rape occurs between people who know each other. Yet even today, it is hard for many men and women to identify sexual assault clearly, because our dating patterns encourage the man to be aggressive and the woman to be accommodating.

Today, some people contend that rape is not about sex at all; it is simply an act of violence. People have said to me, "If I attacked you with a frying pan, you wouldn't call that cooking, would you?" I wish it were that simple.

Unfortunately, sex and violence are so intertwined for men that an easy separation is impossible. Violence is constantly glamorized and sexualized in our culture. The multibillion-dollar pornography industry is the clearest example of how we learn that power and control are tied to sexual arousal. Even in children's comic books, popular music, and magazine advertisements, we are constantly reminded that dominating and subduing women is sexy and arousing. The primary message men receive is that having sexual access to women and having someone sexually vulnerable to you are the quintessential signs of male power, the epitome of success. Women are constantly shown accompanying other signs of male power and success, such as fast cars, fancy stereos, money, and guns.

Some of these images portray the woman as protesting vigorously at first, then finally giving up and enjoying sex. In this way I was taught that women are somehow turned on by the aggression displayed by men. They may protest or say no at first to protect their reputation, but when they relax and enjoy it, they will get aroused by the man's aggression. If they don't, then there is something wrong with them.

The result of this training is that men are given permission to use sexual aggression to control women, to deny what we're doing and then assert that it's no big deal anyway. When I pushed women to have sex when they didn't want to, I assumed this was the way relations between men and women were naturally. If I felt a little remorse or guilt, I blamed the woman.

- She's fucked up.
- She's frigid.
- She's too emotional.
- She shouldn't have said that.
- She knew that would make me angry.
- She asked for it.
- She said no but she meant yes.
- I told her to stop and she didn't stop, so she deserved it.
- She's a tease.

There were so many layers of aggression, blame, and denial in my thoughts and actions that there was no way I could see the effects of my actions on the women around me. Anything they said or did I automatically reinterpreted to serve my needs. In fact, my responses were so automatic that when a woman did confront me with her anger at my behavior, I could honestly say I didn't intend to hurt her. I could then blame her for being too emotional, too sensitive, or too uptight. There was no way I could hear or understand the terror, pain, shame, anger, betrayal, and long-term scars women had from "normal" dating behavior.

My training to be a man made it difficult for me to see that I was acting on assumptions with little basis in reality. I started to listen to women—de Beauvoir, friends, and the wealth of writing from the women's movement. What I discovered was that the information I had received about women was wrong. I also found that it didn't work. Whenever I assumed that women were inferior and tried to dominate one, I was met with resistance, anger, frustration, and a very short friendship. My relations with women were a disaster. Women told me that I was arrogant, controlling, and had thick walls protecting my feelings.

These statements scared me, because they described the qualities I had disliked in my father. I had spent many years trying to be like him, but I was now terrified that I might have succeeded and would end up as isolated as he had become. I wanted to love, trust, and care for people. I wanted a long-term relationship that would create a family and children. Although I did not know how to go about this differently, at least I was beginning to understand what would be required of me.

As I realized the cost of my past behavior both to myself and the women around me, I could see I needed to examine how my training had also influenced my relationships with men. What I found was no less disturbing.

It's painful for men to admit that we have intimidated, pressured, or manipulated a woman to have sex when she didn't want to. We may feel guilty, ashamed, embarrassed, or defensive about our actions. The first step to eliminating violence in our relationships is to acknowledge how we have been trained to be abusive and how we have carried out that training, sometimes unintentionally. Only then can we move on.

The exercises on the following pages can help us acknowledge and reexamine what we have learned.

EXERCISE 4
Our Attitudes toward Women

1. Which of the statements or words from the "I never want to hear again" list on page 43 have you used or thought?
2. Look at the expectations in the Act Like a Lady

box on page 44. Which ones do you still expect
women to live up to?

3. How do you respond when a woman doesn't meet
your expectations?

4. What is one way you have hurt a woman (physically, emotionally, or verbally) in the recent past?
In what ways have you denied your actions?

5. How did you blame her for your actions?

6. How have you learned to express your anger
toward women?

7. In a conversation with a woman, concentrate on
listening to what she is saying and what she means
by what she says. Notice when you get distracted
by your own thoughts or by her body, or when you
feel impatient. *Practice this a lot.*

8. Notice how often during the day your thoughts
or activities are momentarily interrupted by your
noticing women's bodies.

9. Say to yourself, "If a woman says no to sex she
means no." What old learning keeps you from
accepting that?

10. Next time you hear a joke, a comment about
women drivers, or another put-down about
women, speak up and interrupt it. Notice how
scary it is to challenge this kind of male bonding.
How scary it is for you is a small measure of how
dangerous that environment is for women.

11. If you live with a woman, make a list of who does
the cooking, shopping, laundry, diapers (if you
have children), cleaning, and other household
chores. Ask her to look at it, and make changes to
the list together. Talk about the lists.

12. If you are verbally, emotionally, physically, or sexually abusive to even one woman, even occasionally,
get help.

EXERCISE 5 *
Men's Attitudes and the Cost to Women

At the Oakland Men's Project we've developed an exercise to help men see the cost of our actions on the women around us. This exercise is a simple set of statements. After each statement is read, we ask the men in the audience to stand up silently if it applies to them, then silently sit down again.

Most men can stand up for most of the statements. It's a very powerful and emotional experience to look out at the men who are standing and know that they share with you a past of painful and abusive training.

As you read through the following statements, check off the ones that apply to you.

Stand up silently if you have ever
- interrupted a woman by talking louder than she.
- not valued a woman's opinion about something because she was a woman.
- looked at a women's breasts while talking with her.
- interrupted what you were doing or saying to look at the body of a woman going past you.
- put down a woman you were with because she wasn't as pretty as other women.
- made a comment in public about a woman's body.
- discussed a woman's body with another man.
- been told by a woman that you are sexist.
- been told by a woman that she wanted more affection and less sex from you.
- lied to a woman with whom you were intimate about a sexual relationship with another woman.
- left care for birth control up to the woman with whom you had a sexual relationship.
- downplayed a woman's fear of male violence.
- called a woman a bitch, a slut, or a whore.

* Written by Allan Creighton.

- whistled at, yelled at, or grabbed a woman in public, either by yourself or as part of a group of other men.
- used your voice or body to scare or intimidate a woman.
- threatened to hurt a woman, break something of hers, or hurt yourself if she didn't do what you wanted her to do.
- hit, slapped, shoved, or pushed a woman.
- had sex with a woman when you knew she didn't want to.

THREE

Relating to Our Cultural and Ethnic Traditions

Ethnic Identity

Boys in America grow up learning many of the same things—how to be a "real" man, how to be sexual, how to relate to women. But there are major differences between us as well. We come from different classes, races, religions, and families. One of the most important influences in how we relate to male expectations is our cultural and ethnic identity. It took me a long time to realize that my Jewish culture and background had a major impact on how I saw my options as a man, and how I saw other men.

At an exhibit called "Jewish Life in America," there was a photo of a turn-of-the-century bodybuilding club. I asked myself, "What's this picture doing here?" Then I realized the men in the picture were Jewish—Jewish bodybuilders, brazenly physical and strong. My surprised response showed me how deeply I had internalized an image of Jewish men as not being athletic, physically strong, secure, or proud of their bodies. I realized that this had affected how I saw my own body—quick, agile, good at sports, but not strong. I began to understand how I had lost an important part of myself and my culture by internalizing the stereotypical images of Jewish men that mainstream society presented.

I grew up in a Jewish neighborhood, and about 30 percent of the students in the secondary schools I attended were Jewish. I was aware that the area I lived in was successful—full of doctors, lawyers, and other professionals—and that my friends and I did well in school.

When I was growing up I learned that Jewish men were

53

protective of their families, patient to a point, provided much for others, but were angry and wrathful when pushed. Judaism is filled with images of God and man, neither of whom tolerates injustice or disobedience and punishes it swiftly and thoroughly. Jewish fathers love their sons, marry off their daughters, and follow the dictates of God. The image I came to associate with Jewish men was one of cleverness, determination, and passion for freedom and justice. These attributes, not physical strength, gave us victory.

My appreciation of the worth and character of Jewish men was diminished by my American male training to value toughness and strength. Over the centuries, the Jewish people have survived oppression, attempts at extermination, and exile. Being part of that tradition of survival and courage should have brought a sense of pride. But because tales of more recent leaders with personal and political power were lacking, I felt some ambivalence about how masculine Jewish men were. I also blamed Jewish men for not winning—for not protecting their families from exile and destruction. Those of us who are men of minority cultures feel terrific anger at times at the discrimination and abuse we have experienced. I have heard comments, jokes, and put-downs about Jews from people before they find out I'm Jewish. I know the anger, resentment, and sometimes hate that are behind the comments.

As a Jewish man, I am tired of having to fight off people's expectations that I am clever, manipulative, good at business, rich, an expert on Jewish culture, a Zionist, progressive, loud, or from New York. I am angry about the history of violence against Jewish people in this country: the scapegoating, discrimination, swastikas on synagogues and cemeteries, threats, beatings, and firebombings.

Expressing that anger in assertive ways is not part of what we have learned about how to survive. Because of the powerlessness Jewish men feel in this society, standing up for ourselves makes us more visible and often feels too dangerous. All popular images of Jewish power aside, we have not had the power to protect ourselves from discrimination and violence.

Sometimes I take this anger home with me. I was taught that

Jewish men were responsible for their families. When my survival and success in the social world seem threatened, I have the urge to control my family and individual family members by threatening them or by emotionally and physically manipulating them. Where can I feel secure and on top of things if not at home?

Reclaiming my Jewish male history has helped me accept my anger and understand that I have choices. I read the book *They Fought Back** and other accounts of Jewish resistance. These stories helped dispel the myth of "passive Jews." As I read firsthand accounts of Holocaust survivors, both from the camps and from outside, I gained an agonizing understanding of the kinds of choices real Jewish men had to make in completely inhuman circumstances.

Some Jewish men fought back and died. Some fought back and survived. Some hid and survived. Some hid and died. Some fled and were caught; some of those survived. Many of those caught did not survive. They tried everything they could; sometimes it worked and sometimes it didn't. Understanding their choices, I could no longer blame them for their success or failure. This freed me to see my own choices.

There are many things Jewish men have done that I can take pride in and inspiration from. But there are few generalizations I can make that are accurate or meaningful. What we share as men, or as men of a particular culture, is the pressure to conform to certain stereotypes, carry out specific roles, carry on our cultural histories—often histories of oppression. Our diversity comes from our personal and cultural struggle to play out our lives with dignity and creativity. It is our personal response that makes us unique and belies the belief that we are homogenized into groups called "men," or "Jewish men," or "white males." As I learned about the diversity within my own culture, I could begin to see the diversity in others.

While I was in high school, our campus of three thousand received its first African American student, a young man. Everyone

---

* Yuri Suhl, *They Fought Back: The Story of the Jewish Resistance in Nazi Europe* (New York: Schocken Books, 1967).

in the school knew who he was. Since he was a fast runner and a good track-and-field competitor, we soon had all our expectations confirmed. Whoever he might be as a person, as an African American man he was "naturally" an excellent athlete. I never did meet him, but I felt I knew him because we all talked about what he could do on the field.

The other indirect knowledge of African American men I had, besides that gained from the professional baseball, football, and basketball stars I kept track of, was through locker-room talk. I played tennis. As we suited up every day after school with other athletes, there would be tales of "the spooks," how fast and skilled they were, and how dangerous.

There were no African American men in our lives. There was only a generic African American athlete. There were lots of Jewish men—some smart, some dumb, and most in-between—yet what I held on to was that our intelligence made us unique. Every other white male was not quite as smart, nothing special.

I went on to college to actually meet and know some African American men, to see the diversity of Jewish men, and to understand about racial discrimination—within the Jewish community as well as in the larger society.

Now I have worked for over twelve years at the Oakland Men's Project. A few years ago there were three of us on the staff: a Christian African American man, a Christian white man, and me. I thought I had moved beyond all those early stereotypes to treat everyone with justice and without prejudice. Yet looking at that turn-of-the-century picture of muscular Jewish men and recognizing my surprise at the image, I could see that I hadn't really moved beyond anything. I may have gained some pride in my feeling that Jewish men were smart, but I had given up the possibility that Jewish men could be strong and athletic. In imagining all African American men to be athletic, strong, and physically dangerous, I had denied their integrity and diversity. What damage had this done to my relationships with other men?

As the three of us at the Men's Project put our skills together and talked about our lives, I learned that the African American man, Eddie, had gone to college on a football scholarship. I didn't realize at the time that part of me had thought, "Of course, that's how he got into college." This is a man I work with, who is highly intelligent, and whom I respect and love a lot, but in a subtle way I was discounting his intelligence. Then he told me that the quarterback on the team was Jewish. Though I had no immediate images of Jewish football players, his statement didn't surprise me, because the quarterback has to be really smart to guide a team. Afterward, I realized I had assumed the quarterback was not on a football scholarship, that football for him was incidental to his academic career. I had accepted the stereotype that Jewish people have money, are smart, and don't need scholarships. Here I was, recreating the stereotypes in my thinking.

Our other co-worker, Allan, is white. I write about him last because at first I thought there was little to say about him. I thought I could speak in workshops about my experience as a Jewish man and Eddie could speak of himself as an African American man. We had important perspectives to contribute. Our white partner couldn't add much, I believed, because what can a bland representative of the dominant culture say?

In practice, Allan made vital contributions to how we thought about and presented our work on men's lives. Besides, there was a lot that was unique about him—his rural background, intelligence and sensitivity, and resistance to traditional thinking. At first I told myself that he was different from the average white man. Then I realized that the problem was in assuming I knew what the average white man was in the first place.

My stereotypes did not work. I was forced to throw away the lies I had learned and see each man for who he was. I needed to understand our cultural differences without letting them get between us as we worked together. This wasn't easy for any of us. My co-workers had their own stereotypes.

Eddie talked of his own internalized images of African American men as less competent than white men. He found himself continuing to act out of those images, expecting himself to be less capable than Allan or I. And while I was appreciating the valuable and unique contributions of Allan, he was discounting himself and his background, focusing on the importance of African American and Jewish perspectives.

At times it seemed that no matter how far our work together went, we could not get beyond our training. There were always new, more subtle levels of racism, anti-Semitism, and stereotypes that were like walls between us that threatened our ability to work together effectively. I also noticed that we were becoming closer as we shared our feelings, thoughts, and past experiences. We could see that the way we had been trained to assume cultural norms had locked us into fearing one another and destroyed the possibility of intimacy between us. This understanding helped us to avoid blaming ourselves and each other.

Everywhere in this country we see images of rich, white, heterosexual, able-bodied Protestant men in powerful positions. In reality there are very few of them. The rest of us do not qualify, in one way or another, to be part of the elite. Our differences from the dominant culture are liabilities, because we have fewer resources and no models to emulate.

Yet we are judged and we judge ourselves by the same standards of success, as the dominant culture. We might think there is something wrong with us and something wrong with our cultural background. This makes it easy for us to blame ourselves when we hear of violence directed at our people. We end up feeling alone.

If we are white we have been taught that we don't have cultural differences but have somehow all melted together into one homogeneous group. We no longer take pride in our ethnic histories, music, food, holidays, and rituals. We may feel jealous of those who have such identities, or guilty about white homogeneity or blandness. Yet we are unique with specific identities and histories. We may be of Irish, German, Czechoslovakian, or Finnish descent, or a mixture of several cultures. We have cultural heroes and cultural strengths to bring to our lives.

We may not be all the same, but our struggles to retain our dignity are not really all that different. From our personal histories and sociocultural backgrounds we forge our adult identities, visions, and actions. We take our understanding about who men are from our unique background. We then negotiate with the dominant culture about who we can be.

Growing up as a man in this society is a process of confronting one disappointment after another. We all start out as Superman in early boyhood. There is nothing we can't do. Whether it's James Bond, superheroes, movie stars, or professional athletes, we each pick the myths of strength we feel drawn to. And we see these heroes reap rewards of money, women, power, and independence. Our identities become tied into achieving these rewards without questioning them. Because these rewards seem so sweet, and the dangers of not achieving them are so great, most of us experience constant anxiety about who we are and what our worth is based on.

As we grow up, the realities of powerlessness and limits hit us. We can see the compromises the men around us have made. We can see the limited rewards available and how few there are at the top. Every test, grade, paper, evaluation, award, and sports competition defeats a few more of us. The better we are, the better the competition gets. At each level there are very few winners and large numbers of losers. When we are defeated, we do one of two things: (1) We look for an alternative understanding of men and men's lives that is more complex and realistic than the competitive one we were given, or (2) We accept the verdict, self-destruct, become abusive to others, withdraw from the community, and feed our anger and disappointment with violence or drugs.

A friend of mine said recently, "The reason that African American boys have so much difficulty in the world is because their hearts are broken. They are exposed to so much violence, poverty and despair so early that their hopes are crushed and their hearts are broken. How can they make good choices about their lives with broken hearts?"

All of us as men must face the reality of the limits on our

lives. But this process weighs differently on us, depending on our racial and class backgrounds and other factors that give us the education, training, money, and resources to deal with the disappointment.

If you are African American, Latino, or Asian American you might begin to see those limits at age eight, nine, ten, sometimes much earlier. You see how few rich and powerful men there are from your community, as defined by the dominant standards of money and power. You feel the lack of positive expectations from your teachers, counselors, and parents. You suffer the negative expectations and punishment and discouragement from these same adults.

If you are from a poor or working-class family, you quickly learn of your limits and possibilities, and you adjust your expectations accordingly. You see the kind of jobs the men in your community have, the kind of educational opportunities you have available, and the kind of money you can expect to make. Hope fades early, replaced by lowered goals, lowered self-worth, broken hearts, and anger. If you are gay or bisexual your limits become clear as you come out and begin to understand what is off-limits to you unless you seriously compromise your identity.

Adjusted or lowered expectations occur at different times for different people. They occur later for Jewish men who are white than for Jewish men of color. They happen later for middle-class men of color than for men of color from poor or working-class backgrounds. Race, ethnicity, and class influence when and how we meet the limits on our lives. One of the privileges of being in a social group with more power than another is that we can raise our children with more education, more material resources, and more hope for the future.

Unfortunately, we often justify these differences in power and privilege by blaming those less privileged and instilling fear about the less privileged into our youth. I was taught to fear all men. Growing up in Los Angeles I was taught that working-class and Latino men were physically dangerous to me, that African American men were dangerous to white women, and that gay men were dangerous to children. Other men were taught that Jewish men like me were dangerous because of our "international" power. These teachings allowed me to justify the violence that is done to people of color and to cover up the violence that white middle-class men are involved in.

In the middle-class community I grew up in, the physical and sexual assault of children, the rapes and wife battering, and a tremendous amount of white-collar crime were crimes committed by white, middle-class men. But we could ignore that and, in fact, scare women into feeling they needed us for protection by pointing to men of color out there who were "dangerous." The Germans during the Second World War and some Christian Americans today point to Jewish people as dangerous and try to hide the violence they committed toward Jewish people.

This racial scapegoating is an integral part of male violence and protects the real perpetrators of violence. We will look more closely at this phenomenon in the next section.

I still carry around a great deal of cultural baggage about men in general and about how men who are different than I am are "dangerous." Sometimes, for instance, I still find myself checking my wallet when an African American man approaches me on the street. I tend to trust white men more even though I know and fear the greater violence I see us perpetuating in positions of power. My racial stereotypes die hard.

We are all taught lies about ourselves and each other. It takes the slow, painful process of a lifetime to learn the truth. We are taught that differences are reasons to fear, put down, and target others for violence. Everyone is different. There is no normal, majority, mainstream, melted-together American model. It is not easy to value our differences and let go of training that judges and devalues other people. But we can decide now not to pass on the pain of that learning to people who are different than we are.

EXERCISE 6
Cultural, Racial, and Class Background

Cultural and Racial

1. Describe your cultural and racial background. If you are white, be specific. If you don't know, ask someone in your family who does.
2. In this society what are some of the limits that discrimination, violence, and prejudice put on your aspirations and possibilities?
3. At what age did you begin to see these limits?
4. What feelings did you have when you realized what the limits were? How have you coped with those feelings?
5. How have you dealt with those limits in your life?
6. How have your people struggled for freedom, rights, and economic justice against these limits?
7. What can you be proud of in your cultural background?
8. Name one man in your background that modeled positive qualities for you.
9. What are some of the contributions women have made to your culture?
10. Based on your cultural background, what are some of the negative things you have learned about women? Be very specific.
11. If you are white, what is one thing you can do to intervene against the violence directed toward people of color?
12. List three ways you learned to blame men from other cultural groups for the violence in society.
13. What is one thing about your culture you can pass on with pride to a younger person?

Class

14. What is your class background?
15. If different, what is your present class?
16. What did your class and cultural environment teach you about the proper way to control others, specifically women and children?
17. How has your class position—access to education, money, and other resources—helped or hindered your male training to be violent?
18. How does your job and your job security affect your level of anger and violence toward those around you?
19. List three men you might talk with about these questions.
20. List the one you will talk to first.

PART II

Men, Power, and Violence

Growing up male, relating to women, relating to men, cultural and ethnic identities— how do all these pieces of our lives fit together? This next part looks at the social framework of power and violence that we live within. Then we will explore in detail the relationship between alcohol and other drugs, anger, and violence, trying to answer the question, "Why are men violent?"

FOUR

Coming to Understand Men

There are differences among us in gender, racial, and ethnic heritage; age, physical ability, class, religion, sexual orientation, and so on. Some differences are visible, others are hidden. Some we look for automatically, others we may pretend not to see. These differences separate us into groups with varying amounts of power. Some groups have a lot of power. They have access to work, housing, education, physical security, legal protection, and representation in government. These groups often have this power at the expense of other, less powerful groups, whose access to such resources is limited or denied.

One primary root of male violence in the United States is the systematic, institutionalized imbalance of power between groups of people. Each of us belongs to many different groups. Some have more power and some have less power.

All of our interactions take place in this social system of power. Not power from within, but power *over.* In our society

- men have power over women
- adults over young people
- bosses over workers
- teachers over students
- white people over people of color
- Christians over Jews
- heterosexuals over gay, lesbian, and bisexuals
- formally educated over the not formally educated
- rich over poor
- able-bodied over physically challenged
- native-born over immigrants

A chart of this system looks something like this:

Power Chart

Powerful Group	*Less Powerful Group*
men	women
adults	young people
bosses	workers
teachers	students
whites	people of color
Christians	Jews
heterosexual	gay, lesbian, bisexual
formally educated	not formally educated
rich	poor
able-bodied	physically challenged
native-born	immigrant

The list goes on. Our society is based on the fundamental assumption that no two people are equal. Everyone has a place in the hierarchy. It is crucial to one's survival to know where one stands on the scale of power. It is crucial simply because if one has less power, one is vulnerable to violence, including rape, beating, harassment, verbal abuse, job and housing discrimination, police abuse, poor health care, or poverty.

These power relationships are categorical and systematic—all women are vulnerable to rape, all people of color are vulnerable to job and housing discrimination, all workers are vulnerable to low pay and firing, all children are vulnerable to taunting and physical abuse. These violations affect our ability to survive. They push us toward trying to survive at all costs, including passing on our pain to someone who is even more vulnerable, creating an ongoing cycle of violence.

We are taught to believe that this cycle of violence is the way things are and should be. This power imbalance is continually reaffirmed through the training of each generation of young people. All children in this country are raised in one way or another to receive false information about different groups of people—lies, jokes, stereotypes, rewritten history, biased research—which in turn trains us to justify, enforce, and continue the cycle of violence.

The system is reinforced in two ways. One is to blame the victims of violence. Instead of men being responsible for rape, we talk about how women ask for it by manipulating us or dressing provocatively. Instead of business owners being responsible for low pay and dangerous jobs, we say that workers are lazy, untrained, or unwilling to work. Instead of adults being responsible for poor schools, we say that students are unruly, not smart enough, undisciplined, or have low self-esteem. The following are some of the phrases we use:

- They deserved it.
- She asked for it.
- That's all they're good for.
- Some of them like it.
- They're lazy.
- They're too emotional.
- It's for their own good.
- She made me do it.
- You can't trust them.
- She or he should not have dressed that way, talked back, been out that late, acted like that, or pushed me.

The layer of blame we cast on groups of people prevents us from listening to them or understanding who they are. We believe we already know how things are, so we don't need to hear their side of it. We slip into generalizing, saying "they always . . ." or "women are . . ." Other people become objects, less important. If they challenge this order they need to be controlled and "put in their place." This phrase captures succinctly how we come to believe that there is a natural order in the world and that our place is on top. We then use this belief to justify further violence.

The second way power is reinforced takes place when groups of people with less power begin to listen to, and then internalize the lies and the stereotypes that the dominant group continually feeds them. Eventually, if we're on the low end of the power scale we'll wind up blaming ourselves for our powerlessness. As we blame ourselves we feel isolated, separate, and distrustful of others. I described in the last section how my co-workers and I had internalized lies about ourselves and each other—lies that hindered our ability to work together. As we persevered over the years at the Oakland Men's Project and shared our experiences as men of different backgrounds, and as we listened to women and other people from less powerful groups, we noticed some additional important aspects of this power chart.

First, we all fill slots on both sides of the chart. In some relationships we are powerful, in others less so. During a day we might move back and forth across the chart several times. Sometimes we hold power over others; other times someone holds power over us.

I will use a day in my partner Micki's life to illustrate how we move from powerful to less powerful roles and then back again. When our family gets up in the morning, it is immediately clear that the adults have power over the children. We tell them what they can eat, wear, and how fast to get ready. In addition, I was trained to assume control in the family, and Micki was trained to defer to me. Our attempts to balance power in our relationship is a constant fight against our individual training and society's norms.

Micki is a professor at a university. At work she has a department chairperson and an entire university administration with power over her. The men in her department exert more power than the women. Micki, on the other hand, is white and has more power than faculty members of color. She also has power over the department secretary and over her students. Gay and lesbian people have so little power in her department that it is not even safe for them to be "out."

As Micki moves through her day and interacts with co-workers, staff, administrators, and students, she and everyone around her adjust to the power dynamic in each relationship. The conversation of two students changes when a professor walks up; the conversation of two staff, two women, or two faculty members of color changes when a supervisor, male colleague, or white person approaches.

When Micki returns home, she and I have to reestablish our equality because I have received messages all day about how the man should be in charge, and she has had to deal with men who assume that she is less important and deserves less respect because she is a woman. After dinner, when she turns to Ariel and tells him to do his homework, she is clearly in charge. He may resist and argue, but they both know who has the final word.

Micki is also Christian, which means that when she asserts her values and promotes her holidays in our family, they have society's sanction. When I talk about Jewish values, or when we celebrate Jewish holidays, I have to introduce them as something different and explain why everybody doesn't celebrate them. I am well aware that it was a Jewish synagogue in our neighborhood, not a church, that was firebombed recently. When my children see decorations on the streets, they're for Christmas and Easter, not for Jewish holidays. Just like Micki, every one of us is in both powerful and less powerful groups in our society.

The second thing we notice about the system of power is that our training as men to be violent, abusive, and in control provides the tools for maintaining the system of inequality that generates violence. As police officers and soldiers in street wars and foreign wars, our bodies are the tools of enforcement. Women, on the other hand, are taught to be caring, passive, and dependent. Women can be violent, but women are not trained to be violent, men are. Our violence is usually much more dangerous.

We are trained to pass on our hurt and pain to those around us. We learn how to move out of powerlessness by relating to people who are less powerful. Or when that fails, we may turn the violence inward by using alcohol and other drugs or by committing suicide. We create a cycle of violence that all of us, men and women, adult and child, are taught to maintain. We are taught to turn our pain into violence.

As the work at Oakland Men's Project evolved and we explored the meaning of the power chart, we began to see how men can step out of the box, reject the violence they have been taught, and challenge the entire system of power and abuse.

We also came to understand how racial violence and class violence are connected to gender-based violence. All social inequalities perpetuate one another, because each teaches us that it is okay for some people to dominate others. Violence against women and children will not be stopped unless violence against people of color, gays, lesbians, Jews, disabled people, working-class people, elders, and the rest is also eliminated.

The cycle of violence shows us how survivors of violence could be violent themselves. For example, we see how teenaged men sometimes deal with being powerless by being violent toward their girlfriends. We also see that each of us as individuals can choose to carry on the training and pass on the violence or reject the training and stop the cycle. Rejecting the training is the only way to make our communities safer for all of us.

The power chart shows clearly that the system of inequality and violence is maintained because, in our fear of others, we are kept separate, isolated, and unsupported. The assumed model of power is "power over," or control. We believe someone has power only if he or she controls something or someone. Control is *the key issue* in men's lives. We learn early on that the world is a dangerous place. We are constantly vulnerable to violence. Being in control and staying safe are our primary concerns, and the basis for many of our actions. We can see much of men's violence as attempts to establish, reestablish, or retain control over another person or situation, or over the emotions that arise in us when there is conflict or tension. We control our tears, our feelings, and we train ourselves to control our bodies. We learn to hide, cover up, and ignore physical and emotional signals that we are not in control.

We also learn that we must control others so that they will not take advantage of us. Other men are likely to, and probably have at times, put us down, abused us, or used their power to gain advantage over us. We fear that women will unleash emotional intensity and demands that threaten to engulf us. We are afraid that young people will act independently, ignoring our desires and challenging our authority. It feels dangerous to let down our guard, loosen up, and trust that our lives will not get carried away. So we don't. We hold in the fear, pain, hurt, sadness, and excitement—we stay in control by using verbal, emotional, physical, and sexual abuse to control those around us.

Violence is the ultimate attempt to control. It is "power over." Unlearning male training means letting go of the need to control others. It also means redefining what it means to be powerful in the world. Another type of power is "inner power." This is the power we feel when we are successful, strong, or when we feel good about ourselves. Some people describe this as high self-esteem. They assume that if men had higher self-esteem they wouldn't need to assert their power by hurting others.

Inner power is certainly good for people to have, but it does not necessarily lead to less violence. Some men with high levels of self-esteem and personal power routinely beat their wives. Inner power can still make us domineering, arrogant, self-righteous, and insensitive to others.

What we need is a third kind of power, which Starhawk in her book *Truth or Dare** calls "power with." It is the power we gain when we come together *with* other people to make change in our lives—when we recognize that we are a community. At the Oakland Men's Project we speak of becoming allies, working together to make it safer for all of us.

The system of power we live under breaks down when we reject the cycle of violence and build alliances with each other. We gain strength and power by overcoming the isolation, crossing boundaries up and down the chart. There are many ways this can happen. For example, when workers come together they gain power. When workers recognize that women and people of color are also workers, the group becomes even more powerful. When

* Starhawk, *Truth or Dare: Encounters with Power, Authority, and Mystery* (San Francisco: Harper & Row, 1987).

women organize they become powerful. When white women recognize that women of color and working women are also part of their group, they become more powerful.

The hardest alliances to build are across the lines of power. We have been hurt directly by people who hold power over us, and it is hard to trust them. It is also hard for them to change. It is hard for me to become an ally of women because of all the training I have received about gender roles and male/female relationships. As a Jew it is hard for me to trust that gentiles will respect me and not be abusive or unintentionally hurtful. To protect myself from further abuse, I have to see by their actions, not by their words, that they are on my side.

When these alliances are built, they are very powerful. They contradict the entire system and the set of internalized beliefs on which it rests. They break the cycle of violence.

EXERCISE 7
Using the Power Chart (page 68)

1. Locate yourself in the categories up and down the power chart. What do you notice?
2. Pick a category in which you are on the less powerful side and answer the following questions. (If you are completely on the powerful side, then use the category for children, which we have all experienced.)
   A. What kinds of violence happen to your group?
   B. How is your group blamed for the violence?
   C. How have you blamed yourself or others in your group for the violence?
   D. Historically, how has your group come together to be more powerful?
   E. What are you proud of about your people?
   F. List several things you need from people who are on the other side of the chart and have more power than you.

3. For the following questions use the male/female line. If you are a woman use any line in which you are on the powerful side.
   A. List some things that women might need from you. Check these out with women you know.
   B. What is your next step in being a more powerful ally of women? Be as specific as possible.

FIVE

Drugs and Violence

So far we have talked about how the cycle of violence involves others. But there is another part of the cycle that is harder to penetrate because it takes pain and turns it into violence against ourselves. This is what my roommate Ron did.

Ron, another man, a woman, and I, all students, lived together in a house in Portland, Oregon, in 1969. Ron was just back from Vietnam. He had spent eleven months as a grunt, living in the jungle, killing, and being fired on. He had survived, as many of his friends hadn't, and returned to get a college education. He came back to a country and a local community increasingly galvanized against the war and less than honoring of its veterans.

Ron would sit in our living room at night, trying to tell us what it was like—a truly impossible task. Then he would switch. As he watched the lights on the houses across the street flicker through the blowing trees in our backyard, he would reenter the jungles of Vietnam. And he would be crazy for a while, but never enough for us to get scared. He used acid a lot, as he had in Vietnam, and we were used to the craziness of drugs. We not only didn't get scared, we hardly noticed, couldn't understand, and had no way of knowing that he was completely panicked, desperate, and dangerous. We talked about him, sat with him through acid trips, reported it all to the dean. But really, enemy gunfire in Southeast Portland?

One night in October when the wind was blowing through the trees and Ron was watching the flickering light, he panicked, returned to being a soldier, and attempted to rape our housemate. When we intervened, he came at us with a kitchen knife and then bolted down the street. The police found him holding a neighbor hostage. They arrested him and carted him off. All the while he was yelling invectives into the night about women and the dangers of the Vietcong.

A year later he was released, found his way to a gun shop, bought a weapon, and killed himself.

Ron had kept mostly to himself and his nightmares, and few on campus noticed, knew, or missed him. He was a man, had fought and killed, and had attempted to rape a woman. And his last victim was himself. This entire experience frightened me. There is nothing more terrifying than seeing a man you know, live with, and trust suddenly turn violent. At the time I was scared. Later I was angry. Years later, when I returned to my college and thought about Ron, I felt the sadness all over again and started to cry.

War, drugs, rape, assault, and suicide. Violence toward others and violence toward ourselves. What are the connections?

Drugs and violence. The words seem to go together. One image that immediately comes to mind is of an addict so desperate for more drugs that he will resort to any act of violence to get it or the money to buy it. Another image is of a group of people sitting around getting high to further excite and incite themselves, possibly to violence. Still another image is of organized crime units and gangs fighting over control of the drug market. These are all images with some truth but much fantasy in them.

The connection between drugs* and violence is not a one-to-one correlation. A lot of men who are not drug users are violent. Some men who are on drugs are violent when they are not using. Yet about 70 percent of men who hit their partners are on drugs. Counseling professionals recommend that if men who are violent are also drug-dependent they should be in a drug program *and* a program dealing with the violent behavior.

There is a tendency to view people's personal experiences

---

* I am using the word "drugs" to include alcohol, nicotine, and caffeine—legal but addictive substances that have dangerous short- and long-term effects on our lives. If you object to any of these drugs being included, note it and the reasons that come to mind. The exercises at the end of the chapter may address some of them.

either through the lens of violence or the lens of drug use, invoking a medical and psychological model of behavior that describes people as victims, survivors, recovering, abusers, or codependents. These models encourage people to take responsibility for their problem, seek help, and move on to a healthier life. This focus on a single factor as the key to healing, whether from drugs or violence, gives many people a powerful tool that allows them to see a pattern they have been living by and change it.

A lens, however, besides giving greater focus and clarity, also narrows vision. It excludes the complexity of people's daily lives. Drugs and violence intersect, but one cannot explain the other. From a drug treatment perspective, it is hard to understand and deal with violence. Most batterers' counseling programs are not equipped to deal with chemical dependency. Besides, both lenses are too narrow to include an understanding of the social structure we live within, the gender roles we are taught, and the power system we have to navigate. Therefore, they do little to help us understand the social constraints that limit our attempts to change. For instance, there are many culturally specific alcohol treatment programs, but only a few deal with racism and other forms of social violence.

The limits of such a lens became clearer to us recently at an Oakland Men's Project workshop for a drug recovery program. The multiracial group of twenty-five ranged in age from early twenties to late fifties. The building the workshop was held in was conveniently set across the street from a large public park that is a major trading area for drugs. Two-thirds of the group lived in a group home three blocks away.

We started the workshop by looking at female/male roles and relationships. Everyone was very attentive and eager to participate. Their program used a Twelve Step model, so they were used to talking in a group, sharing experiences, and looking at hard issues. Talking about the role of drugs in their lives, they were direct and honest. We soon found that it wasn't so easy, however, for them to talk about violence that was not specifically caused by their drug addictions.

They could easily admit that they had been violent when on drugs or when needing money for drugs. The drugs could be blamed for the violence. But they were more resistant to admitting to violence that wasn't drug-related. At one point, after we had done the bully role play, we gave the following directions to the group: "We'd like everyone to pair up and talk about one time when you pushed someone, abused them, made them do something they didn't want to do. In this exercise everything counts, little brothers and sisters, smaller children in the neighborhood, children at school, your own children now."

A lot of confusion followed these instructions, but some people reluctantly formed into pairs. Five people were sitting on a sofa, silently, so I went up to them.

I asked a large middle-aged man, "Have you ever bullied someone or pushed someone around?"

"No."

"Never?"

"No. I'm not that kind of person."

I asked another man. "How about you?"

"No, I haven't done that."

A woman sitting next to him spoke: "I don't believe you. You've told me how you hit your old lady."

"That was different. I gave her three warnings."

"Say more about that," I added.

"She was nagging me and nagging me and I told her three times to stop. After that I let her have it. I've never hit anyone without warning them. It was self-defense."

"That's what we're talking about, times when you felt pressured and reacted by hitting or bullying someone to make them do what you wanted, in this case to stop talking at you."

"I've done that with my children sometimes," the woman added.

We usually find that after a minute of initial surprise and resistance to seeing themselves as bullies, they all can remember a situation in which they pushed someone else around. But this group was much more resistant than most. It seemed that they wanted desperately to believe that drugs were the problem and staying off drugs was the solution, even to violence. Admitting that violence was a separate issue seemed to threaten how far they had come.

Yet, some admitted that their lives weren't as together as they wanted. Even off drugs they still found themselves being angry and abusive. One man said he thought he was more angry and more dangerous than he had ever been before. Drugs can distract a person from pain for a while. The effect of drugs and the need to get money to buy drugs can preoccupy a person so that the sources of pain and anger are ignored. But what is the interplay of the drugs and the violence?

We continued to keep this question in front of the group as we looked at different kinds of violent interpersonal situations, including bullying, domestic violence, and racism in a job interview. We started off with the father/son role play described earlier in this book. Many in the group had experienced abuse similar to that of the son in the role play. Starting out by talking about violence done to them made it safer to talk about times when they had abused others. When they could acknowledge how they had been hurt by gender roles, racism, abuse, and so forth, they could slowly admit when they had passed on that hurt to those around them.

The role play that created the most discussion and acknowledgment of violence with this group was the scene in which one of the group facilitators plays the white manager of a computer business. The other plays a young African American man coming to interview for a job. In the scene the white boss tries to steer the job applicant to a janitorial job because he assumes the young African American man can't handle the computer work. The scene is filled with subtle and not so subtle examples of racism, and it is clear that the boss is not going to hire the applicant for the job. After a discussion about what actually happened we asked, "Is this a violent scene? Was there violence involved?" These are their responses.

- "No, he didn't hit anybody."
- "Yes, because this guy was hurt."

- "Yeah, but he only used words."
- "It was emotional violence."
- "But he didn't have to respond to it."

We then had an extended discussion of what violence is and how people get hurt. A couple of people denied to the end that any violence had been involved, but most of us agreed that this man was attacked, hurt, angry, and in pain from his experience of the violence of racism and denial of job opportunities in our society.

With violence, as with drug abuse, it is essential that we take complete responsibility for our actions. We choose to be violent to ourselves and others, and we can choose to stop. But if we refuse to acknowledge the social pressures and abuse that push us to pass on our pain to others, we cannot effectively resist those pressures. In this example, acknowledging the effects of racism is a positive and important step toward resisting its effects and resisting drugs and violence. We must understand, not blame, external pressures so that we don't follow the response of the job applicant in the next scene below. After the job interview, people from the group talked with the applicant as if they were his friends.

PARTICIPANT ONE: What's the matter? You look down.

APPLICANT: Yeah, well, you would be too if you had to talk with that asshole.

PARTICIPANT TWO: What happened?

APPLICANT: He was just playing games. He wasn't going to hire an African American for that job. He was talking about how I should apply to be one of their janitors.

PARTICIPANT THREE: Sounds like some shit to me.

APPLICANT: Sure is. Hey, you got anything? I need to get high.

PARTICIPANT FOUR: What do you want to get high for?

APPLICANT: I can't keep doing this, man. I need to get high.

PARTICIPANT ONE: That's not going to help you. It's just gonna make it worse.

PARTICIPANT TWO: We should talk about it. Let's go for a walk or something.

APPLICANT: I don't want to talk about it. I want to forget it.

PARTICIPANT THREE: If you do that you'll mess up your program.

APPLICANT: A lot of good a program's gonna do me if I can't get a job.

PARTICIPANT ONE: You know this cat was a racist. He had an attitude toward you.

APPLICANT: So?

PARTICIPANT TWO: You didn't have a chance.

PARTICIPANT THREE: Don't let him get you like this, man.

PARTICIPANT ONE: Yeah, man, you should stick with it!

APPLICANT: I don't know, you guys, what can I do?

As the participants tried to talk their friend out of using drugs to numb the pain, it became more and more evident how power relationships can produce the pain that leads to both drugs and violence.

We understood that many people would come out of that interview discouraged and angry, looking for a fight, taking it home to spouses, partners, or children, or driving it out on the freeway. We could also see clearly how many others would take it out on themselves.

With this group we did not have to talk about the cost of the drug use. They already knew about that. As we talked about the costs of the violence, they were practically identical.

Costs

Drugs	*Violence*
arrest, jail, etc.	arrest, jail, etc.
loss of family	loss of family
danger from others	danger from others
no pride, low self-esteem	no pride, low self-esteem

friends   friends
jobs   jobs
loss of control   loss of control
lack of intimacy   lack of intimacy
isolation   isolation

We discovered another parallel between drugs and violence as the discussion continued. The participants talked of the tendency to take pain and powerlessness and turn it into anger. From anger it would translate into one of two forms, aggression or withdrawal. They would abuse others through violence or abuse themselves through suicide, drugs, stress-related illnesses, and early death. Often both were involved. The violence or drugs would fuel more pain, shame, or anger, which would continue the cycle.

Both drugs and violence are socially sanctioned ways that we, as men, have been allowed to express anger and pain, to be out of control. "Out of control" in these circumstances means we're not responsible for what we do, not fully conscious and competent. Until recently we have excused men's destructive actions with statements like the following:

- He can't control his liquor.
- When he gets angry he loses it.
- He doesn't remember anything he did last night.
- Something goes off inside and he can't control his anger.
- He just lost it completely.
- Two drinks and he's out of it.
- He has always been like that.
- He grew up in a violent alcoholic family.
- Men are just like that.

We are just now beginning to hold men responsible for what they do regardless of alcohol or other drug use, regardless of whether they lost control or intended to hurt, regardless of whether they remember, feel sorry, ashamed, or guilty.

We cannot avoid responsibility by saying that we have a disease, the wrong genes, or too much testosterone. There is absolutely no evidence that violent behavior is predetermined or irreversible. Our biological and physiological responses may be a factor in our behavior, but as adult males we make choices about what we do.

From this workshop we concluded that drugs contribute to the cycle of violence by allowing us to blame our violence on drugs and by allowing us to withdraw, lock the pain inside, and become self-destructive.

There is no simple description of the connections between drugs and violence. We have found that opening up the discussion of drug addiction to questions of personal and social powerlessness allows us to acknowledge violence in our lives and see how we can take more control over this and other problems. Becoming drug-free and violence-free, then, is not only a matter of personal benefit, it also breaks social patterns of abuse and becomes an important step for making the community safer and stronger for everyone.

EXERCISE 8
Drugs and Violence

Use the following set of drugs for these exercises.

tobacco	caffeine
alcohol	marijuana
tranquilizers	heroin
cocaine	uppers
downers	pain killers

1. Which drugs do you use daily? Which do you use more than once a week? Which ones do you use weekly?
2. What are the emotional and physical effects each drug has on you?

3. What costs from the list on pages 82–83 have you experienced? What other costs not on the list?
4. Have you ever not remembered what you did while you were drunk or high?
5. How does your drug use make you more passive?
6. What kinds of actions do alcohol and other drugs allow you to justify?
7. How do the drugs help you avoid getting close to another person?
8. Have you ever given alcohol or another drug to someone to make them vulnerable to your sexual advances?
9. Have you ever forced yourself on someone sexually while under the influence of alcohol or other drugs?
10. Have you ever used intimidation, manipulation, or violence to get illegal drugs or to get money for drugs?
11. Have you ever controlled, hit, or otherwise hurt another person while using alcohol or other drugs?
12. How has the use of drugs affected your health?
13. In trying to get clean and sober have you ever noticed a lot of anger, violence, or potential violence surfacing?
14. Ask a couple of people close to you to tell you honestly what effects they see drugs having on your personal, family, and work life.

Only you can get help from chemical dependency. Here are some things to remember:
As with violence,
- the problem will probably get worse;
- usage and frequency may increase;
- the damage to you and to those around you will probably escalate;
- you are probably already experiencing serious costs from this in your life;

- you are covering up the things in your life that you
  need to take care of;
- you don't need to live with the pain or the shame—
  life can be better;
- you don't need to do it yourself;
- there is help available;
- it isn't easy to stop using;
- the best time to start is now.

Many of us hope that when we become free of alcohol or other drugs, the violence in our lives will go away. This is usually a false hope. Drugs do not cause violence. We have to unlearn the habits that lead us to use violence. We have to deal with the pressures in our lives. We have to learn to talk with others and respond to the world in new ways that do not rely either on drugs or violence. This work is best done in groups because it is hard, lonely, and lengthy. Both processes can bring up tremendous amounts of anger.

SIX

Anger Is Not the Problem

When we look at men's lives and the effects of our actions on those around us, it can look like anger is the problem. But anger is not the problem, violence is. It is a tragedy that we have been trained to turn pain into anger and anger into violence. We need to harness, work with, and use our misdirected violence and self-destructive anger to rebuild our lives and change our communities.

Anger does not have to be destructive. It can be a guide to injustice, a clue to powerlessness. Anger can excite, mobilize, and bring us together. It is a touchstone of our deepest sense of truth and rightness. It lets us know when we're getting ripped off or when we've compromised too much. Anger can be the force behind revolution, consciousness-raising, pride, and community building.

We have been taught to fear anger because we associate it with violence. It is scary. Therefore, when we feel angry ourselves, we get scared. We might stop it, stuff it, laugh it off, or pretend it doesn't matter.

We like to think of ourselves as nice guys. We want people to like us. We often say yes to requests when we really want to say no. We often say no to our needs when we really should say yes. The result is that we are constantly building up anger and resentment because we are taking care of others and not ourselves—our needs are not getting met.

Most of the time we pretend to ourselves and to those around us that we are not really angry. But there comes a time when we can't take anymore. Then the anger explodes out of us in loud and frightening ways. After the explosion we are so scared that we clamp down again, try harder not to get angry, and begin another cycle.

The power and strength of our anger are frightening because we don't have models of men who

- get angry without becoming abusive or violent;
- can express a range of feelings, including anger;
- communicate their wants and needs effectively in nonthreatening ways.

We can become models of men who do these things.

As men we have two crucial tasks before us in order to use anger powerfully and not abusively. The first is to separate anger from the many other feelings we were never allowed to express. We need to acknowledge, feel, and express the love, caring, sadness, hurt, dismay, affection, gentleness, and hope we carry with us. As we separate these feelings from the anger, the second task becomes understanding where our anger comes from, what we can do about it, and how we can express it in positive ways.

We have been taught to expect women to take care of us, to nurture and support us in the ways our mothers were supposed to. It is easy to blame women and to project our anger onto them. We might feel they've caused our pain and hurt. Women, we must recognize, don't have this kind of power in our lives. Not blaming them and not blaming ourselves as well are part of dealing with anger and recognizing where its roots lie.

Another part is learning to express and talk through anger with the people around us. This means staying connected when we're angry instead of walking away, getting busy, withdrawing, or distracting attention away from the issues that divide us. We must also learn to listen as well as speak to each other. And speaking here means from the heart and mind. We must learn to compromise, give and take, and look for inclusive, more complex solutions. Patience, respect, courage, empathy, perseverance, and commitment are some of the virtues we need to develop for this to work.

Expressing anger fully, directly, and in a nonthreatening way is not easy. We need to know when to blow off steam, walk away, ask for a time-out. A good time-out might be to say to your partner, "I'm too angry to continue. I'm going to take a thirty-minute time-out to walk or talk with a friend so I can come back and continue talking with you without resorting to violence." Then use the time-out to relax or distract yourself or think about the interaction, but not to feed or build your anger. Doing something physical or being alone is necessary before we can continue talking. We also need to distinguish feelings of anger from physical restlessness, tension, or the need for sexual affection and expression. Sometimes dancing, playing sports, or shouting is all we need to do to get over our anger. Other times we may need to hold someone or be held, to touch and talk intimately.

These are skills we can learn and bring to our everyday lives. At the end of this chapter are exercises that illustrate a variety of approaches and some useful starting places.

When we can clear away our other needs, stay with our anger without resorting to violence or blame, and express a full range of feelings, then we can move on to deal with the causes of our anger. This involves identifying the deeper sociopolitical problems that need community attention. Through concerted effort we can find ways to work cooperatively for change. Poor working conditions and low pay, lack of support for parenting, poor housing, poor educational systems, racial and sexual violence in our own past and in our communities, female and male role expectations—these are some of the things that cause pain, despair, anger, and violence. We can develop skills for working with others to eliminate the institutional sources of our anger.

Social change is slow, and the lack of response to our efforts can itself produce more anger and frustration. But if we focus on the work that *we can* do, we can turn that frustration into determination, that despair into hope. Everywhere in our society people guided by their anger are making changes in their own lives and in their communities.

As men we can use our anger to guide us in constructing a more just society. Or we can continue to use it to destroy ourselves and those around us. We each have that choice to make. We need to remember that anger is not the cause of violence.

EXERCISE 9
Skills for Anger Work

These exercises are not meant to be accomplished in one sitting. Each one could take a week or more. It will take you at least three to four months of doing these exercises to learn how to turn anger into a positive force in your life. It is more easily done with others. Find a friend, or better yet, find a small group of men to work with. You don't need to do it alone. If you do some of these exercises by yourself, make sure you write down your responses and your feelings. Having a ready reference will keep you focused and will give you a more accurate measure of your progress.

Self-Awareness Skills
Skill: Ability to know when you are angry.
Exercise: Keep a log and write down the times each day that you get angry. How do you know you are angry? How does your body feel when you are angry?

Skill: Ability to know what triggers your anger.
Exercise: Notice what situations, words, or phrases commonly make you angry. Write them down.

Skill: Ability to know what you are angry about.
Exercise: Each time you are angry, trace the feeling back to the original source. For example, if someone cuts in front of you while you're driving, are you really angry at that or are you carrying anger home from work?

Skill: Ability to know how you express anger.
Exercise: Describe what you do when you get angry. Describe how your parents got angry. What are the parallels?

Skill: Ability to prevent violence.
Exercise: Practice taking time-outs when you notice that you are about to be abusive. Use them when needed.

Skill: Ability to consciously decide how to respond.
Exercise: Each time you get angry, write down three different ways you can respond to the person or situation.

Skill: Ability to identify and express other feelings.
Exercise: Make a list of forty feelings. For a week, notice how many different feelings you are aware of. Each time you get angry, ask yourself what feelings may be behind the anger.

Communication Skills
Skill: Ability to communicate feelings directly.
Exercise: Practice telling your partner and others how you feel during the week. Use simple sentences like: "I'm excited that . . ." or "I'm sad that . . ."

Skill: Ability to listen to others.
Exercise: Practice listening to and then repeating what someone else says.

Skill: Ability to communicate wants and needs nonthreateningly.
Exercise: Practice asking for what you want directly, without threats and without expecting that your needs will always be met.

Skill: Ability to deal with disappointment.
Exercise: Notice how you feel when you don't get what you want. Is it different depending on who is denying you? Record what other choices you have for pursuing your needs.

Skill: Ability to know your effect on others.
Exercise: Ask people close to you how you express yourself to them. Ask them if you are intimidating in any way. Find out how they see you.

Skill: Ability to say no.
Exercise: Practice saying no three times next week in situations that you would normally say yes to. Notice what the experience is like.

Skill: Ability to identify key issues in your life.

Exercise: List those areas of your life in which you experience on-going stress. Identify the root of the problem; make a list of possible courses of action, resources to help you, and people to get support from. Talk with at least one supportive person about each situation. Contact at least two resources you listed.

SEVEN

Why Are Men Violent?

We all know this man. He's friendly, plays with his children, does good work, is fun at parties, and helps out when asked. What a surprise it is when we learn he has hit his wife, molested his daughter, or beat his son. We are almost always shocked to learn that a neighbor, brother, community leader, or co-worker has hit, maimed, sexually abused or killed someone close to him.

We are most surprised and confused if we are the targets of that violence. We know the good side of the man, the side we love and relate to every day. We know the boyish qualities that endear him to us, and the serious, responsible ways he deals with the world. Yet, at some time, we have seen a terrifying vision of desperation and abuse coming toward us that we did not know existed. Even between the outbursts, it is hard to believe so much anger and aggression lives in the same man.

The mystery in our society is not that some men are angry and violent. Looking at our jobs, male roles, and images of violence around us, we might expect that. What is difficult to comprehend is that there is another side to millions of us nice, decent, law-abiding American men—a side carefully hidden that can erupt into physical and sexual aggression which intimidates and destroys family members and others who are close to us. This violence is directed at people we love, people we live with. Like the proverbial bully, we hurt people who are generally shorter, smaller, younger, and less powerful than we are.

We are represented in a group of incest offenders such as the one I co-facilitated for two years. These men had all committed sexual assault against their daughters, nieces, sisters, cousins, or sons. Generally, the survivors were between the ages of six and fourteen, and the incest had occurred over a period of one to four years. A precondition for being in this group was that the men admit to the incest. Some of the participants were in the process of being reunited with their families, others were permanently estranged. This was an ongoing therapy group that met once a week, with the men usually staying in the group from one and a half to two and a half years.

There was Brian, black, early twenties, short-term relationships, short-term jobs. He had molested a cousin, had problems with alcohol, had an upper middle-class background.

There was Don, Filipino, early fifties, heavyset, four marriages, molested a stepdaughter. He had hung out in gangs as an escape from his father's beatings.

Dick, white, early forties, stable family and stable middle-class family background, white-collar worker, second marriage. He'd molested a daughter.

Joe, black, early twenties, newly married with a baby, computer programmer. He'd molested a niece.

Mark, late thirties, came from a poor white farm-worker family, one of several kids, white-collar worker. He'd molested a stepdaughter.

Pete, Filipino, late thirties, wealthy family background, newspaper correspondent. He'd molested a stepdaughter.

Fred, white, mid-fifties, low-functioning, many jobs, illiterate. He'd molested a stepson.

Dick, white, early forties, Vietnam vet and prisoner of war, well educated, electrician, college education. He has three daughters and molested two of them.

John, white, early fifties, minister. He'd molested two daughters.

The men came from diverse racial, economic, educational, and geographic backgrounds. But the same kind of sexual offense had brought them to us. Some had committed only the incest, others were chronically violent. Two of the group members had killed people in Vietnam. Some were very peaceful, law-abiding citizens.

I had been briefed with information about the group members

by the other facilitator, who had been running the group alone prior to my arrival. I arrived for my first session expecting to be able to tell that these men were child molesters. I'm not sure what I expected to notice about them. Their sleaziness? Their smell? Their manner? A deep mark of guilt and crime on their souls? I was looking for something that would confirm what I knew about men and violence.

I introduced myself. They in turn gave me their names and a brief summary of their sexual offenses. I realized immediately that there was nothing for me to grasp, no concrete way to identify them. I could have passed any of these men on the street and noticed nothing. I could have been their friend and still have never known. And I did not know why these men would have turned to the young girls or boys in their lives for their sexual needs. Over the next two years, I looked for clues.

We explored their personal backgrounds, their family histories, the details of their molestations, their relationships with their wives and partners, and their working lives. Why were these men violent? Why was the violence sexual?

This group committed violence toward children, but several of these men were violent toward themselves as well. A couple of them went to bars every Saturday night and got into fights. Some of these men drank, used other drugs, or smoked cigarettes in self-destructive patterns. A couple had simply let their bodies go and were overweight and in extremely poor health. Not every man in the group was self-destructive, but several were clearly shortening their lives by their behavior. The question of why men were violent had to encompass why we were violent toward ourselves.

Suicide, sexual assault, battery, murder—these are clearly violent acts. But alcohol and other drug use, emotional and psychological intimidation and abuse, and dangerous sports and hobbies are also violent. Workaholic patterns that lead to heart attacks, chronic neglect of our bodies that can lead to early death, failure to get help or medical care that lead to preventable deaths, and cutting off wives, partners, children, and friends so that intimacy is destroyed—this is also violence. These are common ways for men to respond to their own pain and abuse.

When we advocate local and national policies that encourage war, prevent people from meeting basic needs, or destroy the environment, we are supporting violent behavior. Some acts of violence are more intentional or conscious than others. But all violence leads to shorter or stunted lives for ourselves and those around us. All violence is life-denying.

Current estimates are that one of every six boys is sexually assaulted and that at least half have been beaten up by a father or other adult.* Essentially, all men were beaten up, harassed, intimidated, sexually assaulted or humiliated at some point in childhood. These men who we know, love, and depend on carry out their childhood pain on others and teach others to do the same.

Understanding this training gives us two handles for working with men. First, if we have learned to be violent, we can unlearn it. And since this learning came from men, the most powerful way to learn other, gentler ways is also from men. Second, if we were hurt as children, we can heal that hurt, work through the anger, and become stronger and more loving adults without retaliating or striking out. Part of the hurt was the shame and humiliation of being young, male, and vulnerable to violence. Working in a group with other men and realizing that we were not weak and that everyone is vulnerable to violence helps alleviate some of those feelings.

The men in the incest offenders group had all experienced violence as children. Several had been sexually assaulted, some had been beaten by fathers, others were involved in street violence. That early training in powerlessness carried over into their adult lives. In some cases, during their incest activities, they achieved some power for themselves. But even this feeling was short-lived because of the furtiveness and desperation of the acts. Most of them felt vulnerable and not in control at work, at home, with

* These figures are based on estimates from child assualt prevention workers. They are very rough, because so few men report sexual abuse and physical violence is often not even identified as abuse.

their children or partners, and with other men. They described their own actions as reactions to pressures and demands from those around them.

Some of them appeared quite successful and powerful on the outside. The male role demands that no matter what our inner state, we must act and appear to be confident, strong, and in control. This contradiction can make us want to control and abuse others to prove that our appearance of power is no facade. The resulting anxiety pushes us toward violence.

We fear that we are marked, that somewhere, someday, someone will discover the shameful secret that we are not all-powerful. In everyday life that fear must be kept secret. The power of a group breaks through the fear, making it safe enough to talk. And we can listen to other men talk about experiences very much like ours.

Some men in the incest group took a year before revealing their own histories of abuse. This revelation of vulnerability and shame was harder for them than describing the circumstances of the molestation they committed. For most of the men it was the first time they had admitted to anyone that they had been abused. We could watch the healing as each began to describe what had happened. These men began to feel less alone, less ashamed, and began to reach to the anger, sadness, and pain of those experiences.

Although we're vulnerable to abuse when we're children, there is no point in a man's life when he is safe from assault by other men. There are many ways we are humiliated or challenged by our bosses, government officials, co-workers—even strangers—and by the assaults on the women and young people we are trained to protect. If we do not respond with manly strength, pride, and aggression—even if it is inappropriate or suicidal to do so—we are subject to the same shame, humiliation, and doubt we experienced in childhood.

Some men look for opportunities to prove their manhood; others avoid it if at all possible. But there is a sense among nearly all of us that we have to be ready to call forth all our anger and physical strength to meet any threat to our sense of self-worth. Teasing,

name-calling, losing in competition, feeling cornered or not respected—even minor incidents like these can trigger the overwhelming panic that tells us we have to prove we are men. We can
never prove it definitively and finally. Each time we assert our
manhood and the world challenges it yet again, we doubt it and
are pushed to assert it more forcefully and more angrily toward
others.

Those "others" are often the people in our lives we expect to
dominate, like the women we live with. The incest offenders in my
group were not able to dominate women verbally or physically
because they either idolized them or were too scared of them. Instead, they molested their children, stepchildren, nephews, or
nieces. This accomplished three things for them. First, it allowed
them to attack their wives indirectly and regain some power in
their marriages. Second, it allowed them to pass on their own pain
to someone more vulnerable. Third, it reaffirmed their ability to
control others, a seemingly essential attribute of manhood.

Since the links between sexuality and violence run so deep in
our male training, issues of power and control can easily get acted
out in sexual ways. The primary message we receive is that having
sexual access to women, having someone sexually vulnerable to
us, is the epitome of male power.

But there is another set of messages in conflict with the first—
that which portrays our role as protectors of women and children.
All of the men in our group hated sexual offenders and thought of
them as scum of the earth. They reconfirmed their own humiliation, shame, and vulnerability to violence every time they committed incest.

The act of incest epitomizes the male dilemma in our society.
The men in this group were able to control others, thereby prov-
ing they were successful. At the same time, they proved their failure as men because they had to hurt someone they loved in order
to assert their control. Hurting those we love destroys our sense
of moral integrity and achieves only a momentary and ultimately
empty sense of respect and control, thus increasing our sense of
failure and pain. The men in this group were caught in a cycle of

sexual abuse that they knew was wrong and that they even abhorred, but they couldn't stop without admitting they were utter failures as men.

These men love their families, including their victims, immensely. They hope to contribute to the world. But they also act out of a history which asserts that children belong to adults and adults can do with them what they want. It asserts that violence toward children is not a crime but part of the adult male prerogative. The men grew up in a society where children were routinely neglected, abused, discounted, impoverished, and violated. They themselves have experienced these kinds of abuse.

Active participation in a group begins to break that pattern. It helps men understand how they have been set up to act aggressively and abusively toward others. It gives them a chance to hear other men share what it is like to be male in our society. By understanding their training they can see the contradictions in the messages they received. Then they can choose different responses to the constant pressure to act like a man. They can begin to step out of the box.

Working with the incest offenders group led me to wonder why some men do not commit violence. As I wondered about this question I reflected on my own experiences with anger. When I am angry or frustrated at work or with my partner, are there ways I take that anger out on the children because I think I can get away with it?

I am sure there are times when I do. When I am very tired and angry, the last thing I can tolerate is noisy children pestering me for attention or spilling a glass of water on my papers. I started to notice how I, and most of the adults I know, dump our frustration onto our children.

Young people do act in ways that make us angry, and sometimes anger is an appropriate response to what they do. But their provocations are often only a lightning rod for the rest of the unexpressed rage and frustration in our lives. Similarly, when someone cuts in front of my car, or maligns my children, or breaks something important to me, I can feel my anger escalate because it is safe. I have an excuse and an easy target for a backlog of anger that I can't express to my partner or my co-workers.

As I see myself and other adults yell at children out of proportion to what they have done, I see a parallel in the ways we have used our anger to cover our pain. For instance, when I am wrestling with my children and I am accidentally hurt, I may yell at them in anger. What I really want to do is to cry out in pain and have someone comfort me. When my children break something important to me, I may yell and punish them. What I really want to do is cry and mourn the loss of a treasured possession. But the anger comes so fast that I do not notice the initial feelings of pain, hurt, sadness, or loss.

Many times a sudden burst of anger seems the more appropriate response from the father and Man of the Family. That was what I was familiar and most comfortable with. Expressing anger is safe because it diverts attention away from my feelings and places blame on the child.

There are other parallels between me and the men with whom I work. I find my children's bodies beautiful. I enjoy watching them move and run and dance and play. I enjoy holding them. I am not saying that I ever wanted to have sexual contact with them, but I have to acknowledge having enjoyed the sensuousness of their bodies.

Working with the group forced me to ask myself about our differences. What kept me from hitting my children, from exploiting them sexually? We all loved our children in very similar ways. But the love, and the anger as well, were framed by prior intent. I had decided not to hit children under any circumstances. I had decided not to exploit them sexually.

I have come close to hitting them. My children have occasionally done things that made me so angry I wanted to pick them up and fling them across the room. I would find it strange if any adult living with young people had not reached that same point of frustration. What prevented me from following through on that desire to reassert control through force was my prior decision that I would not do so. I had decided the harm, danger, and long-term effects to the child and our relationship were too great. I also believe that no person deserves to be hit under any circumstances. Yet even with that decision and belief, sometimes I feel tempted to fall back on being physical because it seems like that is all I have left.

Current approaches for working with violent behavior are based on theories that emphasize psychological and personal background, gender roles, and male socialization as causes of violence. In most cases it is accepted that harm occurred in the past to the perpetrator and that current violence is a result of that personal or social history of abuse.

These theories miss something crucial. The past cannot totally explain why men commit violence. The present is not simply the result of all past experiences and training. Not everyone who was sexually assaulted commits sexual assault. Not every boy who was beaten up grows up to beat his children, wife, or partner.

Men decide to commit acts of violence. Men decide whether to take responsibility for those acts, or to avoid responsibility. There are standard tactics men who are abusive use to avoid responsibility. The first and often primary tactic is *denial*. The batterer says, "I didn't hit her."

If the denial doesn't hold up because of the evidence, e.g. she has a broken arm, bruises, a miscarriage, then the violence is *minimized*. The batterer says, "I didn't hit her, well, it was only a slap." When the minimization doesn't hold up because she is in the hospital, then the batterer's effort shifts to a combination of *justifying the violence* and *blaming the victim*. "She asked for it." "She should have known not to say that to me." If the discussion is more general, then men might make statements like, "Women are too emotional/manipulative, backstabbing." Blaming shifts the focus from the perpetrator of violence to the survivors, subtly blaming them for being inferior or vulnerable to violence. This kind of blaming is common and easy to see in sexual assault cases where authorities question the victim on the appropriateness of where she was or what she was wearing. Refocusing on the responsible person is much easier when we describe exactly what was done by the person who was abusive. He hit her. He broke her arm. He put her in the hospital. We need to keep the focus on the abuser, not on the survivor of violence.

We want to hold adults responsible for what they do. Therefore we must carefully and accurately investigate what happened so that we can stop the violence. However, if we don't look at the overall context and take differentials of power into account, we can be susceptible to the tactic of *redefinition*. For example, he says, "It was mutual combat." "She hit me first." "It takes two to fight." We need to ask questions such as who was hurt and who wasn't? Who is scared of the other's violence? Who is bigger, stronger, or more trained in combat? And what is the longer term pattern of abuse in this relationship?

At this point the individual with more power, who has clearly done something that resulted in some kind of damage, might claim that the damage was *unintentional* and therefore his responsibility was minimal. The batterer says things such as "I didn't intend to hit her," "I didn't mean to hit her so hard," or "Things got out of hand."

Claims of innocence by someone who has hurt you are always suspect. Adults are responsible for their actions and for the results of those actions. "I didn't mean to" is not an acceptable legal or moral excuse for being violent toward another person. In addition, actual intent is often discernible from the pattern of action of the perpetrator. When a man systematically tries to control a woman and then says, "I didn't mean to hit her," he is saying that he hoped to control her by non-physical means. When all else failed he resorted to hitting. The issue is power and control. Intent is clearly evident in the overall pattern of behavior.

Another way men minimize responsibility is by claiming that the violence happened *in the past* and is no longer an issue. The batterer says, "It's over with" or "I'll never do it again." He may finally be claiming responsibility (albeit indirectly) but he asserts that things have changed. Often part of his claim is that the effects of the violence are similarly in the past and shouldn't influence us anymore. The trauma, pain, mistrust, fear, disrespect and vulnerability should just be forgotten. This discounts the seriousness of the violence, blames the survivor for not being able to let go of it and move on, and focuses on the perpetrator's words, not his actions. All we have is his promise that it won't happen again.

Patterns of abuse do not disappear because the abuser wishes them to, or because he promises to do better next time. We need to see concrete changes in closely monitored behavior and not get caught up in the apologies or the promises the abuser might make. Not buying the tactic of *it's over now* means keeping our attention on *her* safety and *his* behavior.

If the abuser is unable to maintain that the violence was all in the past, he may switch to another tactic to make a current situation seem to be the exception. The batterer may say it was only *an isolated occurrence*. Similarly, as a society we may say that it's really only a few men who are like that—it is not systemic or institutionalized. In the case of domestic violence we contend that only a few men are batterers, most men treat women well. However, if 25–33 percent of all heterosexual relationships have an incident of the man hitting the woman—three to five million such incidents a year—then we are clearly talking about a social issue, not the isolated anger of a few men. In an individual relationship the batterer may only hit a woman once, or occasionally—just enough to intimidate her, subdue her, or remind her that he is stronger and could do more serious damage to her. Again, we must look to the larger patterns, both within a relationship and within our society, to see that it is not just an isolated occurrence.

Counterattack and *competing victimization* are also tactics men use to avoid responsibility for violence. When all else fails and responsibility for violence is inexorably falling on the shoulders of those who committed the acts themselves, there is a counterattack, an attempt to claim a reversal of the power relationships. Men usually combine this approach with the final tactic, competing victimization. An individual batterer might say, "She really has all the power in our family." Or, "If I didn't hit her she would run all over me." On a national level there are more and more claims that men are battered by women too, that women win custody and men don't, and that there is too much male bashing.

To counter this tactic we must go back to what happened, who has power, and what violence is being done. Who ended up in the hospital, and who remained in control of the family resources? In the claims above we find that in about 95 percent of domestic violence cases the woman is the victim of a pattern of abuse, and in 5 percent of the cases the man is the victim.* In 80 percent of custody cases the man does not even contest custody. In the remaining 20 percent where the man wants custody, men get custody 63 percent of the time.† The reality is not what men would claim, nor what media reporting would have us believe.

We now have a national discussion of gender in which men are claiming that they are getting mistreated, they have no opportunities to speak without attack, and, in fact, they are the victims of male bashing.

Those with power have many resources for having their view of reality prevail, and they have a lot at stake in maintaining the status quo. Men will employ the above tactics to defend their interests just as white people use them to defend white privilege from charges of racism. We must be aware of these tactics and able to counter them. When unchallenged, they can be used to justify further violence. If we keep our eyes clearly on the power and the violence, we can see that these tactics are transparent for what they are, attempts to prevent placing responsibility on those who commit and benefit from acts of violence. Our strongest tools are a critical analysis of who has power, and an understanding of the patterns and consequences of behaviors and policies. Ultimately we know that individual decisions to change abusive behavior are seldom carried through without social sanctions.

Holding a man accountable for his actions, now, in the present, gives him a clear message.

---

* Women's Action Coalition. *Stats: The Facts About Women.* New York: New Press, 1993. Pps 55–57.
† Weitzman, L. J. *The Divorce Revolution: The Unexpected Social and Economic Consequences for Women and Children in America.* New York: Free Press, 1985.

The deterrent that keeps most men from continuing to hit their wives or partners is arrest. I am not advocating locking up men who hit their wives or partners, or denying them support, counseling, and other aid. I am not even promoting intervention by the criminal justice system in all instances. The legal system tends to attack poor, working people and people of color and locks them up disproportionately. We cannot use violence against women as an excuse for further violence against certain groups of men. The criminal justice system cannot take care of this problem for us.

But as long as we give ourselves the message that sexually assaulting or physically beating a woman or child is not significant, we cannot end the violence. When we don't treat such violence as a crime, men clearly don't take the sanctions against it seriously. We need to confront men's acts of violence.

The threat of arrest is a particularly good inhibitor of incest and battery. The reason the incest offenders' group worked and the men were able to change was, in large part, that the participants had been arrested or threatened with arrest. Few men voluntarily admit to being violent. Few men seek help until the police step in or the woman leaves.

One way to hold men accountable for specific acts of violence is not to accept excuses such as the following:

- I don't know what came over me, but I lost control.
- I couldn't stop myself.
- It was the alcohol, drugs, etc.
- She made me do it.
- I was hit when I was a kid. It didn't hurt me.
- That's the way I was taught to do it.
- I'm too old to change.

Is a man who hurts someone really out of control? All of these excuses are based on the assumption that he had no other choice and that the assault was automatic, natural, inevitable, and therefore acceptable. One effective way to take apart these excuses is to take a recent violent act and to act it out with the man who committed it. Here is an example:

FACILITATOR: John, describe what happened.

JOHN: We were in the kitchen and she was talking to me and I just lost control and hit her.

FACILITATOR: Where were you standing?

JOHN: I was standing here and she was there by the sink.

FACILITATOR: What was she saying?

JOHN: She was talking about how we needed money, and she knows I don't like her to criticize how much I make.

FACILITATOR: What did you do?

JOHN: I hit her.

FACILITATOR: Why didn't you kick her?

JOHN: She is real good at dodging kicks; I've tried that.

FACILITATOR: So you decided not to kick her?

JOHN: Yeah, I hit her instead.

FACILITATOR: Was your fist closed?

JOHN: No, I didn't want to leave a mark; she had to go to work later.

FACILITATOR: So you decided to hit her with an open palm so you wouldn't leave any marks?

JOHN: Yes, and then I left.

FACILITATOR: Did you do anything else before you left? Try to remember all the details.

JOHN: I guess I unplugged the phone as I left.

FACILITATOR: Why did you do that?

JOHN: She called the police the last time and I didn't want to go through that again.

FACILITATOR: So you thought about what she would do next?

JOHN: Uh-huh. And then I went out to the garage.

FACILITATOR: How did you decide to go there?

JOHN: I knew the children were in the living room watching television and I didn't want them to be involved. I thought she would go into the bedroom so that left the garage for me.

FACILITATOR: You knew where everyone in the house was and you decided where to go based on that?

JOHN: Yes.

This kind of detailed reenactment can be very helpful to a man trying to end his violent behavior. It makes clear he was making a series of decisions about what to do. He was in full control of his actions. He may not like accepting this, since at the time he may have felt trapped and without options.

To make better decisions he needs to feel he has more options. Men commit acts of violence partly because (1) there is little critical judgment of our actions, (2) there is denial that we make decisions about what we do, and (3) there is no strong and articulate community holding us accountable for our intentions and our actions. Relying on personal resolve not to hit, abuse, or violate people cannot work in a social environment where assault and interpersonal violence is accepted, extolled, and modeled.

It is only recently that our society has considered rape, spousal abuse, child abuse, incest, and other interpersonal acts of violence serious crimes. Only recently has there been agreement that these acts are wrong even if they take place in intimate family relationships. Oftentimes there is still no serious prosecution of offenders, education in the community, or empowerment of the survivors to challenge the social acceptance of violence. Denial and collusion have been the community's contribution to the violence.

I know that most men do not want to be violent. We walk around desperately trying to control our anger. We are scared of hurting ourselves and others. When our anger explodes we are surprised, confused, ashamed, and embarrassed. We promise and want to believe that it will never happen again. So we try even harder to control our rage. Our anger turns to violence because we have been given no other options, tools, skills, or models.

If we intend to stop being violent we must decide to step out of male roles that encourage violence. In doing this we say that we will not act out the expectations of the community. We will challenge not only the role, but also the structures that the role supports. Martin Luther King, Gandhi, and Cesar Chavez are models of men who stepped out of the box and rejected violence. These men used the love of people, their faith, minds, and voices to become powerful without violence. They did not do it alone. They came together with others, directing their anger toward change.

In stepping out of the box they were called names, attacked, beaten up. Yet they had the courage to develop alternatives to violence.

Yes, some of these men were killed. But many more men die prematurely because of violence. The loss of these men and others through violence diminishes all of us. The question for each of us is not how will we die, but how will we live. Will we be part of the cycle of violence? Or will we break the cycle and take a stand against it?

These men may seem special and their behavior out of reach for you and me. Yet we each know men who have stepped out of the box. And we can think of times when we decided to choose an alternative to the violence presented to us.

It should be clear by now that I am saying men are violent not just because of personality or background, but also because we have created a society in which power is defined as the ability to control others, with violence as the ultimate form of control. Our society still upholds the idea that if you can get what you want by controlling others through verbal or emotional manipulation, financial pressure, or intellectual argument, that is the best thing to do. But if none of that works it is okay to fall back on physical force. And then, of course, it is their fault for forcing us to go that far.

Why are men violent? is a good question. But to end the violence we need to stop explaining it and more seriously confront it. We need to focus our attention on creating a community in which violence is unacceptable. This involves acknowledging the level of violence that exists and the damage it causes. It means challenging men to change and to raise their boys to be different. We need to do in our communities what some of us are trying to do in our families: intentionally create safe, loving, nonviolent relationships and an environment that nourishes, respects, and supports each person's integrity, growth, and creative abilities.

As men there is much that we can do. We each have to take responsibility for our pain, anger, and violence. But personal growth, or even a million batterers' and sexual offenders' groups in the country, won't stem the tide of violence. We heal and change through community action, by accepting our roles as parents, partners, friends, and caretakers of the earth. The rest of this book is about how we develop alternatives to violence.

<hr>

EXERCISE 10
Dealing with Violence

Unlearning male training means letting go of the need to control others through physical, sexual, and emotional abuse and manipulation. While doing the following exercises adapted from Ginny NiCarthy's book *Getting Free,* * think about women, older people or children in your family, neighbors, or co-workers as possible targets of your efforts to control.

Admitting Physical Violence
Use the following list to take inventory of your violent physical behavior. Place a check next to each behavior that applies to you, no matter how long ago it happened.

Have you ever
- pushed or shoved someone?
- held someone to keep them from leaving?
- slapped or bitten someone?
- kicked or choked someone?
- hit or punched someone?
- thrown objects at another person?
- locked a family member out of the house?
- abandoned someone in a dangerous place?
- refused to help someone close to you when she was sick, injured, or pregnant?
- subjected someone to reckless driving?
- forced someone off the road or kept them from driving?
- forced a woman or child to be sexual?

---

* Ginny NiCarthy, *Getting Free* (Seattle: Seal Press 1982).

- used a weapon to threaten or hurt a person?
- "reminded" someone of your ability to hurt them?
- used your physical size to intimidate or scare someone?

1. Now list each way that you are physically abusive.
2. What do you achieve by getting physical?
3. What does it cost you?
4. Do you ever feel afraid that you might hurt someone?
5. List people who you have hurt in the past or are presently hurting.
6. List three preventive steps you can take now to stop the abuse.
7. List three things you can do to stop when you are becoming physically abusive.
8. List three supportive people you can call when you are becoming abusive.

Admitting Sexual Violence

Use the following list to take inventory of your violent sexual behavior. Place a check next to each behavior that applies to you, no matter how long ago it happened.

Have you ever
- told jokes about women, gays, lesbians, or bisexuals or made demeaning remarks about them?
- treated women as sex objects?
- been jealously angry, assuming a woman or a man was a slut or whore?
- criticized a person's performance or adequacy as a sexual partner?
- insisted on unwanted touching with someone?
- had sex with someone when you knew he or she didn't want to?
- withheld sex and affection?
- used names like "whore," "frigid," "fag," or "dyke" to degrade someone you were in a relationship with?

- forced a person to strip when he or she didn't want to?
- publicly showed sexual interest in or had affairs with another person after agreeing to a monogamous relationship?
- forced a person to have sex with you, someone else, or to watch others have sex?
- forced unwanted sexual acts on someone?
- forced sex after beating that person?
- forced sex when a person was sick or it was a danger to his or her health?
- forced sex or hurt a person with objects or weapons?
- committed sexual acts that involved inflicting pain on your partner?
- taken pictures of a person nude or in sexually revealing poses in order to exploit him or her to gain money?

1. Now list any ways you think you might have sexually abused people.
2. Have you ever used sex to get back at, degrade, or manipulate another person?
3. What has it cost you to be sexually abusive?
4. If there are people who you have sexually abused, list them.
5. How do you think your actions have affected them?
6. List three ways you can get your sexual needs met without being abusive.
7. How have you used sexual abuse to prove to yourself or others that you are dominant over another person?
8. What is your next step in treating other people's bodies with respect and integrity?

Admitting Emotional Violence

Many of us are taught to get what we want through emotional abuse so we won't have to assault others physically or sexually. Sometimes emotional abuse is used as a first step in objectifying and justifying violence against another person. Use the following list to take inventory of your violent emotional behavior. Place a check next to each behavior that applies to you, no matter how long ago it happened.

Have you ever

- ridiculed or ignored a person's feelings?
- ridiculed, insulted or otherwise attacked a person's most valued beliefs, religion, race, heritage, or class?
- withheld approval, appreciation, or affection as punishment?
- continually criticized a person, called him or her names, or shouted at him or her?
- insulted or drove away a person's family or friends?
- humiliated a person in private or public?
- kept a person from working?
- refused to work or to share money with a person you were living with?
- took money away from, stole from, or otherwise controlled the financial affairs of another?
- threatened to withdraw financial support from someone who was dependent on you?
- told a person about your sexual affairs in order to embarrass or humiliate him or her?
- harassed a person about affairs you imagined he or she was having?
- raised your voice to dominate a conversation or assert control?
- used your size or body to threaten or intimidate?
- punished or deprived children when you were angry at a woman?
- threatened to kidnap the children if a woman left you?
- abused pets to hurt or intimidate another person?
- threatened to physically hurt a person or that person's family?

The abusive behaviors listed in the exercises vary tremendously in severity. It makes no difference whether you do some once or regularly. The exercise is designed to help you think seriously about how you may have hurt others.

Probably many of the behaviors you check have been directed toward you as well, which means that you know how painful abuse can be. Here, we are focusing on ways we have learned to be physically, sexually, and emotionally abusive to others. Saying that "She does these things to me and worse," or "I only do them in self-defense," or "It's just normal fighting" does not take away *your* responsibility to control *your* actions.

Please write down your answers to the following questions:

1. From the list of emotional abuses in the exercise, note what kinds you have used to control relationships.
2. Where did you learn them or see them modeled?
3. What does it cost you and your relationships?
4. If you are emotionally abusive, does this lead to physical or sexual abuse?
5. What internal physical or emotional signals do you have when you are becoming emotionally abusive?
6. List three ways you can de-escalate an argument to avoid or reduce emotional abuse.

Of the following skills for successful communication and intimacy, which do you have and which do you need to develop? Place a check in the appropriate column.

	Have	*Need to Develop*
• ability to listen to others		
• ability to state needs clearly		
• ability to see choices		
• ability to compromise		
• ability to respect others' opinions		
• ability to share feelings		
• ability to accept outside help		
• ability to admit mistakes		

	Have	*Need to Develop*

- ability to appreciate and
  nurture others
- ability to value myself
- patience
- courage
- honesty

7. List three skills that are a priority for you to develop to prevent further abuse.
8. Make a plan for developing these skills. Make a call to someone who will support you and hold you accountable in these areas.

PART III

Breaking the Patterns

Most of us have spent decades being trained in the patterns and beliefs identified in this book. It might seem nearly impossible to change, but every day people begin changing major parts of their lives. Men stop being violent, men and women let go of the need for alcohol and other drugs, adults change the way they interact with their children and end abuse in their homes.

This next part looks at what we need to do as men to make these kinds of changes in our lives. It begins by looking at how spirituality and religion have influenced our lives. Then our roles as fathers, lovers, workers, and teachers are reexamined and redefined. Finally, we look at how we can give and receive help, and how we can intervene with other men who need our support.

EIGHT

Men, Spirituality, and Religion

Finding Our Souls

There are many connections between male violence and religion. Religious wars, inquisitions, persecutions, witch burnings, and the colonization and destruction of indigenous cultures by missionaries are the most obvious examples of how violence has been commited in the name of religion. The more personal connection is in the ways we attempt to control our spiritual experiences through denial, anger, and authoritarian expressions of belief, missionary zeal, and religiously sanctioned violence toward others.

Violence is the ultimate attempt to control. Men use violence to control women, children, our own bodies, and the natural world. We also attempt to control our spirituality. Why is men's spirituality often expressed through control and violence? Looking at this question may give us some understanding of how we can relinquish control and reconnect with other people, with the earth itself, and with whatever greater life force we might believe in. *

I want to describe my own spiritual odyssey. For me it's a useful starting place when looking at more general issues of manhood and control.

In my mid-teens I became convinced that faith was for the gullible, nonthinking masses. I rejected my Jewish religion, all

* I use *religion* to refer to the organized social structures in which our spiritual experiences are described, shared, ritualized, and preserved. *Spirituality* refers to the unique, intense experiences and understanding people have of a reality greater than themselves, an experience of connection with the totality of things. Some people have such experiences within the structure of a religion, others don't.

117

religion, in fact. I wanted to lead a rational, thinking life. When I went away to college I became interested in the Buddhist tradition of meditation. I needed to center myself in an intellectual, academic environment. Not just any practice would do. I was finally a man, away from home, on my own. I was through being powerless. I was going to tough it out, hold it in, stay safe, and be in control.

Buddhist meditation seemed to offer a perfect practice for staying in control. You could sit forever, attaining no mind or ego attachment to anything—no dependencies, cares or connections. It seemed to me to be a way to attain complete detachment from the world, a way to stay completely in control.

This "spiritual" search was purely intellectual, although it was prompted by the feeling that something was missing from my life. My searching was not based on any spiritual experience, but on a quest for meaning. It was my way to challenge and rebel against the status quo of organized religion.

I thought I was embracing something different from the Western thinking with which I had grown up. But the qualities I attributed to Zen Buddhism were mostly projections of our Western, rational, scientific stance and of my perceptions of what it meant to be a man in our society. My concept of meditation matched my concept of how to be a successful American male—completely in control and not vulnerable to anyone or anything.

Spiritual experiences arise spontaneously. We don't decide, rationally, to have one. They are powerful, overwhelming insights that tear asunder the fabric of control we use to maintain our everyday lives. They offer us glimpses of realities and perspectives that transcend day-to-day life. Because men spend so much effort maintaining control, it is harder for us than for women to have, and acknowledge having, spiritual experiences. It is harder to have spiritual experiences because we have learned how to ignore or reinterpret physical sensations or emotions that have nothing to do with the rational world. We have also learned how to deny or not talk about experiences that might be intense, inexplicable, or otherwise "unmanly."

Since part of our male identity is based on thinking of ourselves as rational and uninfluenced by faith or feeling, we back ourselves into a corner when we have experiences that contradict our self-image. If we put down people who allow themselves to have such nonrational, unscientific experiences, it can be extremely threatening to admit to them ourselves.

I grew up believing that humans were rational beings and should be in charge of managing everything here on earth. Not feeling any connection with other life, it was easy for me to condone polluting and destroying the natural environment. Life was not sacred, rationality and control were. Anything not planned or managed was in the way—whether it was my body, my feelings, another person, a forest, or an animal. I felt responsible for reasserting control and making sure everything was in order.

Ultimately, this thinking led to isolation and loneliness. I didn't have any way to connect with people or the environment. I was good at relating socially, but without acknowledging my soul, my deep inner connections to the life around me, I could not get close to anything or anyone. There were lots of things I was good at, but what was I good for?

Not having a sense of purpose opens the door to drugs and violence. Without an inner sense of connection to a life force greater than our own we may become tremendously isolated, lonely, and angry at others. Without this connection it becomes easy to objectify and abuse others and ourselves. Turning to drugs or violence is an easy way to numb the emptiness and give up. These feelings of isolation are reinforced in our society when material possessions, status, and money matter more than caring for people, the earth, and ourselves.

When nobody else seems to care, we deny that we care. We cover over our hurt with drugs or lash out in violence. When nobody cares we end up violating each other.

In my late twenties I began having some experiences I couldn't explain rationally. I began to feel the presence of nonhuman energy around me. When I became very quiet I could hear an inner voice that seemed to come from beyond my personal experience. This

voice was calm but comforting, offering me insight that I didn't or-
dinarily have.

I also began to feel connections with the environment as I
spent more time outside of cities. I walked among two- and three-
thousand-year-old redwoods that were strong, enduring, and
alive. I sat by rivers and listened to their songs. I saw a beauty
and intelligence in animals that I had never recognized.

At the same time I began to listen to other people. I had never
thought much about listening. It was a passive thing that women
seemed to do better than men. I had spent my time practicing how
to talk and present myself and my ideas. That's how I had learned
that men got ahead in our competitive world. I had believed that
those who listened, watched, or waited would be left behind. But
when I allowed myself to listen to other people, watch the birds,
trees, plants, and other animals around me and wait for inspiration
from outside of myself, I wasn't at all left behind. It was just the
opposite—I felt more a part of things. At the same time, it became
more and more difficult for me to justify controlling anything.

I did not want this to be happening. In fact, at first I pretended
it wasn't. I was pretty good at suppressing feelings and experiences that were uncomfortable, but the force of these experiences
was just too hard to ignore. My first reactions to feeling the loss
of control were worry and confusion. Was I going to hear voices
next? Was I crazy? Would I just flip out all the way?

I felt scared. I couldn't rationally figure out what was happening. One of my fears was that these experiences were softer, more
emotional, more feminine, and that this was an area where
women belonged, not I. I felt I was losing male credibility by believing in something outside myself.

Not all men discounted me when I talked about spiritual experiences, but many did. Most of the men I knew were still where
I had been before these experiences, skeptical and disbelieving. I
had styled myself as Mr. Rational, the logical, scientific thinker
who accepted nothing on faith. I had consistently put down other
people who talked about psychic experiences, connections with
the natural world, or communication with spiritual forces. I had

denied these experiences were even possible and had constructed my life in such a way that I wouldn't allow them to happen. They spoke of too much intensity, too much emotional energy, too much spontaneity, too much passion, too much vulnerability to greater forces.

It was quite embarrassing. Now I found myself on the other side of the discussion. Now I was the one coming off as believing, gullible, naive, and too emotional. Other men were logical and reasonable. At times it was very difficult to maintain my beliefs in the face of such skepticism. I could feel myself losing credibility with men I liked, trusted, and with whom I had friendships.

I was scared and insecure. I needed to convince others that my experiences were real, true, and valid. I became more zealous than my experiences would indicate so that all the doubts I had could be overcome. I also found myself getting very angry with male friends for being so closed to new things, so "reasonable" and in control that they couldn't allow themselves the possibility of new insights. I was angry, of course, because they reminded me a lot of myself as I had been not so long ago.

I realize now that as I tried to convince them of the truth of my experiences it was really myself I was talking to. I was still unsure of the significance of my life and afraid I would discover I had been misled or duped by my feelings.

Since I couldn't just trust my experiences in the face of such skepticism, I looked for books to support me. I read the Seth books and Carlos Castaneda. I read theosophical books and the Bible. I looked at astrology. I reread the Buddhist texts I was familiar with, and I looked up the scientific research available on psychic phenomenon.

Despite the skepticism of friends and my own inner doubts, embarrassment, and confusion, I felt comforted, excited, and connected in ways that I longed for and needed. My experiences were impossible to deny—I just didn't know how to assimilate them into my everyday life. I had only my male training to use as a guide.

Some people believe in God, however God is defined. Others don't. All of us who affirm a connection to some greater reality or

God know the sense of purpose and caring that affirmation brings. As I experienced an immediate and direct sense of purpose, I began to pay more attention to my inner life, my feelings, my body, my friends, and the environment around me. I felt overwhelmed and transformed. I felt reborn into a new world of dazzling complexity and wholeness. Unfortunately, a lot of my early male training was also reborn with me.

My spiritual experiences led me to acknowledge that I was not in control the way I thought I was. I realized there are forces greater than my own influencing my life. One common response for men in the face of such experiences is to give our independence and power to an organization or spiritual leader and become extremely dependent. We might join a cult or rigid religious group. We might connect with a fundamental sect of a traditional religion. There are any number of organized groups that allow us to give up our power and let someone else make decisions for us. Several times when I was feeling confused or overwhelmed I was tempted to do this.

Another factor that reinforces this tendency is that the models we have of God tend to look like either a God of wrath or a God of compassion. A God of compassion is gentle, loving, and forgiving, leading us back to feelings and emotions—women's domain. In the male world, this kind of God looks dangerous and dysfunctional. Men are more likely to connect with a God of wrath, of sternness, authority, moral strictness, and judgment. This is, after all, the model we have for men in authority. This kind of God also lets us continue to identify with our traditional images of male strength and male anger. It also allows us to take a stance of righteous anger toward our feelings, our bodies, our relationships with others, and the world in general if we feel those tenets are being violated. We may look for a group to join that embodies and reaffirms this kind of model of authority and godliness.

A part of me did not really want to give up control to anyone or to be vulnerable to others. I wanted to go it alone, assert my independence, and keep it to myself. I had done this with my meditative practice. Sure, I believed in a reality greater than my own, but I wanted to tuck that away and keep on keeping on, pretending it did not effect the rest of my life. It seemed at times as though I had only two choices—give myself up completely to my experiences and to some group that would guide my life, or hang on to my independence, my control, and try to keep my spiritual life under wraps.

It took me years before I realized I could remain a healthy, autonomous adult, living interdependently with others in a spiritual community. The realization came when I began to seriously question the male role and began to see how deeply my spiritual feelings were conditioned by my training.

The daily facts of men's lives makes spirituality confusing, painful, and unfulfilling. The fears of being less of a man also kept me from claiming and exploring my spiritual experiences. We have seen how living in the box cuts us off from our bodies, our feelings, and from other people. It also cuts us off from the environment and from our own spirituality. We can only reclaim our connection to all life and our delight in the world if we begin to listen and reject our training to be scared, unexpressive, in control, and isolated. Then we can integrate what we learn with our own experiences in ways that steady and strengthen us.

Reconnecting to our spiritual selves does not eliminate violence, end drug abuse, or change our relationship to the environment or to other people. But it does reaffirm our power to reclaim our lives. Such a reaffirmation can rekindle the hope and inspiration we need to become the kind of parents, partners, and teachers we need to be to eliminate violence.

EXERCISE 11
Male Spirituality

1. List any images connected to men and authority, control or violence, that you saw in your religious background.
2. How are men in control in your religion?

3. What did you learn about women through your religious training?

4. What are the images and qualities of a God of wrath and a God of compassion in our society? Are you drawn to either one? Why?

5. Has your religious training ever encouraged you to look down on, exclude, or justify controlling another group of people?

6. Have you ever said or believed that God says some people are inferior to you or deserve to be punished?

7. Name some men who have stepped out of the box in your religious background or in your present spiritual practice.

8. What qualities do they represent that you can use as models for yourself?

9. If you have ever felt connected to a reality greater than yourself, describe what that experience was and what it meant to you.

10. Where were you, who were you with, what time was it? What were the key elements and circumstances that helped create that experience?

11. How has that experience affected your life since then?

12. What might you gain by re-creating those circumstances more regularly?

13. How can you use your sense of connection to the people and the world around you to nurture life and counter the pressure to control, exploit, or be violent?

NINE

Becoming Fathers

I am a father not only at home, but also in the classroom and in workshops. Fathering for me is more than a biological relationship to younger people. It means being a caring, nurturing adult member of the community. Caring and nurturing are the opposites of violence.

I always thought I would be a father. That seemed to be what happened to boys. Yet there were always older, more powerful men who acted fatherly toward me. And my own father was there to remind me that I was still a son. In my twenties I expected that I would be a father one day; I had no sense that I was a father already.

I didn't become a father when my partner and I had our first child. I didn't become a father when my own father died. Perhaps there was no magical moment when I became a parent. But I know the process started earlier than either of those two events.

When I left home for college I entered a much more complex world than I had known existed. As I learned about the problems in that world, I could see my own problems in a more realistic perspective. I grew to care about other people and the problems in our community. I knew that parents cared about the community they lived in. I knew there were self-serving and narrow-minded ways to care, and generous and inclusive ways to care. What marked the role of parent to me was caring for other people.

When I left college I began meeting more people who had children. I spent time with them, baby-sat for them, even lived for a while with children in collective households. I now began to see myself as an adult in relation to young people. I could feel my own power in contrast to theirs. I could feel satisfaction in offering my strength, experience, and support to their lives. I knew that parents cared for children and that there were angry, abusive ways to care and gentle, loving ways to care. Caring for children was another mark of a parent to me.

I also saw that if I truly cared about people, I had to care about the environment they lived in—an environment that had been neglected. My concern had to be strong whether it was glass on the sidewalk, pollution in the air, toxic chemicals in the water, or the threat of nuclear destruction. Our society encourages us to think primarily of our own needs and survival. We are pushed to feel unable to care for anything, even ourselves. We are encouraged to deny our own adult power and act as if we were children, and the worst stereotype of children at that.

This affects men in a particular way. Although we are adult men, we are encouraged to act as if we were still sons, unprepared to take on adult roles and responsibilities. Much of the writing by men about being sons says that we were hurt by our fathers. It is true that many of us were physically and sexually assaulted by them, and many others felt their absence or the coldness, isolation, and distance they handled us with. They are the ones who failed to provide the love, care, and intimacy we needed when we were young. Healing from our relationships with our fathers is important work, and never easy.

Blaming our fathers for the loss allows us to release the anger we feel and to heal from the hurt. As a personal growth process this can be valuable. But getting angry at and blaming our fathers won't help us if that's where we stop the process. By and large, our fathers did what they felt they had to. They fathered us the way they had been taught and showed us love the only ways they knew how.

Traditionally, there were clearer rites of passage. Symbols of power were, in some cases, handed down through each generation. But I don't think fathers were ever anxious to pass on authority and control in the family. Today, we can no more expect parental approval and permission for our lives than we ever could. And we don't need it. As men we need to move into the present. The time of our power as fathers is now.

And we need to expand the "father" role to become a "parent" role shared by men and women equally. There is a profound truth in the role of a parent as a nurturing, providing, active member of a family and community, for whom there is no higher responsible voice, nobody to blame. Our children need us to be adults. So do our partners and adult friends.

EXERCISE 12
Becoming a Father

1. Describe your father, as much as you know or remember about him.
2. What did he pass on to you?
3. If he were standing in front of you today, even if you never knew him, how would you complete this sentence: "Dad, I needed you to . . ."
4. What have you blamed your father for?
5. What have you blamed your mother for?
6. How are your answers to questions four and five related?
7. Say to yourself, "I am responsible for my life today and my parents are responsible for theirs. I forgive them for how they raised me." What feelings come up? What do you give up when you don't blame them?
8. Who were other father figures in your life?
9. What qualities do you think are important in a father?
10. What are ways that a father can nurture younger people?
11. Who are you father to, biological or not, at this point in your life?
12. What do you provide them as a father?

13. What is lacking so far in your fathering?
14. Who are other young people you might provide a father model for?
15. What activities can you become involved in that will improve the lives of the young people in your community?
16. How can you better care for the environment around you?
17. What is the next step you are going to take to become a more powerful and caring father?

TEN

Becoming Partners

Becoming fathers isn't the only task we face as adult men. We also need to become partners with other adults around us. Developing warm, intimate, and loving relationships with other adults promotes cooperation and interdependence.

When I was in my late twenties, I got to know a woman I had met through my sister. She and I shared a lot of interests and had fun together. As our relationship grew, talk of living together and having a family came up. We were both clear that we did not want to do it as we had been taught. We had each been part of too many couples that had run aground on traditional male and female expectations. Neither of us wanted a relationship that recreated the subservience expected of women or the rigidity expected of men.

During this period my sexual life changed substantially. For the first time I felt secure sexually. My partner, Micki, was steady, mature, and responsible. I could relax. This allowed me to start taking in pleasure from her in ways that were completely new to me.

I found myself less preoccupied with orgasms and enjoying lots of other sexual sensations in my body. As we experimented with different sexual activities that did not involve intercourse, the importance of my maintaining an erection diminished. Sex itself became much more intense, exciting, and fun because the challenge of and responsibility for making it all happen were balanced between us.

Our relationship continued to grow. Other lovers in our lives became less important. We began to share dreams of having a family together. As our talk progressed, our intimacy grew.

Sometimes I was terrified by our closeness. I would say to myself, "Oh my God, this is serious! Am I ready for this? Is she the one, the one and only, my enchanted princess, the special lifelong mate I have been looking for?" When the physical and emotional connection to her felt so full, so complete, so encompassing, I would escape the intensity and the intimacy by retreating into my head with questions. Fortunately, the reality of our closeness was greater than my fear.

Acknowledging the depth of our relationship, Micki and I talked about and wrote down our ideas and expectations. Talking would help us know our feelings better and bring agreement on major issues. Writing it down would ensure we both understood each other clearly and would help us anticipate difficulties that might arise.

It wasn't easy to establish our lives together in ways that did not re-create patterns of male dominance, female economic dependence, or specialized emotional or domestic roles. Micki was strong, financially independent, politically experienced, and unwilling to settle for anything less than complete equality. She kept challenging the assumptions I would make about women. And I was beginning to understand the importance of listening to her and respecting her insights. The more we talked about creating a new kind of relationship, the more I could see that I had lots of personal growth to do.

My belief that women were not very smart was deeply entrenched. There was a tone of condescension that I had to work on eliminating. I didn't know how to pay full attention to what Micki was saying. Instead of listening I would prepare what I was going to say next. I also "knew" that her thoughts were blurred by her emotional reactions to things and that I had to be prepared at any time for an emotional outburst.

Since I wasn't paying complete attention to what she was saying, my mind would wander, and I would notice her body. I felt safer paying attention to that. When she would get animated and excited during our discussions, I would find her very attractive. I would begin to notice her breasts or her legs and start thinking how I might maneuver us to bed. It was easy to sexualize her presence. It was not easy to learn how to fully respect her intelligence and understanding. It was not easy to listen to her ideas and not feel the need to reassert control.

I started to notice my feelings and thoughts. Sometimes Micki would comment on my lack of attention or poor listening. Often, I would find my thoughts drifting off to other subjects. The process was quite discouraging, and I felt terribly guilty. I was doing all the things that feminists accused me of. I did treat women, including my partner, with condescension and lack of respect. I did view them as sexual objects.

Honestly recognizing these patterns did seem to give them less power. I didn't try to fight what I was doing. By just admitting how I was acting, I could pay more attention to what Micki was saying. Every time I noticed my attention drifting to her body I could refocus on the conversation.

The process of talking about and writing down our values meant I couldn't get away with not listening. We had to work out common ground or we had no future relationship. For the first time, it became crucially important for me to change. I needed to listen to her, respect her, and talk about my own feelings so we could build a solid foundation.

I started noticing other feelings. Sometimes I wanted sexual contact with Micki to have her prove she cared deeply. Other times I just needed to be touched or held but couldn't seem to ask for that. I noticed feelings of insecurity, loneliness, sadness, affection, contentment, nervousness, and excitement. I had always translated these feelings as either sexual desire or anger—the two emotions I had seen men have.

I couldn't immediately start to express all these feelings. I would feel sad and have the urge to cry. Then my training would kick in and I would keep the feelings inside and keep the tears from flowing. After a while I learned to breathe deeply and relax so that I could stay with the feelings longer. Even today, when I am about to cry, I look around first to see who is watching!

As Micki and I talked about how we wanted to lead our lives

together, I could see myself becoming more emotionally articulate. I noticed how much better I was able to listen to her. We could both feel the strength, mutuality, and importance of what we were building. When we wrote up a final version of our agreement, I was happy and proud. I said to myself, "Well, that's it. We just have to check back once in a while to see how we're doing." I thought the hardest part was over.

But this was only the beginning.

Micki and I moved in together and in the next year had a baby. Our sexual life changed dramatically. We both were getting a lot of sexual satisfaction from holding and feeding and carrying the baby. This was a great surprise to me, because it had nothing to do with orgasms or sexual contact. It had more to do with glowing, full, rich sensations of affection, deep intimacy, love, and vulnerability that I had only experienced before with a lover, and usually in a sexual setting.

Micki was back at work after three months' leave, and I looked after our son for nine months before returning to work part-time. Micki was often tired and not interested in sex. We fell into a pattern in which I made the first moves and tried to arouse her. Sometimes I was successful; other times she fell asleep.

Occasionally, especially on weekends when the baby was napping, she was aroused and initiated lovemaking. A couple of these times I wasn't particularly interested. It was the middle of the day and there were other things I wanted to do. But I didn't know how to say no to her. And because her sexual arousal was much rarer these days, I felt I had to respond to it so as not to discourage her. I had never even conceived of the possibility that she would want sex and I wouldn't. How could a man say no to sexual opportunity?

It wasn't hard to become excited and enjoy lovemaking, but it wasn't quite what I had wanted to do. One time I decided to say I just wasn't interested right then, maybe later. She was taken aback. I had suddenly breached both of our expectations about my sexual responsiveness. She was not only disappointed, she was also a little unsure whether this was about her desirability or my needs. I was unsure whether it was all right not to be interested all the time. Was I giving up a good opportunity? Was I drying up at the ripe age of thirty-two? I had heard that lots of men reach their sexual peak at twenty-two, women at thirty-two. Maybe this spelled the end.

All my fears about not being man enough to satisfy her came up again. We spent that evening talking about our reactions to my saying no to sex. It took courage and honesty to talk about what was happening. Rather than it being the end of my sexual drive or our relationship, this was the beginning of my being able to say no sometimes, while encouraging her to be aggressive and sexual when she wanted to. We ended our discussion by reaffirming that there was still a lot to learn about sexuality, and by making love.

We also paid a lot of attention to changing gender roles in our family. But about two years after Ariel's birth, after a miscarriage, we noticed how our relationship had developed. It certainly wasn't the traditional man-at-work, woman-at-home-with-the-children family. It looked more like a caricature of a traditional one than something personal and healthy for us. Micki had a high-pressure, professional career in the male-dominated university world. She worked late, brought work home, and identified strongly with her work. I worked a flexible, part-time job in community education. I spent more time with our son, did the housework and most of the cooking. We had simply reversed the male/female roles.

At first I found it satisfying and new to be taking care of the baby and doing the housekeeping and cooking. I enjoyed the unpressured pace of the day, the time to sit in the park with the baby or watch television while I fed him. Soon, however, I became worried and guilty that I wasn't doing enough. I was "just" taking care of the baby. So I started to do a million cleaning and fix-it projects and every household chore imaginable so that at the end of each day I could feel I had accomplished something.

I also had that proud, pat-me-on-the-back-because-I'm-liberated feeling that allowed me to look down on all other men who were not doing what I was. Of course, I ignored the fact that

I had the financial security to take the time off. At the same time I felt lonely, isolated, and exhausted by all the baby babble, drool, and poop. I envied "working" people's ability to go out and meet people and do interesting things. I became jealous of Micki's working life, restless and dissatisfied with the lack of stimulation in my own.

Now, after two years, I wanted to work more outside the house and cut back on child care and housekeeping. We started to question our family roles. But by ourselves we were unable to see a way to balance our work and family life more equally. Micki's job didn't seem to give her much flexibility, and somebody had to stay home when the baby was sick, do the laundry, shopping, and other household work. After several unsuccessful attempts to work out a solution, we decided to see a counselor.

Getting help wasn't easy. I had been raised to handle things by myself, like a man. Personal matters, sexual or not, weren't for public exposure. It was painful enough talking with Micki about these problems. I wasn't anxious to air our dirty linen in front of someone else. I also felt embarrassed because it seemed to indicate we weren't together enough to handle it ourselves.

We had discussed the possibility of needing help when we first got together. In our contract we had stated that if one of us wanted to get outside help, we would both participate willingly. It was easier to get help now because we had talked about it earlier. Now we needed help. Both of us wanted to have another child, but I was feeling stuck at home and afraid of becoming even more locked into the traditional woman's role—taking care of everything but my own needs.

We found a good counselor and worked with her for a few sessions. It helped us through this hard period, and it set a precedent for going back to her when we had other problems.

Micki and I continue to talk about our relationship, revise our contract, rebalance our family and work roles, and seek counseling when we need to. This work is not easy, but the rewards are great—intimacy, trust, support, sharing, and pleasure.

During my life I have had two images of men growing older. One is of a man going through a mid-life crisis, leaving his partner and children for another, usually younger, woman. The other image is of a man who becomes more and more passive in his relationship as he resigns himself to the uneasy patterns established in the early years of a couple's time together.

I am not advocating that anyone stay in a relationship that is unhealthy or not working. But all too often we are encouraged to give up and leave or give up and stay. We don't need to give up. Struggling through the difficulties, being willing to change our attitudes and habits, listening to our partners, and sharing our most private excitements and fears—these are the qualities of a healthy partnership.

EXERCISE 13
Becoming Partners

1. Whether you are homosexual, heterosexual, or bisexual, write down for yourself and describe to a friend your history of intimate relationships.
2. What patterns do you notice?
3. Have you ever had a partner say he or she wanted less sex and more intimacy, closeness, or communication from you?
4. What is one expectation from the Act Like A Man box that keeps you from becoming closer to the other adults around you?
5. Pay attention to the ways the men around you avoid intimacy. Notice the ways they are intimate without admitting or talking about it.
6. How can the lack of intimacy lead to violence?
7. What are your ways of avoiding intimacy?
8. List three things you talk about in place of the personal parts of your life.

9. What might you lose if that continues?

10. What would you gain by being closer to the special adults around you?

11. What is your greatest fear in telling your partner your hopes, fears, or desires?

12. Is it embarrassing for you to listen to someone cry or share something personal or painful? Why?

13. List three things you would like to talk about but don't know how or are scared or embarrassed to.

14. If you have a partner, pick a time that is not sexually charged and talk about your sexual relationship. Listen attentively and respectfully to what he or she has to say and communicate caringly what you have to say.

15. What excuses immediately come up to avoid doing the work in question fourteen?

16. Who is one person in your life that you would like to be closer to in a nonsexual way? How can you make that happen?

17. Choose one man you care about. Tell him that you care about him. Talk with him about some of these exercises and how you've responded to them.

ELEVEN

Becoming Workers and Teachers

Most of us are workers. Many of us are teachers or have jobs that serve others. How do our work lives fit into the cycle of violence we have been discussing?

Our economic system is set up to keep some people on call for periodic low-wage labor, others for regular low-wage labor. Still others are left out of the labor market completely. In order for the economy to work as smoothly as possible, there needs to be a way to contain the potentially restless and explosive power of the people whose labor is worth less to the economy and who have to survive in poverty.

In order to understand this dynamic better we need to look at the economic system in which we live. On the following page is a simplified version of what the economic pyramid looks like. Our current American concentration of wealth among a ruling class is one of the greatest that we know of among a ruling class at any time in the history of the world. Although anti-Semitic stereotypes would have us believe there are many Jews at the top of the pyramid, a careful look at the distribution of wealth, and at political and corporate leaders in this country would reveal few Jews. Those at the top are primarily white and primarily Christian.

In a previous section we asked ourselves, "What is my class of origin?" and "What is my present class position?" You might want to look at the pyramid and revisit those questions.

If we add up the top two groups we realize that 20 percent of

THE ECONOMIC PYRAMID*

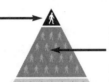

Rich: Owners

1% OF THE POPULATION
HOLDS 48% OF U.S. WEALTH

Independently wealthy
Over $3,000,000/household net worth
Average income $400,000/year

**Upper-Middle:
Professional/Managerial**

19% OF THE POPULATION
HOLDS 46% OF U.S. WEALTH

Work for owners
Over $500,000/household net worth
Average income over $100,000/year

Lower Middle

40% OF THE POPULATION
HOLDS 8.3% OF U.S. WEALTH

Work for professionals/managers
$79,500/household net worth
Average income $35,500/year

Working/Poor

40% OF THE POPULATION
HOLDS MINUS -2.3% OF U.S. WEALTH

Low- and minimum-wage workers,
unemployed, welfare, homeless
Minus -$6,000/household net worth
Average income $11,000/year

---

* From Lawrence Mishel, ed., *State of Working America, 1996 to 1997* (Amonk, N.Y.:
M.E. Sharpe, Inc., 1997), 275–86; and from Holly Sklar, *Chaos or Community? Seeking Solutions, Not Scapegoats for Bad Economics* (Boston: South End Press, 1995), 10.

the population controls about 94 percent of the wealth of the country, leaving the other 80 percent of us to fight for the scraps—the 6 percent that is left over. Six percent of the available resources doesn't go very far divided by 80 percent of the population.

Obviously, many of us live near or on the bottom of this pyramid, barely able to survive, struggling to put food on the table, to clothe ourselves and our children and to keep a roof over our heads.

Many of the rest of us, through our family history, our own efforts, our educational and work opportunities, are in a section of the pyramid somewhere in the middle, in a set of jobs and professions which were historically set up by the people at the top (who we might call the wealthy, the rich, the ruling class) to control people at the bottom. These professions were set up to serve as a buffer zone to protect the power and wealth of those at the top. Social workers, counselors, teachers, police, security guards, deans and principals, and many other occupations fall into this grouping. We could call this the containment part of the economy.

The containment part of our economy has four components, and all of us in the middle class are instrumental in maintaining it. The first component is hope—the belief that the system is flexible and that anyone can make it up the ladder of success. The second is self-blame, which leads people to believe that if they don't succeed it is because of their individual failure. The third component is a welfare system that provides poor people with just enough so that they can stay alive, relatively healthy, and just sane enough not to disrupt the rest of society. The backup component to these three is the physical and legal enforcement of the roles and relationships when the first three break down. Those of us who help others have a role in maintaining all four components.

For people to think they or their children have a chance to escape poverty, unemployment, low wages, high rent, and the violent conditions in their lives, they need to see a few people make it from their situation to a better one. Regardless of the reality, they need to believe that if they have it together, work hard, and persevere they can succeed. Success in this way often becomes synonymous with escaping from family, class, ethnic, racial, and neighborhood backgrounds. One of our assignments as workers and educators is to choose the best and the brightest from disempowered groups and push them up the ladder. We are supposed to encourage them to stay in school, study hard, and become leaders. Education is the key.

The reality is that those who do make it out of poverty often leave their communities to join the middle class, which leaves their communities unchanged.

These few individual success stories foster the illusion of hope and keep our work focused on helping people escape, one by one, from lack of economic opportunity. They also distract us from understanding why there is unequal economic opportunity in the first place.

These stories of individual achievement serve another purpose—they provide a way to blame those who don't make it. It appears that success goes to the hard-working, disciplined, competitive, smart, and self-confident. Those who don't succeed must, therefore, be lazy, unskilled, dumb, and lacking in self-esteem. Self-blame is reinforced by the many professionals ready to step in with training in self-esteem, assertiveness, self-management, and other achievement skills. The fact that the economic system is set up to allow only a few people through the gates to success is kept carefully hidden.

We live in a society in which women are told they are not as smart as men. People of color are told they cannot compete with whites in the classroom. Working-class youth are told to go only for vocational skills and basic education. Increased self-esteem and other personal skills are going to help only a few people stand up to the constant harassment, stereotyping, low expectations, and limited opportunities available to them.

The hope fades for some before or during early adolescence. For others it happens later in adult life. It makes no difference whether they blame themselves, their family, community, or cultural group. Angry and hurt, they just try to survive.

Yet surviving economically takes so much time, energy, and emotional resources that people are often unable to take any action to change the circumstances that produce the lack of opportunity in the first place. Those of us in the middle class who dole out the food stamps, welfare benefits, social security benefits, and health care, often do so in such a way that recipients are left exhausted and drained from the bureaucratic gymnastics and all the monitoring they are subjected to. Very little organized resistance to the economic system is possible under these circumstances.

The social service sector, as broadly as I have defined it, encourages hope, corroborates failure, and sustains life. These three functions, properly fulfilled, keep the system of power and money very stable. In case of malfunction, some of us are trained to enforce the system by punishing and monitoring the "troublemakers." Deans and principals, probation officers, child protection agents, welfare investigators, and police—each are empowered to intervene punitively in the lives of people who are disruptive.

It is not accidental that women hold jobs in the first three categories and men hold jobs in the enforcement area. Women are trained to take care of people, to nurture and support, to be helpers. Men are trained to be tough and aggressive and to use violence to control others. Both roles are useful in maintaining a system in which a small group of people control most of the wealth in our country, leaving the rest of us with very little. There is nothing biological in these functions.

As men there are particular ways that we allow ourselves to become distracted from this economic reality. Besides the factors listed above our attention gets diverted by alcohol and other drugs, by spectator sports, by pornography, by fights and other forms of violence, by blaming women for our problems, by blaming people of color if we are white and recent immigrants if we were born in the United States. We each need to look carefully at our own behavior not just to see whether we are abusive, but to notice any ways we get distracted from working with others to challenge the economic injustice of the system in which we live. If we have some economic security, or a job in the buffer zone, we have to be particularly conscious of this dynamic.

Each of us who does not want to play out our preassigned role has to explore how we can work to change an economic structure that consigns so many of us to poverty and impoverished lives. We must constantly remind ourselves that we are all in this together. Any temporary middle-class privilege, power, or status we have is very fragile and based on inequality. A major medical crisis, a disability, or cash-flow problem can quickly remind most of us of our economic vulnerability.

It is also important to acknowledge that we have social power over people's lives. Some of us can, through our work, take children from families, provide or deny benefits, allow or prohibit access to various programs and community resources, and recommend people for jobs, housing, or academic placement. Let's be up front with ourselves and those we serve about this fact. Let's use the power we have in the best interests of those whose lives we affect, as they define "best interests."

We can help people have better lives, but unless we are part of a social movement for change, we are not moving towards a more equitable and economically democratic society. We must question all the assumptions we have about the people we serve so that we don't inadvertently carry out an upper-class agenda. We don't want to put people down or blame them for the results of the economic, racial, and gender-based distribution of resources and opportunities. We help confront people's internalized self-blame, self-destructiveness, and violence by not excusing such actions and by helping them understand the costs.

If we incorporate education about the political system of power into our work we break the cycle of self-blame. It helps tremendously when we can empower groups of people to work together. We can enable students to see themselves as allies rather than competitors and enemies. We can help welfare recipients organize themselves for greater strength and mutual support.

Finally, it is important that we examine our own needs for power to ensure that they are not acted out against the people we want to help. Whatever our job, there are many ways we can hurt and abuse the people we work with. We must not let our own feelings of anger, frustration, or powerlessness lead us to hurt others.

Sometimes people come to us for services involuntarily and with tremendous ambivalence. They know the power we have over their lives. We can be their allies by responding to their needs. We can tell them what resources and services we can provide, and then let them decide what they want us to do for them. We must constantly ask ourselves whose side we are on.

We are also vulnerable and dependent because we too need jobs, references, and benefits. The system uses the same three tools of hope, self-blame, and controlled distribution of benefits to keep us playing our roles. We each must heed some authority over us, which may encourage us to pass on abuse to those who have less power than we do.

We can stop this economic cycle of violence only if we build alliances with co-workers and those we serve in the community. First we have to see that what is happening to others is also happening to us. Then we can organize not just for higher wages and better health care, but also for the power to change the way people are able to meet their needs.

Many of us were drawn to our work because we wanted to do something in our communities. If we keep a wide perspective, balancing our personal needs with working together to build a different kind of society, there is much we can do.

EXERCISE 14
Becoming Workers and Teachers

This exercise is for anyone who has a job in which he or she has power over co-workers, clients, students, patients, or the public. Such jobs include teachers, medical personnel, counselors, social workers, police, supervisors, managers, and probation officers.

Looking at the economic pyramid,

1. Who are you in solidarity with—people on the bottom or people on the top?
2. Which group of people benefits from your work?
3. What power over people do you have in your job?
4. What power do people above you have over you?
5. How might the pressures of your job push you to mistreat people under you?
6. How have you seen co-workers mistreat people?
7. List any ways that clients or others get blamed for being mistreated, poor, needy, not formally educated, or otherwise unsuccessful? How are they made fun of, laughed at, or discounted?
8. What stereotypes or comments about groups of people do you encounter at work?
9. What keeps you from intervening more often when you hear or see these kinds of interactions?
10. Has there ever been a time when you mistreated someone because that was the policy and you feared that not doing so would mean the loss of your job?
11. How do you and co-workers help people despite the rules?
12. What are ways you and co-workers can change the rules to be more respectful of the people you serve?
13. How could the clients, students, or workers under you be more involved in making decisions about your work? How could they have more power?
14. What do the people you have power over need the most?
15. What is one thing you can do to become a more powerful ally for them in your workplace?
16. In your personal life, what activities distract you—that is, what takes up your time and energy, keeping you from becoming more involved in

community efforts to challenge the distribution of wealth? Are any of those distractions unhealthy and/or unsatisfying? Which ones keep you isolated from your family or your community?

17. Which activities could you cut down on?
18. What is one community project you could use that extra time to participate in?
19. When will you start?

TWELVE

Getting Help for Ourselves

There have been many times when I needed help but didn't ask for it. These are some of the things I said to myself:

- I don't want to bother anyone.
- It really isn't that important.
- No one would understand.
- How could they help me anyway?
- I'm embarrassed to admit it happened to me.
- It will probably go away or get better.
- I don't want to cause a problem.
- I should take care of it myself.
- Other people's problems are much more serious than mine.
- They might laugh at me.
- I don't know how to talk about it.

Why don't men ask for help? The climate of individual responsibility and self-blame we live in sets us up to remain isolated and vulnerable. Most of us think of our problems as "personal" problems. This phrase makes them sound unique to us and not as important as social problems. In reality, most of our personal problems *are* social problems. Our economic situation, our health, the violence in our lives, family tension, the lack of good education and educational opportunities, a polluted environment—these are the root causes of most of our "personal" problems. And yet, if I am robbed or raped or unemployed I am often still seen as being responsible for having brought it on.

The Protestant ethic implies that our lives reflect our moral worth. New Age spirituality teaches that we create our own reality. The mythology of capitalism says that the hardworking move up and the lazy move down. Our belief systems reinforce the message that we are individually responsible for all of what comes at us.

If we try to get help we are pushed to admit that on some level we have failed to create a healthy life or to work hard enough to achieve success. Having learned throughout our lives that we are to blame for whatever happens, it is hard to reach out for help and not feel embarrassed, guilty, cautious, and unworthy.

Men have particular difficulty asking for help because part of the message of the Act Like a Man box is that we don't make mistakes, that we aren't vulnerable, that we are strong. So we go it alone and never ask for help.

We become masters of denial and will avoid, at all costs, admitting a mistake and asking for help. Sometimes when facilitating a workshop I will ask women to give examples of ways men avoid asking for help. Listening to women do this is both embarrassing and useful for men. Invariably there are stories of men driving for hours, completely lost, refusing to ask for directions. Women describe men who try to fix cars and appliances, make a big mess of the situation, yet are still unwilling to admit they need help. Then there are always examples of men refusing to see doctors or get medical treatment for serious conditions.

Behind these examples is the fear that in being vulnerable we will be taken advantage of. The fear that if we are not in control, we are out of control. The fear that if we give up a little, we will lose everything.

Our inability to ask for help maintains our isolation. In addition, popular culture bombards us with stories of successful and glamorous people having very dramatic, Hollywood-sized problems that are more significant than our own. Or we come to believe that everyone else has it together, that our problems are badges of failure, or that our problems are so small they're not worth talking about. If we are working-class or poor; if we are people of color, Jewish, or gay; if we are older or physically challenged, we know that the dominant culture already expects us to fail. Having a problem that we need help for just confirms to them and to us that we are what they say we are—not quite good enough to make it by ourselves.

This situation is reinforced by a social system that creates a hierarchical structure of helpers and people who need help. We have entire occupational categories of people who help others. We call them the helping professions. This creates a situation in which giving help is a paid job, not a common human endeavor. An individual comes to an office to receive help from a "professional." This creates a one-on-one situation in which we feel unique, regardless of the millions of us with the same problems.

Millions of men have problems with anger and violence. Millions of children are victims of violence. Many of us have experienced street violence, racial or economic violence, or sexual harassment. We are not alone in having problems and needing help.

That social problems are blamed on individuals, that getting help is difficult and has pejorative connotations, that giving help has become professionalized—these are political statements. Reversing these patterns is a powerful step in recreating our communities, building alliances, healing from the violence, and beginning to change the injustices that caused the violence.

It can be hard to reach for the phone or ask a friend to listen. It is also a much more powerful step than we can imagine. We don't need to ask for help with guilt, self-blame, or embarrassment. We can be proud that we are ready to change, proud that we are survivors. We are worthy of all the love, respect, and support we can get.

Nothing makes us feel more powerless and vulnerable than being in pain and having problems that seem unresolvable. Getting help can be an empowering first step in breaking down social isolation, building alliances, and healing.

Before we can give help, we may need to get help ourselves. Before we can get help, we need to be able to admit to problems and mistakes.

EXERCISE 15
Getting Help for Ourselves

1. Acknowledge to yourself a mistake you made recently. What did you learn from it?
2. Notice how rarely you say the phrases, "I'm wrong," "I'm sorry," and "I made a mistake." What is hard about saying them?
3. Think of two people you need to apologize to for something you said or did. Why haven't you? When are you going to?
4. When you do admit to a mistake do you hedge it ("I'm sorry, but . . .), make a joke about it, blame someone else, or otherwise downplay it?
5. Do you feel angry at people to whom you owe an apology?
6. Is it hard for you to ask for directions when you don't know where you are going?
7. Do you feel pressure to know the right answers when your partner, children, or co-workers ask you a question?
8. Can you admit your problems to your partner? To your children? To your parents?
9. Do you have any health problems or concerns you need to see someone about?
10. Do you know of any man who died or had a situation deteriorate drastically because he refused to get medical help?
11. Are you avoiding getting help for a problem with violence or drug dependency?
12. Are there social or cultural factors that make it hard for you to ask for help?
13. Do you think that family problems should stay inside the family? Why?
14. Name one area of your life in which you have

a problem you really should talk with someone about. What are you afraid would happen if you asked for help?

15. Who is a friend or family member that you can talk to about your situation, and who can help you get help?

16. How can you find out about sources of help available to you in your community? List several such sources below. Contact them and find out what services they offer.

THIRTEEN

Helping Others Get Help

Getting help for ourselves and seeing why sometimes we don't get help when we need to can lead us to more effective strategies for intervening with other men who need help. All of us live with and know male friends, family members, co-workers, and neighbors. What can we do when one of them is violent?

Intervention is never easy. In a society in which interpersonal violence is taken for granted, it is risky for us to get involved—as if we weren't already involved, as if we didn't already lead lives of fear because of the prevailing levels of violence. Next time it could be one of us who needs help.

Family intervention is most delicate. The privacy and sanctity of the family, the feeling that what they do among themselves is their business—all these ideas prevent us from being involved. How much is it "their business" when our neighborhoods are disrupted, our medical and legal systems are overloaded, people are killed and lives destroyed daily from the results of family violence?

Nevertheless, when interacting with violent men, we must remember that safety comes first! We must be safe from immediate danger and retaliation before we can ask someone to accept responsibility for his violence or offer support to him.

Confronting a man who is violent means letting him know clearly and directly that the violence is unacceptable and cannot continue. Let him hear that violence is illegal, dangerous, and will not be allowed to continue. He may also need help seeing the costs to himself in lowered self-esteem, pain, despair, and the brutalization added to his own life and surroundings.

We can provide him with this information through one-to-one

dialogue, group discussion, legal intervention, or public confrontation. Since confrontation is always risky, no one can judge how much someone else should say or do. But we become complicit with the violence if we don't take some steps to confront it. This can be done by police, friends, neighbors, and other family members. Effective confrontation decreases the level of violence. Our primary responsibility is to stop the immediate violence and to support the person attacked.

Support

Individual men who are violent need our support to make positive changes. Support should not be confused with collusion; the violent situation cannot be allowed to continue. Support must be conditional on the violence stopping.

To support a violent man we must

- confront his violence;
- separate his violence from his worth as a person;
- help him understand that his violence comes from his hurt, pain, and powerlessness;
- help him see that violence is dangerous, self-defeating, and ineffective in getting his needs met;
- make a commitment to caring for him over time, providing a compassionate and empathetic ear to his experiences of violence, hostility, anger, and despair;
- recognize his training to be male and his unique place in the power hierarchies of our society, including those based on class, race, sexual orientation, and cultural background;
- help him understand that violence is learned and an unnecessary behavior that can be changed;
- address that part of the man that does not want to be violent and that does not want to hurt others;
- help him admit he has a problem;
- help him ask for help—perhaps one of the hardest things for a man to do.

Personal Clarity

In order to confront another man's violence and to support his changing, we must also have some clarity. We need to

- acknowledge, understand, and at least partially heal from our own past experiences of violence;
- feel confident enough to make ourselves vulnerable to another man's violence;
- acknowledge our fear of further violence;
- acknowledge and understand our own gender-based training to be violent;
- recognize our anger at his violence and understand that anger can help keep us from colluding with him.

Nearly everyone in this society has been bullied and been the object of violence. Nearly everyone has bullied someone else. Acknowledge this commonality of experience with a violent man and use it to talk with him effectively.

Alternatives and Resources

We know that a violent man needs to

- know change is possible and that he does have alternatives;
- know specifically what those alternatives are and where to find out about them—how to start the process and what community resources are available;
- learn other ways to deal with anger;
- learn how to express other emotions, including pain, hurt, sadness, and frustration;
- learn to get his needs met and to resolve conflicts without resorting to hitting, intimidation, or abuse;
- get help in examining his gender training;
- get help in more deeply understanding his personal and family history;
- be shown the resources for dealing with other issues such as drug abuse, health problems, and unemployment;

- know that we expect him to use these resources to
  eliminate his violence.

We don't have to be crusaders or self-righteous missionaries.
We can make our presence felt by intervening in safe ways and
completely respecting the people involved. It becomes safer for all
of us when we recognize men's violence as a community problem
and support each other in dealing with it.

EXERCISE 16
Getting Help for Others

1. Do you know of any situations in your family or
   among your friends in which a man is beating,
   controlling, molesting, or otherwise hurting someone else?
2. What is dangerous about this situation for the
   people involved?
3. How might it be dangerous for you to intervene?
4. Besides the danger, what reasons have you used for
   not getting more involved?
5. How could you caringly confront the person
   who is abusive?
6. What kind of support can you give the person
   being abused?
7. Who can you talk with to get support for intervening more strongly?
8. Do you know any men who have a problem with
   violence and refuse to get help?
9. How can you be a friend to him and support his
   stopping the violence?
10. What are three things you could do if you see a
    man hit a woman in public or a group of people
    attack another person?
11. Why would doing these things be scary or danger-
    ous for you?

12. Why is it important for *you* to intervene?
13. How will you feel about yourself if you don't do anything?
14. What are some things you could say when you see a parent abusing his or her child?
15. What are some ways to interrupt harassment of women, gays, lesbians, bisexual people, or people of different ethnic groups?
16. What do you gain if our communities are safer for women?

PART IV

Men's Work: To Stop Male Violence

As men we have two responsibilities. The first is to eliminate our own abusive behavior in whatever form it takes. The second is to be a community worker. We began talking about community responsibility in the last chapters on helping and getting help.

This part looks at the Oakland Men's Project, which for many years has worked to challenge male violence and to develop effective alternatives. During these years we have had to reevaluate our ideas substantially so that we did not reproduce the abusive relationships we were striving to change. We had to go deep into our own lives and experiences so that we could talk with other men. As people in the workshops and others doing this work challenged our assumptions, we had to continually rethink and question our understanding of the issues.

The work of the project is exciting and challenging. We have seen thousands of men begin the process of change. We have seen many men take this work into their family, job, and community lives. This part chronicles that work and describes some of the specific ways we work with men to challenge the violence.

FOURTEEN

The Oakland Men's Project

We began the work of the Oakland Men's Project in 1979 with a multitude of personal motivations, not the least of which was that the male roles we had been trained to follow didn't work. Even without identifying it as a box, we knew we wanted out.

The women's movement and a 1978 national conference in San Francisco on violence against women were our immediate inspirations. For years, women's groups had been responding to the needs of women survivors of male violence by operating shelters and rape crisis centers. One result of this organizing was to make the public aware of the tremendous need for shelter, counseling, advocacy, and legal intervention. During this period the devastating effects of the violence on women, children, and even on men became more and more visible.

Some men began to see that we could no longer discount sexual harassment, battery, and rape as women's problems. These were clearly part of a nationwide social problem. We could see that the effects of past violence and the threat of future violence was keeping women off the shop floor, out of the corporate office, and out of public office. It was keeping them in dangerous marriages and in poverty.

Some women said, "You're doing the violence. You are men. Take responsibility for your actions and address other men." There was a lot of attention paid to the question, "Why are men violent?" Some people argued that men are unalterably aggressive because of their genes, hormones, chromosomes, or just because all males are "that way." None of these "theories" had any scientific legitimacy, however. Male behavior is immeasurably variable.

159

Most feminists wanted to hold men responsible for their actions and looked to male power and male socialization as sources of male violence. The huge amount of violence promoted in popular culture led them to the conclusion that boys learn male roles, and violent behavior was part of that learning.

Women were hurting from the violence. They were angry at the men who committed violence and the men who condoned it by their silence. We assimilated much of their anger. Partly motivated by self-hatred, we took the anger directed toward us and directed it at other men for not seeing what was happening to women. We used that anger to encourage other men to acknowledge their complicity in the violence.

A group of us developed a slide show to be shown to men's groups. We took images from pornography, record covers, magazine ads, and comic books. Most of the images we showed were pictures of women being humiliated, bound, beaten, or raped. Our motivation was to convey horror, shock, and outrage at how violent the images were.

As part of our presentation we read the following poem by ntozake shange:

with no immediate cause*

> every 3 minutes a woman is beaten
> every five minutes a
> woman is raped/ every ten minutes
> a lil girl is molested
> yet i rode the subway today
> i sat next to an old man who
> may have beaten his old wife
> 3 minutes ago or 3 days/ 30 years ago
> he might have sodomized his
> daughter but i sat there
> cuz the young men on the train
> might beat some young women

* ntozake shange, *nappy edges* (New York: Bantam Books, 1978). Reprinted with permission.

later in the day or tomorrow
i might not shut my door fast
enuf/ push hard enuf
every 3 minutes it happens
some woman's innocence
rushes to her cheeks/ pours from her mouth
like the betsy wetsy dolls have been torn
apart/ their mouths
mensis red & split/ every
three minutes a shoulder
is jammed through plaster & the oven door/
chairs push thru the rib cage/ hot water or
boiling sperm decorate her body
i rode the subway today
& bought a paper from a
man who might
have held his old lady onto
a hot pressing iron/ i dont know
maybe he catches lil girls in the
park & rips open their behinds
with steel rods/ i cdnt decide
what he might have done i only
know every 3 minutes
every 5 minutes every 10 minutes/so
i bought the paper
looking for the announcement
there has to be an announcement
of the women's bodies found
yesterday/ the missing little girl
i sat in a restaurant with my
paper looking for the announcement
a yng man served me coffee
i wondered did he pour the boiling
coffee/ on the woman cuz she waz stupid/
did he put the infant girl/ in
the coffee pot/ with the boiling coffee/ cuz she cried
too much
what exactly did he do with hot coffee
i looked for the announcement

the discovery/ of the dismembered
woman's body/ the
victims have not all been
identified/ today they are
naked & dead/ refuse to
testify/ one girl out of 10's not
coherent/ i took the coffee
& spit it up/ i found an
announcement/ not the woman's
bloated body in the river/ floating
not the child bleeding in the
59th street corridor/ not the baby
broken on the floor/

>   "there is some concern
>   that alleged battered women
>   might start to murder their
>   husbands & lovers with no
>   immediate cause"

i spit up   i vomit   i am screaming
we all have immediate cause
every 3 minutes
every 5 minutes
every 10 minutes
every day
women's bodies are found
in alleys & bedrooms/ at the top of the stairs
before i ride the subway/ buy a paper/ drink
coffee/ i must know/
have you hurt a woman today
did you beat a woman today
throw a child cross a room
>   are the lil girl's panties
>   in yr pocket
did you hurt a woman today

i have to ask these obscene questions
the authorities require me to
establish
immediate cause

> every three minutes
> every five minutes
> every ten minutes
> every day

This is a very upsetting poem. You may feel angry, guilty, or ashamed after reading it. When presented with facts about the costs of male violence against women, as we are in this poem, we cannot escape the horror of the reality. I don't spend any time in this book citing statistics because the numbers only mask the reality. We need only open the daily newspaper to read the stories. We need only listen to the women we know talk about their experiences to know the truth.

Men must listen to women's pain and anger. The fact that it is safe enough for women to publicly express that anger is an indication of important change in our society. It means that women are challenging male perceptions of sex, gender, rape, exploitation, and abuse. They are describing parts of our common reality that are tremendously destructive to all of us.

But if we just accept those perceptions without confirming them through our own experience, we will eventually reject and turn against the source of those perceptions—the strong women around us. This happens when we respond to women's anger with guilt, shame, or defensiveness. In many cases these feelings eventually lead to a backlash against women. The defensiveness becomes counterattack; we blame women for the powerlessness of men or try to protect the power that men have.

Instead we need to take the pain and anger in ntozake shange's poem as a probe into a reality we often deny. We need to look at our own lives and experiences. We need to grapple with the issues, not the anger, until we can understand the truth of what shange says—not because she says it, but because we have confirmed that she is right. Then, and only then, do we become committed to making personal and social changes because we know what is at stake for women *and* for us.

Evoking this kind of response from men called for an entirely different educational approach than reading angry poems and showing slides of women being brutalized. It meant we had to come together and, with absolute honesty, share and compare our experiences growing up and living as men, analyze women's experiences as *they* described them, and piece through the causes and costs of our violence.

But the old methods of lecture and slide presentation were hard to let go. They made us the "good" men with the "right" ideas and allowed us to feel powerful by attacking and berating other men. We became the best liberated men on the block, and that became another way of winning women's approval and attention. It also allowed us to feel self-righteous toward other men.

We took our presentation with its slides and poem and testimony to many different men's group. Some men were shocked and outraged, others weren't. Shock and outrage did not necessarily lead men to sustained commitment and action to end violence. Nor did it help our audiences understand how the system of male violence worked, *or how it affected them personally.*

We told men they were powerful, privileged, and responsible for the violence. The men we talked with did not agree. They told us they felt angry, hurt, vulnerable, and powerless. We didn't believe them at first, because we had a lot at stake in being right. After all, we were the teachers and they were the students. We were supposed to have the right answers.

Then we took the workshops to some junior high classes, bringing the message that men were strong and powerful in the world and women weren't. The young men said they were trying to be powerful and weren't. The young women refused the label of victim. Both the men and women thought that women were not as vulnerable as we were saying they were. We couldn't hear them either.

Over the next two years we looked at what wasn't working in our workshops. People loved discussing the slides, but they didn't buy what we were saying. We finally had to acknowledge that teen men are not powerful in our society. They are primarily victims and survivors of family, community, and institutional violence. We had to acknowledge as well that the young women, while vulnerable to violence, were not passive victims but survivors trying to make it in a hostile environment.

We came to see that boys and girls are hurt as children, violated, and rendered powerless. They are recipients of adult, primarily male, violence. Boys are taught to pass on the violence to others. Girls are expected to become victims of this violence.

All men were victims of the system as young people. So the key to doing effective work with men was to understand how we had been trained, the pain we had suffered, and yet still hold ourselves accountable for the violence we perpetuated. We had to create a way to understand the connection between social training and individual responsibility. We did this through a process of trial and error.

During that period we learned that men who speak out and take actions against sexism contradict the lies that men are inevitably abusive to women, that men will never change, and that they can't be trusted by women. We found that when we made mistakes, said the wrong thing, or acted out our own sexism inadvertently, women got angry at us. Having invited their trust, we ended up hurting them. Sometimes this made us very cautious. We were reluctant to antagonize women or to be incorrect.

To be a true ally to women we had to hear their anger and understand its source in their feelings of hopelessness and experiences of violence. We learned how to listen, take criticism, and make changes while continuing to take risks. We were doing this work to reduce the violence. It was not just another way to wrangle women's support, approval, or gratitude.

We also experienced anger from men as we spoke out. Some of them felt deserted, unfairly blamed, or saw us as hypocritical. To counteract this anger we learned that it was crucial not to fault or attack other men for the lies and training they have received. By caring for and accepting them, while confronting their beliefs and attitudes, we were able to demonstrate the strong and loving alliances against injustice that are possible between men. The next sections show some of the ways that the staff at the Oakland Men's Project have tried to model this kind of approach.

As we developed the role plays, the power chart, and other

exercises we use in workshops, we also developed a way of relating to people, of being teachers, that we felt was consistent with the content of our work. The basic educational methods of Oakland Men's Project developed as we grappled with the issues of power and violence, gender roles, and racism. Over time the goals and mission of the project grew into the following statements.

The Oakland Men's Project
Mission Statement

Abuse of power and violence are taken for granted in our society and dominate our lives and relationships. We are trained that the way to get power is to wield it over someone who is, within the social milieu, less powerful. Hurting others through physical and sexual assault, harassment, exploitation and discrimination, or hurting ourselves through suicide, drug and alcohol abuse, and other self-destructive behaviors creates a cycle of violence, pain, and hurt.

Social institutions and individual practices maintain this cycle, producing violence, lack of equality, poverty, and physical and mental disability for all of us. As men, we are particularly trained to perpetuate violence, domination, and oppression.

The Oakland Men's Project's mission is to challenge the cycle of violence and the social structures that perpetuate it. All people can learn to be powerful without being abusive. Together, we can develop alternatives to violence. We can change the institutions that perpetuate violence. The Oakland Men's Project provides the information, support, resources, and training necessary to build violence-free, equal, and respectful relationships and communities.

Goals

1. To CHALLENGE the cycle of violence through active intervention in people's assumptions of continued abuse and victimization.
2. To EMPOWER individuals to come together and reach beyond/out to each other to build community responses to violence and oppression.

3. To UNDERSTAND men's unique training to perpetuate violence, and to challenge each of us to unlearn that training.
4. To SUPPORT the struggle of each person to overcome pain, hurt, and learned helplessness, to heal and become a more powerful community member.
5. To PROVIDE young people with the information, support, resources, and encouragement they need to create violence-free relationships and communities.
6. To UNDERSTAND and make connections between all the complicated ways power and abuse are worked out in our lives and in society.
7. To PROMOTE a variety of powerful and effective alternatives to violence in social and personal situations.
8. To CONFRONT the violence of local institutions and social practice.
9. To MODEL, in all of these areas, the powerful role that men can take in breaking the cycle of violence.

We also developed an understanding of how the issues of power, violence, and oppression need to be translated into an approach for working with people that does not further the violence, but instead contributes to people's liberation. The basic ideas are set forth in the appendix of this book.

These are dry principles, hard to use without concrete examples. The descriptions of workshops and thoughts about men's lives throughout the rest of this book are intended to give a fuller understanding of what we do and why we do it.

Confronting Sexism

We now need to talk about the third level of "men's work," confronting institutional sexism and other forms of exploitation and violence.

The first level of men's work involves looking at our own lives and eliminating any controlling or abusive behavior toward others, and toward ourselves. The second level is reaching out to other men and challenging abusive behavior wherever and whenever we see it.

The third level involves acting at the institutional level, seeing the big picture. Why are women vulnerable to violence from men? Why are men trained to be violent? In what other ways are women systematically disempowered, abused or exploited by institutional patterns? These are the questions we must ask ourselves.

Institutional patterns are difficult for us to see in a society in which we are encouraged to focus on individual behavior. Sexism is often described by how individual men treat women. We might think that the central question of men's work is, "Am I abusive to women?" This is an important question that the first part of this book has helped us look at. But what if I am a perfect "gentleman" and the staunchest ally to women around me—yet exploitation of women continues? If I take no action I am both enjoying the benefits of sexism and colluding in its maintenance.

What are the benefits of sexism to men who don't hit their partners? Some of the most obvious are that we enjoy better educational, job, and housing opportunities, better police protection and better health care than women around us. We are charged less for services and products and when we walk into a room we are treated with more respect and listened to more attentively than women are. The existence of these benefits has been documented extensively by comparative studies throughout the country. Even in 1998 there are huge gaps in the way that men and women of comparable status are treated in classrooms, during job interviews, when applying for housing, in the boardroom, on the shop floor, in doctor's offices, in the courthouse, and on the street. Again, I am talking about comparable women and men. For example, in many situations men of color are treated much worse than white women, but better than women of color.

We should not be surprised to find men benefiting from the system, because if we look at any institution in this society we will find that it is run by men and men are given favored status. Even jobs and professions which are traditionally the domains of women, such as teaching, nursing, and counseling usually have men in the top administrative positions accruing greater power, money, and status. And at every comparable level women still make about 76 cents to each dollar that men make, experience more sexual harassment, more limits on their upward mobility, and less job security.

Most men find it difficult to acknowledge the benefits we receive from sexism and the disadvantages that women experience. We may even believe that women have gained so much in the last twenty-five years that they now have it better than we do! We may confuse the fact that because some women have it better than we do that therefore all women enjoy the same benefits. (Or we may hold those successful women up as examples to avoid confronting the devastation that sexism wrecks upon all women's lives, particularly those with fewer financial resources.) The exercise at the end of this section will help you look at the benefits we enjoy from being men, regardless of our personal attitudes. In addition, we can look at the institutional policies of our schools, the corporate economy, the criminal justice and health care systems and every other institution in our society to see how men are advantaged and women systematically disadvantaged.

The systematic and devastating effects on women from sexism is most clear when we look at the issue of violence. In situations of domestic violence few men voluntarily stop battering or go for help. They may stop battering their partner if the woman leaves or if the police and court system step in. If we seriously want to stop battering then we need to shift our focus from stopping some men from battering their partners to enabling all women to avoid or to leave abusive relationships. This shift in focus requires us to create a community response which gives a clear message that battering is absolutely unacceptable.

Women cannot avoid abusive relationships if they don't have information about domestic violence, if they don't have good job opportunities, if they don't have assertiveness and self-defense skills, if they don't have safe neighborhoods and safe housing available. Once in a battering relationship a woman often can't leave because there are not enough shelter spaces, not enough support groups, not enough well-paying jobs, not enough affordable alternative housing and child care opportunities, and not enough police protection and criminal justice sanctions against male violence. These are community and institutional issues. These needs should lead us to provide funding to shelters, accessibility of services, child care centers, access to affordable housing, strong, enforced criminal justice protocols on violence, better training for police, prosecutors and judges, and increased access to decent jobs. Women will continue to be vulnerable to male violence as long as they are second class citizens in our society.

Therefore, the third level of men's work is to challenge gender-based inequality throughout our society. We need to work for the implementation of policies and procedures that ensure fair and equitable treatment of women and men. How are women treated at your workplace or school? Are they paid comparably with men, do they have the same hiring and promotion opportunities? Do they face sexual harassment? Are they supported, encouraged, and mentored as well as the men are? These are some of the questions we need to ask ourselves to guide our action in this level of men's work.

In every community there are women, both individually and collectively who are resisting inequality and injustice. Women have always resisted and organized. Women would not have gained the vote, access to jobs, laws against sexual harassment, rape crisis centers, and battered women's shelters if they hadn't been outspoken, active, and organized. There have always been some men who have been strong allies of these women and have worked with them to make those changes. There have also been many of us who have resisted those changes, blaming women for causing problems rather than supporting their attempts to find solutions to those problems. The key question for each of us to answer is are we strong allies to women—are we doing men's work—by supporting women's efforts to build gender justice?

We must also look at public policy issues. Are women's and

girl's programs (athletic, job training, counseling services, treatment facilities, after school programs, recreational services) funded as well as men's and boys'? Do women have opportunities to represent themselves in decision making bodies at all levels? Which women? At which levels? Are women visible and accessible as role models and mentors for younger women? Are programs which benefit women such as welfare, child care, health services, or affirmative action being cut back or eliminated? Are particular groups of women such as welfare recipients, immigrant women, or teenage mothers being blamed or scapegoated for social problems for which they are not responsible?

Sexism works to keep women the focus of our blame and men the locus of control and decision making. We will only be able to change institutional sexism when women share fully in the decision making and those who perpetuate inequality and violence are held responsible for it. If we refer to the economic pyramid on page 138, we can understand how only a few men enjoy large scale benefits from sexism. Most of us have little to lose and a lot to gain from uniting with women for gender justice.

EXERCISE 17
The Benefits of Being Male

Please stand up if:

1. Your forefathers, including your father, had more opportunities to advance themselves economically than your foremothers.
2. Your father had more educational opportunities than your mother.
3. The boys in your extended family, including yourself, had more financial resources, emotional support, or encouragement for pursuing academic, work, or career goals than the girls.
4. You live in or went to a school district where the textbooks and other classroom materials reflected

men as the heroes and builders of the United States, and there was little mention of the contributions of women to our society.

5. You attend or attended a school where boys were encouraged to take math and science, called on more in class, and given more attention and funding for athletic programs than girls.

6. You received job training, educational, or travel opportunities from serving in the military.

7. You received job training in a program where there were few or no women, or where women were sexually harassed.

8. You have received a job, job interview, job training, or internship through personal connections with other men.

9. You worked or work in a job where women made less for doing comparable work or did more menial jobs.

10. You work in a job, career, or profession, or in an agency or organization in which there are few women in leadership positions, or the work has less status *because* women are in leadership positions.

11. You live in a city or region in which domestic violence and sexual assault are serious problems for women.

12. You generally feel safe when hiking in the woods, in the mountains, on the beach or in other rural settings. (This one will obviously exclude most men of color.)

13. When you turn on the TV you can routinely see men in positions of leadership, male sports, men portrayed as heroes and in a wide variety of other roles.

14. When you have medical procedures done to you, or take prescribed medicines and other health

treatments you can assume they were tested and proven safe on men.

15. You have seen or heard men in positions of authority belittle women's contributions, women's writing or music, women's intelligence, or women's physical strength, or make other comments suggesting that women are inferior to men.

16. You know where you can have access to sex from women for money in the city or region where you live.

17. You have easy access to sexually revealing images of women, whenever you want them, from magazines, the Internet, bookstores, video stores, or pornography outlets.

18. You have taken advantage of women earning much less than you do for childcare, cooking, cleaning, clerical services, nursing, or other services.

19. In your family, women do more of the housecleaning, cooking, childcare, washing or other caretaking than you or other men do.

20. In your community it is harder for women to get housing loans, small business loans, agricultural loans or car loans than it is for men of similar qualifications.

21. In your community women are routinely charged more for haircutting, cleaning, cars, or other services or products.

Questions

1. Which of the benefits listed above have you experienced?

2. In what ways have you denied these benefits, or minimized the costs to women of sexism?

3. What are current public policy issues where women are being blamed? Which groups of women in particular?

4. In what areas of public policy are services to women being cut back?

5. What are examples of institutional sexism against women in schools or programs you have attended?

6. What are some examples of institutional sexism (policies, practices, or procedures which either disadvantage women, or unfairly benefit men) in your workplace or places where you have worked?

7. How might you work with others to address these issues?

8. Name a man you know or know of, either contemporary or historical, who has been a strong ally to women at the community or institutional level? What did they do? (Some historical examples are Cesar Chavez, Martin Luther King, Jr, Chief Joseph, Frederick Douglas, Mahatma Gandhi, and W.E.B. DuBois.)

9. What are ways that women in your community are organizing to protect themselves, to gain access to services, to change organizational policies, or to challenge institutional discrimination and inequality?

10. What is one of these projects you can support with money, time, or other resources?

11. How can you challenge other men to support these efforts?

FIFTEEN

Going to Prison

I always feel uneasy doing a workshop in a prison. It's not the men; I enjoy working with them. But by the time my co-workers and I have cleared security, been searched, left our keys and valuables behind, and then walked through the fourth set of ironclad doors, I wonder if they'll let us out.

We generally work with men in prerelease programs. These are workshops designed to prepare the men for reentry into the community. The men we work with are very interested in what we are presenting. They have spent much time thinking about the costs of violence. Many are almost desperate to figure out alternatives to going back to prison. We have three hours with seventy-six men doing a workshop we call "The Roots of Male Violence." We start out doing some of the exercises I have already outlined in this book.

We all know how unsafe it is in prison. The men are vulnerable to violence from other inmates and from the guards. When one of our workshops was filmed by a prison team, they could not show the faces of the participants because whatever personal information the men revealed might be used against them later.

I remember the first time I was inside a prison. After we did the father/son role play, I looked around, and some of the men were in tears. Many others were visibly moved. Some of the men told stories of how they had been raised. Others nodded in understanding. Rarely do men get to talk about the deep level of violence we experience. Throughout the workshop, with seventy-five other inmates around him and guards and wardens looking on, each man continued to participate, questioning, sharing, challenging us to be absolutely direct.

Nowhere was the challenge more evident then when we came to the two role plays that deal directly with men's expectations of and violence toward women. One deals with sexual assault and the other with battery.

Dating Scenes

We began this section with the following role play.* One of us plays a man, the other a woman. The scene is set in her apartment at 11:00 P.M. on a Saturday night. He has taken her to dinner at a nice restaurant, then dancing. Now he is planning on settling in and spending the night with her. She likes him, but has to get up early the next morning and doesn't want him to stay. She doesn't want to have sex. (M = man, W = woman.)

> M: You really look hot in that dress. Come over here
>   and sit next to me.
> W: Okay. The dance was fun. Did you see who Carol
>   came in with?
> M: Yeah.
> W: Hey, what are you doing?
> M: Just trying to be friendly.
> W: Well, okay, but take it easy.
> M: Hey, I like you. Don't you like me?
> W: I had a good time with you tonight.
> M: You're not acting like you like me. Loosen up a little.
> W: Wait a minute, not that way, please.
> M: You're not uptight, are you? I'm not a rapist.
> W: Look, I know you're a nice guy, but I have to get up
>   early tomorrow and it's getting late. Maybe you
>   should leave.
> M: Leave! Are you crazy? I just got here. Don't play with
>   me—I showed you a good time. Relax, you'll enjoy it.
> W: Get your hands off me. No. Stop it.

* © Oakland Men's Project.

We freeze the role play here. We begin the discussion by asking the men what is going on with the guy. (P = participant, F = facilitator.)

P1: He wanted to get a piece.

F: A piece of what?

P1: A piece of action.

P2: He was horny!

P3: He spent a lot on her and she was supposed to pay him back.

P4: He was frustrated because she invited him back to her place.

F: Early on in the conversation, she clearly said she wasn't interested. What were the pressures on him to keep going, to not hear her no?

P1: He had put out a lot of cash and wanted something in return.

P2: He might've had some friends who knew he was going out with her and would ask him what happened.

P3: Women say no but they really mean yes.

F: That's something I was taught when I was growing up—women say no but mean yes. I know now that it isn't true. For example, this woman was clearly saying and meaning no.

P4: There's pressure from his body. He needs release.

F: He's turned on. Does that mean that she has to sleep with him?

P5: If she's the cause of it.

F: If I walk down the street and see a beautiful woman and get turned on, does that mean she caused it and should sleep with me?

P6: There's pressure on him to prove he's a man, that he can score.

F: These are all pressures we feel. So what happens is that we keep on pushing, hoping she will give in, say okay, and we can get what we want. Even though she

is clearly saying that she doesn't want sex, we ignore
that and keep on trying.

By this point they are visibly trying to figure this out. They recognize she did not want sex but find it hard to accept that the man
should not have pushed her. They are confronting the reality that
they might have forced a woman to have sex. We ask the participants if there is anything the man in the role play did that reminded them of the Act Like a Man box.

P1:   All of it.
P2:   Be in control.
P3:   Be aggressive.
P4:   Don't make mistakes.
P5:   Be insensitive.
 F: Okay, what's going on with her?
P1:   She wants to get rid of him.
P2:   She's tired.
P3:   She has to say no.
 F: She has to say no?
P3:   If she said yes, she would look easy.
 F: That's a hard one, isn't it? We're taught she should
      say no even though she means yes. This teaching
      keeps our sexual relationships impossibly frustrating
      and confusing. It can also set up violence. Is this situ-
      ation dangerous for her?
P1:   If he gets bent out of shape by being rejected, he
      could get angry.
P2:   He could decide to stay and not leave.
P3:   He's probably bigger than she is.
 F: How does that influence how she acts?
P4:   She was smiling a lot and trying to take care of him.
P5:   Yeah, if she really told him what a creep he was that
      might blow it.
P6:   And he might take what he wanted.
P7:   Right. Or smack her.

F: If this is dangerous for her, and we all know that it can be, she has to change her behavior. We've seen how he's under a lot of pressure to act in certain ways—to be a man as we have defined it in the box. We see now that she's also under a lot of pressure from him to act in ways that protect her and don't make him angry. He ends up being more aggressive, pressuring, and trying to be in control, and she ends up being more polite, smiling, and trying to please him without giving in to what he wants.

Even if they started out trying not to act out the roles, the pressures force them to act more and more like they're in the box. They can't just talk together as two people who like each other. What would it take for that to happen? For them to work this out as equals?

P1: They'd have to talk about it.

P2: He couldn't be in control.

P3: Someone has to be in control.

P4: Yeah, the guy.

P5: No, then it can't be equal.

P6: The woman is in control anyway. She can say yes or no. She has the power.

F: Who really has the power here? (Everyone is talking at once about who has the power—some say the man, some say the woman.)

F: Let me ask it a different way. Who is it dangerous for?

P7: Her.

F: When it comes to physical control, who has the size advantage? Who is vulnerable to violence?

P8: (reluctantly) He has the power.

F: When we really come down to it, he has more power over what happens. If he doesn't like the way it is going, he can yell at her, hit her, or rape her. She has to protect herself from him, not the other way around. She is always aware of the possibility that he may get angry. She

has to be aware of her vulnerability to violence. He may
be a very nice guy and have no intention of abusing her,
but we've all had experiences with men who were great
to be around until something got them ticked off. Then
they exploded violently. And we know that according
to FBI estimates, a woman is raped in this country every
five minutes. One out of three women will be raped in
her lifetime, and one out of four girls is sexually assaulted before she turns eighteen.

   This is a simple dating scene involving two people,
but it also mirrors the power relationships between
men and women. We can see how this situation is
a setup for frustration, anger, and, potentially, for
violence.

By this point some of them begin to understand the frustration
and anger built into the relationship. They are experiencing those
same feelings trying to figure out what he should do. Many of
them, however, are still distancing themselves from the scene.

F: Let's assume that he did get angry with her, decided he
     would take what he wanted, and forced her to have
     sex with him. Maybe he just refused to leave. Maybe
     she got tired and just gave up. Maybe she got scared
     and decided to give in. In any case, he had sex with
     her knowing that she did not want to.

At this point we get four or five of the men to come up and participate in the scene.

F: The situation is that you know him and you know
     her. She called you this morning, very upset, and said
     that he raped her last night on their date. Now you
     want to talk with him. (BF = boyfriend, M = other
     male friends.)

BF: What's up?

M1: I hear you went out with Sally last night.

BF: Yeah, we had a good time. We went out to dinner, dancing, the whole bit.

M2: That's not what I heard. You think she had a good time?

BF: Sure. I think so. She seemed to enjoy herself the whole evening. Of course we ended up getting it on. I know she enjoyed that!

M3: That's not what I hear from her. She said she didn't like it at all. In fact, she didn't want to have sex.

BF: She said that? Are you telling me she called you up? Well, you know how women are, they can change their minds anytime. She really liked it while it was happening.

M4: She's pissed off and upset this morning. She said you pushed her down, called her names, and forced her.

BF: Look, I'll take care of it. She was okay last night. Maybe it's something else. Let me handle this.

M1: Was she drinking? Were you drinking last night?

BF: We had a glass or two of wine, nothing much.

M2: Sally says that she told you real clear she didn't want to have sex with you.

BF: Hey man, you know how women are. They may say no but they mean yes. Sure she said no, but they all do. You know how they want it.

M3: No, man, it doesn't work that way. When a woman says no you have to take her at her word. Forcing yourself on her is rape. You really hurt her.

BF: I didn't mean to hurt her. I just wanted to get something going. I knew she would like it in the end. You guys have been there before. You know how it goes.

M4: Yeah, we know. But you can't force yourself on her, that's going too far. You better hope she doesn't press charges!

Sometimes during this conversation the men really understand why what he did is wrong and argue from conviction. At other times the men say what they think they should say. In either case they are practicing something completely new, challenging another man's violence. The other men in the room are watching this being modeled.

We continue the discussion, looking at the effects of his actions on her, what she needs, and what other issues are involved. Each workshop is different. This is only one example of the discussion that might take place. The men are not just given information; they are challenged to look at their own past actions and assumptions and are given a chance to break down patterns of collusion with male violence. These role plays allow men to realize that we each have a role in breaking patterns of violence. It models how to do that in situations we often avoid involving ourselves in because they are "private."

This new role of male friend and confronter is clearly awkward for some men in our prison group. They don't know what to say and are easily stymied by the boyfriend's responses. At the same time they are learning a new and powerful way to confront male collusion with violence. They can understand how difficult, but necessary, it is to intervene. They can now feel how pitiful the excuses and defense of the boyfriend really are.

There are many more complex issues that could be unraveled from a role play like this one. Men need more than one workshop to lay a strong foundation for eliminating violence. Unfortunately, the reality is that there are tremendous amounts of money spent in locking people up in our society and precious little spent in preventing future violence. Most of these men will be back on the streets. It is in our best interest as well as theirs to give them the skills to lead violence-free lives before they return to the outside.

In a workshop we can only start a process that must be continued by each man and by the entire group, preferably with institutional support. If the money were available, we would continue to work with them. Sometimes we are able to work with the staff so that they can facilitate further work. We do know that the process we have begun with the men goes on, that the role plays and discussion are so powerful that the men continue to analyze and apply this work to their lives. As one man wrote to us recently after our workshop,

> Well, you might not know it but you sure helped a couple of us guys here. . . . I just want to say thank you for sharing the information with me, as I can't talk for another man. I came here to my cell and thought about the day and all that was said about different ways to avoid anger and violence. I didn't think anything about it until the last act. You people must really care to come from Oakland to share these things. I want to be the first from here to let you know that you opened some eyes here. . . . Maybe one day I'll too be able to help someone!
>
> P.S. Tell all those youngsters this isn't where it's at!

Many of the men are eager to understand these situations in ways that will work better for them in the future. Usually nothing provokes so much discussion as this next scene we do.* This is the "last act" referred to in the letter above.

Spaghetti Again?

(H = husband, just coming home from work. W = wife, cooking dinner in apartment.)

H: (coming in and sitting down) What a day! (Pause) Why is this place always a mess?

W: Have a hard day, honey? So did I. I just got home. Just sit and relax for a few minutes until dinner's ready.

H: How can I relax when I have a stack of papers to do tonight? The boss was on my case from the moment I walked in this morning.

W: That's too bad. Here, have a beer.

H: What's for dinner, anyway?

---

* © Oakland Men's Project.

W: (hesitantly) Spaghetti.

H: Spaghetti again? We just had spaghetti. (He gets up.)

W: I know, honey, I didn't have time to fix anything else. Tomorrow night I'll fix you something special.

H: I won't eat this crap. Fix something else. Don't make me angry.

W: I can't. I've been called for a shift at the hospital tonight, and I have to leave real soon.

H: You've what? You're telling me you're leaving? You aren't going anywhere. I've had a hard day at the office and I want you home with me tonight. (He calms down a little.) I'll tell you what. Let's not get into a fight about it. I'll go down and get a bottle of wine, you pull out some steaks from the freezer, and we'll have a quiet dinner together.

W: I can't. Tomorrow night I'll fix you a nice dinner. Tonight I have to go in to work or they'll fire me.

H: Call in sick. It's a hospital. They understand that.

W: We need the money.

H: Oh, so it's my fault. (He is getting angrier by the minute.) Don't push me too far.

W: That's not what I mean.

H: You are not going anywhere! (He grabs her arm.)

W: I have to. Here's your dinner. I'm leaving now. (She turns to go.)

H: You're staying here, bitch! (He slaps her; they freeze in place for a moment.)

When he hits her, there is some nervous laughter in the group. We immediately ask what is funny about what happened. The men admit that it isn't so funny in real life. But we have also been trained not to take it too seriously, to think of her getting hit almost as a joke. We ask what gets us to the point where we can be so insensitive to the humiliation and abuse that she is experiencing. One of us begins to facilitate the discussion. (F = facilitator, P = participant.)

F: What's going on with him?

P1: He's tired.

P2: The boss has been on his case.

P3: He's angry because there are leftovers.

F: Is this really about leftovers?

P1: No, it could have been anything. He was angry
     when he came in.

F: Okay, he was angry when he got there. What
     assumptions is he making about the situation,
     about her role, about his?

P2: He's the boss.

P3: She should take care of him.

P4: His needs are more important.

P2: She should take care of the cooking and the cleaning.

P1: She shouldn't argue with him. She should do what
     he says.

F: Does any of this remind you of the Act Like a Lady
     box? His expectations are simply what he was taught
     about women. We're all taught this. What does he
     do when she doesn't live up to his expectations?

P3: He gets angry.

P4: He's frustrated.

P1: He knocks her about.

F: How many of you have ever seen a man get angry and
     frustrated with a woman and hit her? (Every hand
     goes up.) Many of us have lived this scene. Just about
     all of us have seen it happen. It is estimated that some-
     where between 25 and 50 percent of all male/female
     relationships have had at least one incident during
     which the man hit the woman. It is very common.

At this point, we again get four or five men to come up and talk
to the man in the role play.

F: We're going to pretend that this is an apartment and
     you live down the hall from them. You've just heard

the fight and are concerned. He's just stepped into the hall for a breather. (H = husband, N = neighbors.)

N1: What was that all about?

H: What are you talking about?

N2: All that yelling.

H: She and I just had a little fight, that's all. You know how it is.

N3: Sounded pretty serious to me. You look upset. What happened?

H: Nothing much. Look, it was just a family argument, and I've taken care of it.

N4: Anybody get hurt?

H: No. She was about to throw a pot of spaghetti at me but I stopped her.

N1: Did you hit her?

H: Who me? It was just a little fight. (Pause) I may have slapped her is all.

N2: I could hear her through the wall. She sounded pretty scared.

H: Hey, look! I'm sorry if we made too much noise. We'll try to keep it down. You two were going at it pretty bad last week, weren't you?

N3: Yeah, I know what it's like, coming home tired and things aren't the way you want them. But hitting her is not the way to handle it.

H: What am I supposed to do, let her walk all over me? I warned her not to push me too far. You make it sound like I did something wrong. Don't tell me you're so innocent yourself!

N4: It is wrong to hit her.

One of us steps in to facilitate the discussion.

F: What's hard about talking with him?

M1: He denies everything.

M2: He isn't listening.

M3: He's defensive.

M4: He is just thinking about himself.

F: Can you tell us one thing about him that reminds you of yourself?

At this point there is some painful silence as the men realize they have been talking with some version of themselves.

F: He's clearly acting like a man, just as he's been trained to. He's hard to talk to. Maybe because he reminds each of us a little bit of ourselves when we've been confronted with something we did that was wrong. (Turning to the whole group.) What did the neighbors do that got through to him?

M1: They challenged him.

M2: But they didn't jump all over him.

M3: They wouldn't let him deny what he did.

M4: They wouldn't go away.

M5: They showed they cared.

F: They were strong and clear. They challenged the violence, but in a caring way. As men this is a very powerful way for us to be there for each other. We can confront the behaviors, expectations, assumptions, and still not give up on each other. This could be a dangerous situation, and we're not suggesting that you necessarily go up to the next violent man you see and confront him. But there are many ways we can intervene to stop the violence. We can call the police. We can talk with her. We can talk with him. If we don't do anything, what are we telling him?

M1: That it's okay.

M2: That we don't care.

M3: That she's not important.

F: One more question before we go on. What does he need from us?

M4: He needs to know we care.

M5: He needs to know the violence is not okay.

M6: He needs friends.

M7: He needs to control his anger.

M8: He needs to take a walk.

F: He needs all of these things. He also needs to know
     the costs and dangers of what he is doing. You know
     what those costs are, you can talk to him about
     them. He needs to know he is doing serious emo-
     tional and physical injury to her. Intentionally or not,
     he could maim or kill her. It happens every day. He
     needs to know that it is destroying his relationship
     and his family. She could leave at any time. He needs
     to know that it is illegal. He could be arrested and
     sent to jail. He also needs to know that he is destroy-
     ing himself. We all know this is not how he wants to
     live. Finally, he needs to know there are alternatives.
     You've learned today some of the alternatives—
     time-outs, listening to her, communicating his feel-
     ings, dealing with his anger from work, changing his
     expectations that she will serve him. You become an
     ally of his and help all of us stay a little safer by let-
     ting him know that he can get help and change. Let
     him know he can eliminate the violence from his life,
     and you will help him do it.

At this point the men have some tools to work with, a framework to understand the issues, and a sense of how the dynamics
of everyday situations and traditional gender roles set up violence.
We have started a process that each of them must continue to end
the violence in their lives.

We thank the men who came and wind up the workshop with
a summary of what we have covered and a closing circle in which
the men get to identify their next step in stopping the violence.

As we leave the prison, checking out through massive gate after massive gate, I think about the tremendous amount of money

we are spending on new prisons and how little there is to support violence prevention. To stop male violence we must lobby, agitate, and organize to get the money appropriated for the prevention work that is needed. These men need to be met at the gates with jobs, low-cost housing, health care, parenting and relationship classes, and counseling and retraining programs. Each one of us can play a part in initiating and supporting these kinds of programs, and in pressuring our governments to provide the necessary funding for them. In the long run this will save money. More importantly, it will save lives.

SIXTEEN

The Violence of Racism[*]

One of the most difficult topics we discussed in our workshops is racism. As with all issues of violence, there is large-scale denial of the extent to which racism devastates our lives and affects every relationship. Racism is the institutionalization of violence and inequality of power based on skin color. In our society, white people have the economic, legal, political, physical, and emotional power to exploit, control, or violate people of color. It doesn't matter that most white people don't consciously or actively seek such power. By simply being white, one has material advantages and privileges unknown to most people of color. These advantages include better schools; safer neighborhoods; more money for comparable work; recognition in the courts and representation in government; better health care; near-universal representation in radio, television, and the print and film media; and more respect when one speaks. White people are also protected from the everyday racism that people of color experience, such as stereotyping in the media, police brutality, job, housing, and school discrimination.

It is important for white people and people of color to be able to identify how racism operates in their lives and affects them day by day. The results of racism—the continuation of prejudice and discrimination— need to be understood so healing can begin. In our workshops we try to help participants understand the social system as well as their personal experiences with racism.

Some white people have experienced mistreatment or prejudice

---

* This section benefited from editing by Allan Creighton.

from people of color. Sometimes white people use this claim to justify the mistreatment of people of color or to level charges of reverse racism. But because racism is institutional, the power is always on the side of the institutions, which favor white people. Anyone from any group can have personal attitudes of prejudice toward others. These attitudes are wrong and dangerous, whoever holds them. But racism is more than prejudice; it is based on power and inequality. And in American society only white people are placed in positions to enforce racism and benefit from it.

Power + Prejudice = Racism

Racism trains white people to be prejudiced just as sexism trains men to treat women as sexual objects. All men are trained to be sexist; some of us are trying to unlearn what we've been taught because it doesn't work. It produces violence, inequality, and disrespect. Similarly with racism, all white people have been trained to view people of color in certain ways, to discriminate against them and then to blame them for the racism. As with sexism, the training is everywhere and is so complete that it becomes nearly instinctive for white people. We learn it from our parents, friends, schools, comic books, television, advertisements, movies, and government and religious institutions.

Some of the obvious effects of racism are direct violence, economic exploitation, and the destruction of the cultures of people of color. These result in the following:

- shorter life spans for people of color
- higher infant mortality rates and poorer health care in general
- less access to education and jobs, lower wages, and more dangerous working conditions
- more vulnerability to physical violence
- loss of many of the tremendous contributions that people of color can make and denial of the contributions they have made to society

- fear, mistrust, anger, and violence between whites and people of color
- disillusionment, despair, fear, and hopelessness among whites and people
- denial and suppression of cultural differences among white people
- the near extinction of many Native American peoples and cultures

---

EXERCISE 18
Exercise on Racism for Racially Mixed Groups *

One of the exercises we do in racially mixed groups to help white people understand the costs of racism begins with everyone sitting down. People of color are asked to rise whenever one of the following statements applies to them:

- Your ancestors were forced to come to this country or were forced to relocate from where they were living in this country, either temporarily or permanently, or were restricted from living in certain areas in this country.
- You have heard or overheard people saying that you or your people should leave, go home, or go back to where you came from.
- As a child, you were the intermediary between your parent(s) and store clerks or public officials (social workers, school officials, etc.) because of language or other differences.
- You have been called names or otherwise ridiculed by someone you didn't know because you are, for example, African American, Latino, Asian American, Native American, or Arab American.

* Adapted from Allan Creighton.

- You have been ridiculed by a teacher, employer, or supervisor because you are a person of color.
- You have been told by a white person that you are different from other people because of your racial or ethnic group.
- You have been told that you didn't act (Black, Latino, Asian, Arab, Indian . . .) enough.
- You have received less than full respect, attention, or response from a doctor, police officer, court official, city official, or other professional because of your race or ethnicity.
- You have felt ashamed, embarrassed, or angry over the way that your racial or ethnic group was portrayed on television or in the movies.
- You have tried to change your physical appearance, mannerisms, or behavior to avoid being judged or ridiculed because you are a person of color.
- You have been told to learn to speak "correct" or "better" English.
- You have been discouraged or prevented from pursuing academic or work goals or have been placed in a lower vocational level because of your racial or ethnic identity.
- You have been mistrusted or accused of stealing, cheating, or lying because you are a person of color.
- You have picked up that someone was afraid of you because of your ethnic or racial background.
- You have been stopped by police because of your racial or ethnic identity.
- You have been refused employment because you are a person of color.
- You have been paid less, treated less fairly, or given harder work than a white person in a similar occupational position because you are a person of color.
- Your religious or cultural holidays were not recognized where you worked or went to school; for

example, meetings and work time were scheduled during those periods.

- You have been refused housing, or you have been discouraged from applying for housing, or you have had to move from where you lived because of racial discrimination.
- You have felt conspicuous, uncomfortable, or alone in a group because you were the only representative of your racial or ethnic group.
- You have felt uncomfortable or angry when a remark or joke was made about your race or ethnicity, but it wasn't safe for you to confront the person or people who made the remark or joke.
- You have felt the threat of violence because of your race.
- You or your close friends or family have been victims of violence because of your race.
- You have been told by a white person that you are too sensitive, too emotional, or too angry when talking about racism.

Seeing the majority of people of color who stand up for most of these questions is a sobering experience for those of us who are white. Generally, we who are white are able to ignore the effects of racism on people of color except when we are confronted with them. This is one of our privileges. This exercise is a painful reminder of the costs of racism. It can make us feel embarrassed, guilty, or angry at people of color for bringing it up again. We can blame them for being too angry, too impatient, too pushy, not appreciative enough of what they have or of what we do for them.

We need to acknowledge and then put aside these feelings and listen closely to what they are describing. Then we need to examine our own experiences and see how they confirm the truth of what people of color say about racism.

It can be hard for those of us who are white to recognize the costs of racism to us. One exercise we use at the Oakland Men's Project to make this clear is the following.

EXERCISE 19
Stand Up Exercise for White People *

Please stand up if any of the following apply to you:

- You don't know exactly what your European/American heritage is or your great-grandparents' names are, or you don't know what regions or cities your ancestors are from.
- You grew up, lived (or live) in a neighborhood or went to school or a camp that, as far as you know, was exclusively white.
- You grew up with people of color who were servants, maids, gardeners, or baby-sitters in your house.
- You did not meet people of color in person or socially before you were well into your teens.
- You grew up in a household in which you heard derogatory racial terms or racial jokes.
- You grew up in a family in which you heard that people of color were to blame for violence, lack of jobs, or other problems.
- *(For this category, after you stand, stay standing if the next item applies to you.) You have seen or heard people of color described or pictured in the following ways (this includes movies, television, radio, magazines, or music):*
  Mexicans depicted as drunk, lazy, or illiterate
  Asians depicted as exotic, cruel, or mysterious
  Asian Indians depicted as excitable or "silly"
  Arabs depicted as swarthy, ravishing, or "crazed"
  African Americans depicted as violent or criminal
  Pacific Islanders depicted as fun-loving or lazy
  American Indians depicted as drunk, savage, or "noble"
  Any character roles from nonwhite cultures acted by white actors

* Adapted from Allan Creighton.

- You were told not to play with children of a particular race or ethnic group when you were a child.
- You felt that white culture was "Wonderbread" culture (empty, boring) or that another racial group had more rhythm, more athletic ability, was better at math and technology, or had more musical or artistic creativity than white people.
- You felt that people of another racial group were more spiritual than white people.
- You felt nervous, fearful, or felt yourself stiffening when you encountered people of color in a neutral public situation (for example, in an elevator or on the street).
- You have been sexually attracted to a person from another racial group because it seemed exotic, exciting, or a challenge.
- You have been in a close friendship or relationship with a person of color in which the relationship was affected or became stressed or endangered by racism between the two of you or from others.
- You are not in a significant relationship with any people of color in your life right now.
- You have been in a close friendship or relationship with another white person, including members of your immediate family, in which that relationship was damaged or lost because of a disagreement about racism.
- You have felt embarrassed by, separate from, superior to, or more tolerant than other white people, white friends, or members of your family.
- You have worked where people of color held more menial jobs, were paid less, or were otherwise harassed or discriminated against.
- You have belonged to an organization or a work group or attended a meeting or event that people of color protested as racist or that you knew was racist.

- You have heard degrading jokes, comments, or put-
  downs about people of color made in your presence,
  but you did not protest or challenge these remarks.
- You have felt racial tension or noticed racism in a
  situation, but you were afraid to say or do anything
  about it.
- You have seen a person of color being attacked verbally or physically, but you did not intervene.
- You have felt angry, frustrated, tired, or weary about
  dealing with racism and hearing about racial affairs.
- You live in communities where, for whatever reason,
  no people of color are present, so that some of these
  statements don't apply.

Answering these statements honestly and acknowledging how
racism affects us can enhance our ability to fight it actively and effectively. Decreasing white people's prejudice toward people of
color and decreasing people of color's internalized racism toward
whites are important components of this work. But this is not
enough. Eliminating racism calls for people to work together, for
white people to support people of color in taking strong and effective social action.

The following section of a typical workshop we do at the Oakland Men's Project is structured to identify racism clearly and
provide options for responding to it.* It also reinforces issues
raised earlier in the workshop: issues of self-blame, levels of violence, and our role as friends to each other. This particular version
occurred in a racially mixed high-school class. (F = facilitator.)

F: In this next role play one of us is going to play an
      African American teen male, about eighteen, who
      has just finished a math and computer training pro-
      gram and is applying for a job. The other person will
      play the white manager of a computer company. He's

---

* © Oakland Men's Project.

conducting this interview, which takes place on a high school campus. *(Scene starts with manager [M] sitting, looking through some files. Applicant [A] enters.)*

A: Hello, I'm here for the job interview. *(Reaches out to shake hands but manager doesn't extend his hand.)*

M: *(Points to a chair.)* Okay, sit down. *(Looks at watch.)* You're on time? I'm impressed.

A: I'm always on time. And I really want this job.

M: You're going for one of the building maintenance jobs we have available?

A: No, sir. I am applying for the computer programming job.

M: You are? That job takes lots of training, lots of math.

A: I'm very good at math.

M: You mean school math. On-the-job math is much harder than what you learn in school, Charles.

A: My name is Robert. I think I'm well qualified for this job.

M: Yes, Robert. Well, I want to be direct with you. Can I speak directly? This is a demanding job. It calls for hard work every day. You have to be on time, here every morning. Frankly, I don't want you to get your expectations too high. Maybe you should start in building maintenance and try to work up to computers. We have had good success with you there, Robert.

A: Sir, I am not interested in building maintenance. I have been trained for computers. You can see that on my application.

M: Yes, yes, well, we'll be getting back to you. Keep that other job in mind, will you? *(Turns back to folders, clearly indicating that interview is over.)*

A: Please read my application carefully. Good-bye.

F: (to group) Let's step out of the scene for a few minutes. What was happening here? What did you see?

(P = participant.)

P1: The manager wouldn't even look Robert in the eye.

P2: Wouldn't shake his hand.

P3: Prejudice.

P4: His attitude. He wanted him to be a janitor, and he kept referring to "you people."

P5: The manager didn't believe Robert could do the math and computer work.

F: How did you feel watching this scene?

P1: Upset.

F: Why?

P1: Because he wouldn't give him a chance.

F: Okay, other feelings.

P2: Angry.

P3: Sad.

P4: He shouldn't have put up with it. If it had been me I wouldn't have just sat there.

F: What would have happened if he had struck out at this man?

P2: He should just forget it and go find another job.

F: Is this a violent situation?

(Several noes and yeses from around the room.)

F: I'm hearing noes and yeses. Let's hear from a couple of each. Who said no?

P1: The boss didn't hit him or anything like that.

P2: I don't think it was violent. It was only talking.

F: How about those of you who think it was violent?

P3: The boss hurt him with words. It was emotional violence.

P4: It was violence because he wouldn't give him the job because he was African American.

P5: By not remembering his name and not shaking his hand, it attacked his self-esteem. He attacked his group too.

F: Very often we think of violence as physical or sexual assault. But there are other ways of hurting someone, and they aren't always physical. This manager was abusive. He attacked Robert, and Robert felt hurt and angry about it. One of you said that if you were treated that way you would want to strike back. It feels like an attack. Robert is also being denied a job. This white person is part of a system of violence that keeps people of color from getting good jobs. Where else have you seen racism?

P1: At school.

P2: Yeah, with teachers.

F: Sure, it can happen at school. Where else?

P3: At stores. Where they follow you around if you're African American, or ask you questions.

P4: Sometimes with the police too.

F: You're right. These are all instances in which because of the color of their skin, people are denied basic rights and are subject to abuse. Some of these situations also get physically violent. For example, sometimes the police beat or shoot men of color without provocation. More people of color get disciplined in the schools or arrested, not because they act worse, but because the system is set up to see them as dangerous and to blame them first for any violence that happens.

     It can be difficult for those of us who are white to know how to be strong allies for people of color in scenes such as this role play. Let's see how one white person might respond. Let's pretend that this scene just happened. The interviewee is angry and not sure what to do next. He walks down the hall and meets a teacher who is white and wants to help.

(I = interviewee, T = teacher.)

T: Hey, Robert, how's it going?

I: That honky! He wasn't going to give me no job. That was really messed up.

T: Hold on there, don't be so angry. It was probably a mistake or something.

I: There was no mistake. The racist bastard. He wants to keep me from getting a good job; he'd rather have us all on welfare or doing maintenance work.

T: Calm down now or you'll get yourself in more trouble. Don't go digging a hole for yourself. Maybe I could help you if you weren't so angry.

I: That's easy for you to say. This man was discriminating against me. White folks are all the same. They talk about equal opportunity, but it's the same old shit.

T: Wait a minute, I didn't have anything to do with this. Don't blame me, I'm not responsible. If you wouldn't be so angry maybe I could help you. You probably took what he said the wrong way. Maybe you were too sensitive.

I: I could tell. He was racist. That's all. *(He storms off.)*

F: *(turning to audience)* What did you notice about this scene?

P1: The teacher was trying to help.

F: How was the teacher responding?

P2: He was concerned.

P3: He was defensive. It seemed like he was feeling attacked for being white.

P4: He was uncomfortable with Robert's anger.

P5: He was downplaying what happened. He suggested that maybe it was a mistake or that Robert was too sensitive.

P6: He threatened to get him in trouble if he didn't calm down.

F: How do you think Robert was feeling?

P1: Angry.

P2: Frustrated with the teacher's response.

P3: Like he wasn't being heard.

F: Was he being heard?

P4: No, the teacher was focusing on his anger and didn't listen to him say what had happened.

F: This teacher is concerned, he wants to help. First, he's feeling uncomfortable with the anger Robert expressed. Second, he's feeling defensive and guilty about being white and is taking the interaction personally. Because of these feelings, he really can't be of much support for Robert. He doesn't believe it can be racism, even without hearing the whole story. He is also reluctant to challenge another white person. Instead, he focuses on how Robert expressed his anger rather than on what actually happened. He ends up blaming Robert for being too angry, too sensitive, and too out of control. How could he have given Robert more support?

P1: He could have asked him what happened.

P2: He shouldn't have taken it so personally.

P3: He could've tried to do something.

P4: He should've shown more understanding.

F: These are all good suggestions. Let's see how they might look in action. We're going to replay the scene using the ideas you came up with.

T: Hey, Robert, what's happening?

I: That honky! He wasn't going to give me a job. He was messin' with me.

T: You're really upset. Tell me what happened.

I: He was discriminating against me. Wasn't going to hire me 'cause I'm African American. White folks are all alike. Always playing games.

T: This is serious. Why don't you come into my office and tell me exactly what happened.

I: Okay. *(They move to office.)* This company is advertising for computer jobs, and I'm qualified for the job. But this man wouldn't shake my hand, and then he tried to steer me toward a janitor job. He was a racist bastard.

T: That's tough. I know you would be good in that computer job. This sounds like a case of job discrimination. What do you think you want to do about it?

I: I don't know. I want to get that job.

T: If you want to challenge it, I'll help you. Maybe there's something we can do.

F: *(Second facilitator steps in.)* What's different about the scene this time?

P1: The teacher wanted to hear what Robert had to say, and he believed him.

P2: Yeah, he took him seriously.

P3: He didn't get defensive or take it personally.

P4: He focused on the problem.

P5: He let him be angry.

F: The teacher was being a strong, supportive ally for this young man. He accepted his responsibility to confront the racism and to support the person being attacked. He recognized that it was an example of job discrimination and that it needed to be addressed as such. Those of us who are white can each be the kind of powerful ally that this man was.

We cannot be effective allies if we believe that racism is over. Nor will we be able to step in if we don't see the benefits we have gained from racism as white people, if we still believe that there is a level playing field and everyone has an equal chance.

It is not necessarily a privilege to be white, but it certainly has its benefits. That's why so many of us gave up our unique histories, primary languages, accents, distinctive dress, family names and cultural expressions. It seemed like a small price to pay for acceptance in the circle of whiteness. Talk about racial benefits can ring false to many of us who don't have the economic privileges that we see many in this society enjoying. But just because we don't have the economic privileges of those with more money doesn't mean we haven't enjoyed some of the benefits of being white.

It is not that white Americans have not worked hard and built much. We have. But we did not start out from scratch. Much of the rhetoric against more active policies for racial justice stem from the misconception that we are all given equal opportunities and start from a level playing field. We often don't even see the benefits we have received from racism. We claim that they are not there. For the final part of the workshop we did an exercise with the white people in the group to help them see the benefits they had from racism, regardless of whether they wanted them or not.

Look at the following benefits checklist. Put a check beside any benefit that you enjoy that a person of color of your age, gender and class probably does not. Think about what effect not having that benefit would have had on your life.

White Benefits from Racism

My ancestors were legal immigrants to this country during a period when immigrants from Asia, South and Central America or Africa were restricted.

My ancestors came to this country of their own free will and have never had to relocate unwillingly once here.

I live on land that formerly belonged to Native Americans.

My family received homesteading or landstaking claims from the federal government.

I or my family or relatives receive or received federal farm subsidies, farm price supports, agricultural extension assistance or other federal benefits.

I lived or live in a neighborhood that people of color were discriminated from living in.

I lived or live in a city where red-lining discriminates against people of color getting housing or other loans.

I or my parents went to racially segregated schools.

I live in a school district or metropolitan area where more money is spent on the schools that white children go to than on those that children of color attend.

I live in or went to a school district where children of color are more likely to be disciplined than white children, or more likely to be tracked into nonacademic programs.

I live in or went to a school district where the textbooks and other classroom materials reflected my race as normal, heroes and builders of the United States, and there was little mention of the contributions of people of color to our society.

I was encouraged to go on to college by teachers, parents or other advisors.

I attended a publicly funded university, or a heavily endowed private university or college, and/or received student loans.

I served in the military when it was still racially segregated, or achieved a rank where there were few people of color, or served in a combat situation where there were large numbers of people of color in dangerous combat positions.

My ancestors were immigrants who took jobs in railroads, streetcars, construction, shipbuilding, wagon and coach driving, house painting, tailoring, longshore work, brick laying, table waiting, working in the mills, furriering, dressmaking or any other trade or occupation where people of color were driven out or excluded.

I received job training in a program where there were few or no people of color

I have received a job, job interview, job training or internship through personal connections of family or friends.

I worked or work in a job where people of color made less for doing comparable work or did more menial jobs.

I have worked in a job where people of color were hired last, or fired first.

I work in a job, career or profession or in an agency or organization in which there are few people of color.

I received small business loans or credits, government contracts or government assistance in my business.

My parents were able to vote in any election they wanted without worrying about poll taxes, literacy requirements or other forms of discrimination.

I can always vote for candidates who reflect my race.

I live in a neighborhood that has better police protection, municipal services and is safer than that where people of color live.

The hospital and medical services close to me or which I use are better than that of most people of color in the region in which I live.

I have never had to worry that clearly labeled public facilities, such as swimming pools, restrooms, restaurants and nightspots were in fact not open to me because of my skin color.

I see white people in a wide variety of roles on television and in movies.

My race needn't be a factor in where I choose to live.

My race needn't be a factor in where I send my children to school.

I don't need to think about race and racism everyday. I can choose when and where I want to respond to racism.

What feelings come up for you when you think about the benefits that white people gain from racism? Do you feel angry or resentful? Guilty or uncomfortable? Do you want to say "Yes, but . . ."?

Again, the purpose of this checklist is not to discount what we, our families and foreparents have achieved. But we do need to question any assumptions we retain that everyone started out with equal opportunity.

We ended this particular workshop section with a discussion of institutional racism, the systematic effects of these historical developments and policies, and by connecting it all back to the power chart and the role that allies can play.

Throughout this book I've discussed the important role we each can take in stopping the cycle of violence by becoming allies for people with less power: men becoming allies for women against male violence; white people becoming allies for people of color against racism; middle-class people becoming allies for poor and working-class people against economic exploitation; and heterosexual people becoming allies for gay, lesbian, and bisexual people. There are many excuses we use for not being involved. Each workshop we do is designed to make participants acknowledge the excuses and the fears behind them, and then take effective action.

It should be clear by now that guilt, shame, embarrassment, defensiveness, and taking things too personally get in the way of our being better allies. Pretending that racism doesn't exist anymore, or that everyone is equal, or that these are problems for people of color and not those of us who are white, or that the victim was at fault— these are also ways that we avoid getting involved. We can't just say, "I didn't hit anybody," or "I'm not prejudiced," or "I don't see color, I just see people," or "I don't see what this has to do with me."

The costs of gender-based and racial violence affect each of us in important ways every day. At the same time, every day we have the opportunity to be allies and break the cycle of violence.

As adults, we have a particularly strong role to play as allies of younger people. Young people need us to model alternatives to violence in our families and communities. The last part of this book is about how we can pass on alternatives to violence to the next generation, the young people in our lives.

PART V

The Next Generation

Ending our own abusive behaviors, reaching out to other men, supporting women's struggles for power and equality—these can seem to be huge tasks, demanding all of our time and energy. But it is not enough. Unless we reach out to young people and present them with better choices, with alternatives to violence, we will not have broken the cycle of violence.

This last part of the book describes my work and the work of the Oakland Men's Project in reaching out to young people to develop alternatives to violence. Some of us are parents, many of us have younger family members, all of us relate to young people in our community. Our responsibility to those younger than we begins with our role as parents in the community and continues through the kind of work done by the Oakland Men's Project and described on the following pages.

SEVENTEEN

Visiting Junior High

During the first year of our work we started to take our presentations into junior and senior high schools. Working with young people has always been a priority for us. Nurturing the next generation is inspiration for our work. We need only remember the lack of support in our own youth to realize that young men and women need us to be there as they try to sort out the choices they have to make. How limited those choices can seem was brought out during a visit we made to a local junior high.

There is no missing the school—a faded stucco building and a long wire-mesh fence enclosing the asphalt playground. Several portable bungalows are lined up at the far end of the campus.

The main entrance is closed off for security reasons; it is easier to monitor the students that way too. We walk up to the small side entrance used during class hours.

I notice how dark it is as I enter the hall. There are steel lockers along the walls, long halls, and almost no windows. The security guard is sitting, monitoring movement down the halls. She directs us to the main office to check in and tells a student headed that way to guide us there. He looks at us and says, "Weren't you guys here last year?"

"Yeah, we're from the Oakland Men's Project."

"I remember you guys coming in."

"What do you remember?"

"You did this scene where a father hits his son, and then this Act Like a Man box."

"Uh-huh."

"There's the office."

211

"Thanks, take care now."

It is encouraging that he remembers us and some of the content of the workshop. We know we are noticed and remembered because teens approach us all over the city—on the streets, at the drugstore, when I'm swimming in the public pool with my children—and they say, "Hey, weren't you in my class last year?" What else they remember is harder to determine; it's difficult to tell what kind of long-term effect we have on them.

We check into the main office and sign the visitors' book. We are issued little numbered name tags so that guards can identify us as officially registered visitors. When I check into a prison I'm always a little scared and intimidated; in a school I'm usually depressed. The unlit corridors, the somber atmosphere, the constant adult surveillance—it reminds me that part of our work is to counteract the prevailing tendency to treat students as being either vulnerable to violence, needing protection, or dangerous. I remember the way adults viewed me when I was a teen, always with suspicion. This thought makes me eager to get in and talk with the students.

When we get to the classroom the teacher informs us that there is going to be a "lockout" when the period starts. I do a slight double take: I thought he said "lock-down," and I assumed there was still some difference between jails and schools. He explains that when the bell rings for class all teachers are instructed to lock their doors. Any student caught in the halls is immediately sent to the office. He expresses his satisfaction with this policy. He tells us it is necessary because the students are unruly, not too bright, and in need of tight control (which he had obviously relinquished long ago). He is white; most of his students are African American and Latino. Some of his comments are blatantly racist, and all are condescending. Many of the wardens at Juvenile Hall, where we also work, are considerably more sensitive and unprejudiced than he is.

In fact, the parallels with Juvenile Hall are striking. Teens are sent to both places. In both environments they are shuffled back and forth between a series of rooms at the discretion and monitoring of adults. They have no chance to go outside except during closely supervised gym and lunch periods. Many of the adults are burned-out, long-term employees who have their own struggles over work conditions, pay, and supervision.

An even more striking parallel is the tremendous exuberance and vitality of the teens in both places. No matter how bleak the environment, how decrepit the buildings, how arbitrary and callous the adults, the amount of energy bristling in the halls and in the rooms is astounding. Students literally bounce into the classrooms, shouting at each other, pushing, throwing things, passing around novel objects, dancing on the tables, singing, and doing stunts. A lot of this energy is tied into maintaining image, impressing others, and challenging authority. How could it be otherwise in a place where they are given no power, no responsibility, and no chance for self-expression or self-determination?

Most of their songs and raps, passes and pushes, are directed at each other. They wade through the schoolwork and dance around the teachers; their community is each other. They are seen or not, respected or not, supported or not by their peers. Peer interaction consumes most of the time, energy, and creativity of each day. Adults are more than just a part of the environment because of the power we have over the students, but we are not the main show.

So here we are, two adult men, one African American, one white, about to spend one class period for two days with them. What role do we have? What can we do? Can we cross the gulf between our concerns and their daily experience?

Our presence in the classroom is immediately noticed. Students come up and ask who we are, why we're here, what our names are. They introduce themselves, show off some, ask about our clothes, my earrings (they wonder if I'm gay, but don't ask directly), and anything else that comes to mind.

On the one hand we are adults, set apart from them by age, experience, dress, purpose, and our collaboration with the adults who hold power in this institution. On the other hand, we're a little outside the formal lines of authority. We're there to talk with them, listen to them, and address the issues they want to talk about. Between these two positions we have an opening, a slight gap between our roles and our purpose. We have to get through the gap quickly, showing respect for the students and sensitivity to their concerns, or the opening will close.

They are eagerly attentive for the first few minutes, though not necessarily quiet. I am aware that we are being seriously evaluated, quickly and effectively. Are we dangerous? Are we interesting? Are we relevant? For their own survival, students have to check out how we are going to use our power as teachers and adults. Are we going to intimidate, disrespect, or threaten them?

These students are forced day after day to listen to boring adults talk about boring subjects. Adults are not very interesting to younger people because we do not talk about what interests them. We do not listen to them. We avoid the pertinent topics. We talk too much. And there is an element of coercion in most of what we do say. They have developed many ways to tune out what's boring and focus their attention elsewhere. Elsewhere may be inside their heads, in other conversations, or in what little physical activity is possible in a guarded classroom. It may be in reading something else, and it may be in going numb and empty inside. If we don't keep their interest they will simply drift off elsewhere.

They will also drift off if the material is too painful or if they feel unsafe. Since the subjects we're there to discuss are family violence, sexual assault, bullying, and power, some of their responses will be triggered by pain and fear, not by boredom. We have to be sensitive to that.

The students are also judging how relevant we are to them. I don't just mean that they are judging whether or not what we talk about connects to their lives. They are wondering how serious are we about their participation? How relevant are we to *their* problem-solving, *their* decision making, and *their* empowerment?

We start out the class with a few words about why we are there, and then immediately go into the father/son role play. The students watch intently because the scene is so familiar: an adult yelling abusively at a younger person. Many feelings are coming up. We have turned the scene from just another passive media experience, as powerful as that may be, to one that the students are asked to participate in. At the end of the role play the person playing the son turns to the class, still as the son, and says, "You're my friends, what can I do?"

This opening role play and dialogue does several things. It pulls the group into the situation, giving them choices to make and making them full participants. It also elicits a variety of statements we've been trained to tell victims of abuse, such as giving advice ("Why don't you . . ."), blaming the victim ("You should study harder. . . ."), and fantasy ("You should run away, beat him up, etc."). This segment also identifies feelings we might have if we've been abused, such as fear, anger, sadness, confusion, and wanting to protect the abuser, or blaming ourselves. Finally, this role play begins to touch that part of the students that stood alone and powerless when a parent, older sibling, relative, teacher, or anyone bigger than they were pushed them around, abused, or humiliated them.

After the group talks with the son, the facilitator (F) who played Dad steps back in. (P = participant.)

F: That's hard, isn't it? It is hard to know what to say to this son. You had some good suggestions for him. He needs to talk to someone. What feelings came up for you while you watched that scene?

P: I think . . .

F: I just want feelings, give me one word—
     what did you feel?

P: Sad.

P: Angry.

P: At the dad.

P: Angry at the son; he shouldn't watch television. He should study more.

F: Okay, other feelings.

P: Scared.

P: Powerless.

F: A lot of different feelings come up in a situation like
       this. Some of them come from similar experiences
       we've had. Some come from what we've learned
       from others. Let's see what the son is learning. He's
       learning a lot from his dad. What's the last thing his
       dad yelled at him before he left? "Act like a man!"
       What does that mean? What is this boy learning
       from his dad about being a man?

From here we do some exercises that reconstruct the Act Like
a Man box presented earlier in the book. We ask the class to identify what boys learn. We ask the class to look at what they've
learned about what men are like. They become engaged with us as
we reflect on our lives.

Every response from a student is affirmed, repeated, and written down on the board. It takes courage for many of them to
speak out. If someone says something we cannot let go unchallenged because it is untrue or disrespectful, we turn to the rest of
the class and ask, "What do the rest of you think about what he
[or she] just said?" We try to get them to analyze for themselves
and challenge each other.

These students are a community. They live in the same neighborhood and attend the same classes. We're just a couple of visitors to their daily reality. Our role is to help them become a
stronger community by enabling them to look at issues that keep
them apart.

We move through the section on growing up as males, including a discussion of powerful men, such as Martin Luther King, Jr.,
who have stepped out of the Act Like a Man box. Then we look
at girls' training. We ask each young woman to state one thing she
never wants to hear from a man again, and we list it on the board.
We construct the Act Like a Lady box and talk about the names
girls get called.

The contrast between the women's box and the men's box is
noted. The group is asked to describe what might happen if a
young man and a young woman who act out of the roles get into

a relationship: what if they have a disagreement? All the time we are asking the group to identify their own experiences, to acknowledge the pressures, and to look at the choices they have.

At this point we enact the following role play:*

(B = boyfriend, G = girlfriend.)

B: Hey, girl, I've been looking for you.

G: Just got out of class, what's up?

B: I have some great new tapes. Come cruising with me.

G: I'd really like to but I have to study for this math test. I told Rhonda I'd meet her at her place to study.

B: The test can wait. I want to spend time with you.

G: I can't. My father said he'd ground me if I mess up in math again. How about tomorrow?

B: Today. You're my girl, aren't you?

G: Sure I'm your girl.

B: Then show me by how you act. (Grabs her by the arm.) Besides, the girls in fourth period said you've been talking to some dude.

G: That's not true! I don't know what they're talking about!

B: Then show me you're mine! You're coming with me!

G: I can't. Let me go! I'm going home!

B: No, you're not, bitch! (Slaps her across the face. They both freeze for a few seconds.)

We immediately get three or four guys from the class to talk with the boyfriend (who is played by one of us). This part of the workshop is very important. It allows young men to practice intervening and questioning the assumption that violence is okay. I am always tremendously moved by the ways that young men,

---

* © Oakland Men's Project.

when given a chance, step forward and support the boyfriend, but seriously challenge his violence.

About halfway through the class this particular day, we are beginning to look at what teen women can do when confronted by violent men. Three young women come to the front of the room for a role play. They are to help a young woman friend of theirs, played by one of us, tell her boyfriend that she is leaving him because he hit her. As we are about to start, another young woman is called out of class. As she passes the front of the room she calls one of the young women "four-eyes." The offended student runs after her into the hall and throws her against a locker. They begin to fight. The other students rush into the hall and watch as both girls are quickly sent to the principal's office. After the class files back into the room, we talk about the incident.

The students are upset because they feel the fight was over something small and the offended girl shouldn't have responded so aggressively. But when I ask the class point-blank, "Is that realistic? Can you really walk away around here when someone calls you a name?" The entire class responds with a loud "No!" They all agree that is the most dangerous thing you can do, because word gets around. Then you become a mark, a target for other youth. In their opinion, the safest thing to do, the only thing to do, is fight—to the death if necessary.

We can talk about alternatives to violence, but it may not be until some other point in their lives, when the costs are more immediate, that they will use what we were offering. The students want alternatives. Objectively they can see that it doesn't make sense to fight over being called a name. But when it comes to the bottom line they say, without a dissenting voice, that if someone threatens your dignity by calling you a name, you have to fight. If you don't, your safety will be continually threatened.

We continue our discussion by looking at other situations and alternatives. The animated vocal participation also continues. By the end of the class period the students share choices and discuss alternatives to violence that some of them will be able to use in the future. We hope we have challenged the roles and expectations they've brought to the class.

But we have to be humble and realistic about what we can do in a school. The abuse, the lack of power, the physical confinement, the lack of safety, the limited options—these are the realities of their lives. Our brief presence can offer them hope, alternatives, and models of adults as their allies. But after we leave, they must go on together working out solutions to the everyday occurrences confronting them.

After one class presentation we got a letter from a young man:

> Believe it or not, yesterday my friend was put in the exact situation you had rehearsed in our class. Her old boyfriend came up to her and started harassing her. We were a group of people and made our presence known to him. Thanks a lot for the advice.

As we leave the class and walk down the halls we hear the familiar names—"wimp," "fag," "punk," and "bitch." Maybe some of the students in our workshop now understand how we use these names to pass on violence to those around us. Maybe some will decide to avoid a fight because of that understanding.

I look down the hall. The guards are loud and present, herding the students toward their classes while cajoling and threatening them. There are hundreds of students and only a half dozen guards. *The students could take this place over in a minute,* I think to myself.

We sign out at the main office, walk down a final hall, and we're outside. I notice that it's cool, a bright autumn day with the smell of fallen leaves in the air. There is no way the students will know that for another four hours, when they are permitted to leave.

EIGHTEEN

Teens and Power

After a visit to a school like that, it seems clear that whatever the personalities or achievements of particular students or teachers, the schools themselves need a major overhaul. Without understanding the institutional nature of a problem, we always come back to blaming the victims—in this case, young people.

Why do so many young people do poorly in school? Why do teens use drugs, or hang out on street corners, or get pregnant? A common answer to these questions is that many teens have low self-esteem, which is generally defined as having a poor sense of self-worth or ability—a lack of confidence. Literature written by professionals about teens, the priorities of social agencies, and those who fund educational programs, emphasize building self-esteem.

When I think back on my years as a teenager I realize how much I wanted to do, and how little power I had to do it. I wanted to go places I couldn't go. I wanted to try activities I wasn't supposed to do. I wanted to influence my environment, my classes, community, and neighborhood. And I wasn't able to. I never had the money, wheels, friends, influence, or credibility to make a difference.

There were lots of promises from adults. They promised me a life filled with power and privilege if I studied hard, worked hard, stayed clean, stayed safe, didn't have sex, didn't drink, and didn't goof off. . . . But the promise of power ten or twenty years in the future was not convincing. Meanwhile, few adults listened to me or allowed me to participate in things that mattered to me; they neither trusted nor noticed me and my friends and fellow students.

That can make anyone's sense of self-worth deteriorate. If one is hit, put down, arbitrarily punished, and belittled—or molested or raped—self-esteem drops even lower. But the problem is not low self-esteem. *Young people simply have no power over their lives.* Without the power to protect themselves, they are constantly abused by adults. At home, at school, in stores, at work, on the sports field, on the streets—adults have the authority to decide how youths should dress, how they should talk, where they can go, and with whom they can socialize. Busy adults label them irresponsible, immature, lazy, underachieving, and stupid, and blame them for "failing" until teens end up blaming themselves for not succeeding.

In reality, we—adults, the system—have failed them. We discriminate against teens, keep them unemployed, vulnerable to violence and drugs, and uninformed about health and reproductive issues. Then we blame them if they get strung out, pregnant, or if they drop out of school and get picked up for hanging out.

Teens internalize the blame, and it keeps them from helping themselves as a group. Because the lack of personal power and success is seen as a personal problem, each teen views every other teen as more successful or more popular than he or she is. It becomes embarrassing and shameful to admit to not "making it." Other teens become dangerous competitors for the few rewards there are. Teens become divided and are unable to see their common bonds and issues.

Besides a lack of power, personal and social abuse prevents teens from succeeding. The rates of neglect and emotional, physical, and sexual abuse toward young people are horrifying. A young person's past experiences of violence drastically limit his or her ability to succeed in the future. Such violence fosters self-doubt, mistrust, and self-destructive behavior.

Teens also perceive that if they are a person of color or a woman, if they are gay or lesbian, or if they are from a poor family, their opportunities to achieve are severely limited. Females of all races face lower expectations from others than men, as well as sexual harassment. African American and Latino males face higher rates of discipline, suspensions, and arrests. Gay and lesbian teens have to deal with verbal assaults, intimidation, and violent physical assault. Teens learn to blame themselves for this abuse. Our high rate of teen suicide is the direct result of the powerlessness teens face and the self-blame we foster in them.

When we only help them to develop higher self-esteem, we lie to them. We reinforce the belief that they are the problem and they are to blame. We mislead them into thinking that personal virtue, effort, perseverance, and skill can completely change their lives. The brutal reality is that many will fail. Their chances of surviving and succeeding are increased when they know what they are up against. Then they can work together, with adults as allies, to change the odds.

Most of us remember the pain and confusion of our teen years. We can use our experience to help individual teens move through this rough period of their lives. We can pick selected groups of young people and work with them intensively. We can see changes in their self-esteem, their performance at school, and their ability to hold jobs, and we can hope for a good future for them.

Those of us who are trained in social occupations have been taught that individual change is all that is possible. The educational, economic, and family systems are a given, and we're supposed to refine the tools to help people find their way through these systems. Our entire focus is on individual pathology, individual history, individual growth, and personal achievement. In many cases society has rewarded us with good jobs and community respect because we're able to enhance personal development in those we serve. This is important work, but it is not enough.

By seeing teens as a series of individual cases who we can help, we focus on the one we can reach and ignore the ten who are being beaten down. In other words, we don't confront the reality of systematic abuse and disempowerment. By keeping our vision narrow, we avoid facing the greater challenge. Because of a lack of community, we are not able to see that we can also measure change and sustain hope by what we are able to do together on a larger scale.

An important reason some of us talk about self-esteem, rather than organizing young people to fight for change, is that we have internalized our own lack of power and have blamed ourselves for our failures, lost dreams, and the abuse we take. It's as if *our own* self-esteem is the issue. If we understood that teens need to organize to claim power and that we could support them in that struggle in the school system, the job market, and the family structure, we would recognize that this is also our task as workers, women, people of color, and community members. Fighting for teens to gain power would mean fighting for our own power. It is much safer for us to see young people's problems as individual ones and to see their problems as different from our own. These views permit us to continue our lives without confronting our own fears, failures, and unrealistic hopes.

Sometimes we limit ourselves to the area of developing self-esteem because we don't know how to talk about, much less effectively intervene, in situations of domestic violence, drug abuse, sexual assault, and discrimination against young people. We owe it to young people to learn how to address and support them in dealing with these issues. (See the suggested reading list in the back of this book.)

We can raise young people's self-esteem—and our own—by helping them build the power to protect themselves and make meaningful choices. That is what we as adults seek to do. Young people seek no less, and they deserve our support as allies in doing so.

One of the most powerful ways to be an ally to young people is to *take the time* to listen to what they are saying and to help them articulate their questions. What follows is a list of things we try to keep in mind at the Oakland Men's Project while we work with young people.

What Teens Need from Adults

Be an ally. Teens need to see us as strong, reliable, and completely on their side, knowing that we trust them, respect them, and will tell them the truth.

Provide information about power. Teens need us to tell them honestly about how power is used and abused in this society. They need help to develop strategies for becoming more powerful.

Provide information about violence. We need to help them identify the social violence directed at them because they are women, people of color, gay or lesbian, physically different, or poor. We need to help them use this information to help stop the violence.

Support healing. We need to let them know that it is not their fault when they are assaulted, and that it happens to many of us. And we need to give them skills for avoiding further violence in their lives: self-defense skills, communication skills, and alternatives to violence in everyday situations.

Promote history. Young people need information about our struggles and achievements so they can take pride in and build upon them. (It does not mean using lines like, "When I was your age . . .") This enables them to feel part of and responsible for their communities.

Be a partner. Teens need us to be willing to share power with them.

We can be better allies if we shift our emphasis from raising teens' self-esteem to increasing their power. That, in turn, will allow the exuberance, insight, and creativity of young people to contribute to bettering all our lives.

EXERCISE 20
Teen Power

1. List any ways you can think of that you had power as a teen.
2. List any ways you lacked or were denied power as a teen.

3. List major concerns that you had about your sexual orientation and sexual performance.

4. What experiences of abuse or violence did you have as a teen?

5. Did you abuse alcohol or other drugs during that period? Describe major incidents and how they affected you.

6. What was the most difficult thing about being a teenager?

7. What was the most exciting thing?

8. What fears or hurt do you still carry with you from those years?

9. Who was the friend that you could talk with?

10. Name an adult who was an ally of yours.

11. What did the friend and adult provide you?

12. What do you need to do so that your experiences as a teen don't cloud your ability to work with teens now?

13. What experiences and insights from that period of your life can you draw upon now in your relationships with younger people?

14. List some teens who are part of your life right now. What is your relationship to each of them?

15. What prevents you from setting aside time to give them attention and an opportunity to talk about some of the concerns raised in the questions above? How can you overcome these obstacles?

16. What kinds of skills, experience, understanding, or other support can you offer teens?

17. Why? Is it difficult for you to talk with young people?

18. What might be difficult for them in talking with you?

19. Name one teen who you are going to spend more time with, talk with, and offer support to.

EXERCISE 21
Checklist for Working with Teens

- Do I love, acknowledge, and respect young people and tell them that at least once a day?
- Do I avoid blaming them for their mistakes and their youth?
- Do I avoid taking out my own anger, frustrations, past hurt, and present disappointments on them?
- Do I challenge them and expect them to be as powerful as possible?
- Do I talk clearly and straightforwardly about power with them, including the power in my relationship to them?
- Do I share power with them?
- Do I encourage them to develop the inner power to be strong, proud, and whole; develop the assertive power to take care of themselves and achieve their goals; develop the group power to improve our communities?
- Do I talk with them about the costs of using power abusively over others?
- Do I talk about racism, sexism, and economic oppression and help them understand and deal with the specific manifestations of these social factors in their lives?
- Do I acknowledge the personal abuse they have experienced and provide information and support to help them heal?
- Do I help them feel connected to their racial, ethnic, religious, and cultural traditions and our common tradition of struggle for change and improvement?
- Do I help them work together and support each other?
- Am I working with young people to change the structured powerlessness in their lives and to end the personal and social abuse that comes at them?

NINETEEN

Taking the Time

What young people need the most from us is not information or advice. They need us to take the time to listen to their questions and concerns, and then to respond as honestly and directly as we can.

It is difficult, if not impossible, to explain a way of conducting a classroom workshop that respects people and gives their education full range and power. The assumptions from which the Oakland Men's Project operates can offer only an inkling of how the project staff tries to be present for students.

No two workshops are alike. What is perhaps most important to note in the following dialogue is the way the discussion is facilitated around the key issues, how people are involved at every step, and the assumptions about community education that are at the base of the methods we use. Unless workshop participants are asking themselves the pertinent questions—hard, awkward, and embarrassing questions—they won't feel safe about getting to their real fears. Fear will keep them locked into acting-out patterns that don't work for them, and the workshop will be unsuccessful.

As you read the dialogue, notice how group members are gently pushed and challenged to go more deeply into how they feel and how they understand what is happening in their lives. It takes patience and willingness on the facilitator's part to stand next to a person and encourage him or her to say a little more. Although we have a big agenda for each workshop and never enough time, we have to be able to stop to let the group respond to its own needs. We have to be able to let one person have some time to articulate what he or she wants to say, to let the group move in a different direction than we intended, or to stop to further explore an issue that we were ready to move away from.

Here's an example from a junior high school group talking about the Act Like a Man and Act Like a Lady boxes. We have just done the father/son and father/daughter role plays. A young woman in the back asks, "How come when a guy gets a girl pregnant they're not treated the same?" This was definitely not on our agenda and seems to be a distraction. (F = facilitator, YW = young woman, S = student.)

F: What do you mean, "not treated the same"?

YW: Well, if your son got someone pregnant you'd be angry at him, but you probably wouldn't do too much. You might say you feel sorry for him because when her father catches him it will be all over. But you wouldn't do much. But if your daughter got pregnant you'd be all over her. You would be so angry, and you would treat her worse than you did your son.

F: Are you saying you think we should be equally angry at both of them?

YW: You wouldn't be, I bet. You would be more angry at her. What would you do if it was your daughter or son? Do you have children? I mean for real?

F: We both have children. Do you think we should be angry at them?

YW: Sure, they both messed up, and I just want to know which you would be most angry at?

F: So if teens mess up and get pregnant, adults are going to come along and be angry with them. You want the anger to be fair, equally on the man and the woman?

YW: Yeah.

F: If a young woman is pregnant, what does she need from her parents? *(Addressed to the entire class.)*

S1: Support.

F: What kind of support?

S2: Advice, love, someone to be there.

F: Does she need someone to be angry with her?

YW: If she messed up!

F: If she's pregnant, it's too late for advice about that, isn't it? I agree with you that she needs support, and he needs support too. If they were my children I would try to love them, help them decide what they wanted to do, and support them however I could.

YW: Wouldn't you be angry at them? Be real now!

F: I might be angry or disappointed or worried about them, but they don't need to hear that. I would try to be supportive, and if I was angry I would talk with my partner or my co-workers and get support from them. I might call up Eddie here that night and say, "I need to talk with you. My daughter's pregnant and I'm upset, hurt, and angry. I need some help." If I yell at my daughter or son and get real angry and punish them or call them names, doesn't that remind you of the father/son role play?

It turns out that her concern about these pregnant teens is not only relevant to the discussion on male/female relationships, but is also actually unfinished business from the opening role play and the power that adults have over young people. She has always assumed that young people mess up and adults get angry and punish or discipline them for their own good. She was taking our idea that there are other, better ways for a person with power to communicate, and she was trying to see if it could fit into a difficult family situation. She was also checking out how honest we were about the sexual equality we were discussing.

Not all comments are so relevant or so easily connected as this young woman's. At the Oakland Men's Project we find that our tendency is to want to move past the questions and hard situations in order to get things done, to move through our agenda and cover everything. In the process we may miss the concerns, fears, and questions that keep people from moving forward in their own growth, and we end up leaving lots of them behind. We are always reminding each other to "take the time" to listen and respond to their concerns. Then we become their allies and can help them reclaim some power in the classroom and in their lives.

Discipline

It is a sobering experience to walk into a room with thirty teen mothers and pregnant young women: Latina, Asian American, African American, White, and multiracial women who have been catapulted into adulthood and parenting at the ages of fifteen to eighteen. A few male partners have come *(Where are all the others? I wonder),* and there are a handful of babies. One couple has twins. Parents of twins at sixteen!

We are here to do a workshop titled "Male Violence, Dating Relationships, and Gender Roles." Many of these women have been or are in dating relationships in which they have been abused. Many have experienced other kinds of physical, sexual, and emotional abuse in their lives. Some of them are at high risk for hitting their children in the future. We are here to look at the origins of the violence and work out alternatives.

We are both parents, both middle-aged men. We are experienced enough to know that we need to listen a lot, help healing to take place, and offer some information. We also know that we need to draw out the experiences of the group to help everyone find the alternatives to survive in the future.

They are survivors. They have survived beatings, other abuse, and were denied the information and power they need in their lives. For them, survival is a day-to-day concern, not a philosophical question.

We start off with the father/son role play. We talk about how boys are trained to be men, and then we look at girls' training to be women/ladies/good girls. Then we look at relationships and particularly how violence arises in a teen relationship. We do a role play: a boyfriend gets angry at his girlfriend for not coming with him and ends up hitting her. At the end of the discussion we ask, "Is there any situation in which a woman deserves to be hit?"

There is a chorus of noes. Then we ask, referring to the father/son role play, "Are there any situations in which a child deserves to be hit?" A few noes, and a lot of silence.

We ask if they are saying that sometimes children deserve to be hit.

"Not hit, but disciplined."
"Sometimes you have to do it for their own good."
"Just a little slap on the booty."
"Yeah, you have to set limits."

The group is much more animated now than it had been during the opening role plays. Everyone will agree that hitting people is bad and you should never do it. For example, men regularly say to us that you shouldn't hit women. But when pressed, they say that in some circumstances it is okay. They usually mean that when all else fails, when there is no other way to maintain control, it is okay to hit.

This group had agreed in the beginning that it is bad to hit children, and we had discussed the costs of doing so: how it scares children, lowers their self-esteem, teaches them that aggression is okay, and destroys trust and intimacy. But the group holds on to its reservations, so we ask them to describe those situations in which a child deserves to be hit.

"If a child doesn't stop when you ask them to stop again and again."
"If the child won't listen."
"If the child is disturbing other people [adults]."
"If the child is calling people [adults] names and using bad language."
"If a child is doing something dangerous and won't stop."
"If a child is challenging you."

In each case the use of force is justified because all else failed. These young people were talking about children from one to six years old who are clearly not a physical threat to them. We decide to take some specific situations they suggest and act them out to see if there are alternatives. In the first, a three-year-old is banging a chair up and down, making noise. A student comes up and tries to talk the child into stopping. The child stops for a few minutes and then resumes banging. The only other thing the parent can think of doing is hitting the child to enforce the quiet. We ask for alternatives. It is suggested that the child could be punished by taking away something it likes. "What if the child still doesn't stop?" Someone else suggests taking the chair away.

We come up with a few more alternatives and then ask what was really going on in the situation. The students are clear that the child wanted attention, and the group talks about ways to give the child attention. Then someone says, "What if you have just come home from work, you have no energy to give attention, and the child still won't stop?"

I can understand that! I face it at home with my own three children. I also appreciate this group pushing us because it forces us all to see the dynamics more clearly.

Other alternatives are suggested, such as turning on the television, distracting the child with a toy, bribing the child, or threatening the child with punishment. Someone suggests explaining the situation to the child and enlisting cooperation. Most feel this is inappropriate or unnecessary.

The picture being painted is one of children who are fundamentally irrational, uncooperative, too emotional, nagging, demanding, unresponsive, and incapable of self-control. They aren't supposed to intrude when they're not wanted, nor should they question our need for quiet time. They must simply accept our decisions or face the consequences. This picture looks familiar. It's a picture men paint when they talk about women they have hit. Although drawn with different details, the underlying assumptions about who is in control, about the maturity of the other, about the prerogative of quiet in our hard lives, about the accommodation of our needs, and about the legitimacy of ultimately resorting to violence ("discipline"), the pictures are almost exactly the same.

For this group of young people it is almost inconceivable that they should not fall back on force to exert their control. It is also difficult for them to see that young children can participate in a more responsible way in the interaction, and that they, as adults, can work out alternatives that are nonviolent and healthy for all involved. They also have trouble seeing that force does not work and that it does great harm to everyone to subdue people into obedience. Men tend to have the same difficulties in understanding their tendencies toward violence and their assumptions about women. In each case we end up talking about *them,* blaming *them.*

We are talking with a group of young people, many of whom are not so many years past being "disciplined" themselves. They have come to believe that they deserved to be hit, that ultimately it was for their own good. I have talked with hundreds if not thousands of adults who believe the same thing. They have internalized the assumptions about young people so well that they can't imagine that it was wrong for them to have been hit. They can't imagine that no one has the right to hit another to gain control.

It can be scary to acknowledge that those who hit us were wrong, especially if they were people we loved or were dependent on, such as our parents. It may mean looking at anger and pain we haven't wanted to admit or deal with. It may mean looking at attitudes we have carried from childhood. But in order to be caring adults to the young people around us, we must be able to say to ourselves that it was wrong that others hit us, teased us, put us down, or abused us in any way. We were not "bad" and we did not deserve it.

It can be difficult for children to be clear about who is responsible because the physical power parents hold over them is immediate and intimidating. But as adults who are no longer fearful of parental abuse we must reevaluate our pasts. It isn't easy for the teens to do this; they haven't been encouraged to reconsider the role of abuse in childraising because their education is run by adults, and they are still not safe from adult power. Many of them, trying to be adults as quickly as possible, are giving us adult justifications for abuse. As one young man says, "My father never hit me after I was five. All he had to do was look at me in a certain way, or raise his finger, and I froze. I knew that look, and I never got hit anymore."

This young man goes on to admit that he doesn't feel particularly safe with or close to his father. Yet he maintains that the hitting had been appropriate because he was a troublemaker. A troublemaker at three or four or five? He is offering this story as an example of the effectiveness of spanking. But the group interprets it as an example of fear and intimidation, and the desperation of adults to maintain control.

We do come home tired, frustrated, and upset. If we have decided there are some circumstances under which it is okay to hit "our" children or "our" woman, there will come a time when we will do that. Because we cannot make our best decisions when we are stressed, the only protection we have against acting violently is to be absolutely clear ahead of time that hitting is never okay. Otherwise, if we are in situations of panic, we will act out of that panic and end up hitting those we love. We know that when we've done it once, it is a lot easier to do it again.

The class turns to a discussion about whether there is a difference between hitting a child and slapping, yelling, or calling the child names. We return again and again to the role play in which the guy had denied he hit her: "It was no big thing, we just had a fight," and "I didn't hit her, I just slapped her." We talk about how it affected us when we were called names by someone close, when we were hit lightly but with the threat of greater force. We also continue to talk about specific alternatives in each situation, because we must see alternatives to break the cycle of violence.

Understanding that we have alternatives is crucial. When we leave this class we want every single person to know that he or she can be more powerful. Everyone can understand the pressures and training to be violent and can resist.

Sometimes I am tempted to see teen parents as a special case. But I know that the *subjective feelings* of vulnerability, powerlessness, and lack of self-confidence are as strong for adults as they are for teen parents. Each one of us feels the pressure to keep the cycle of violence going. That is why, although individual awareness and change are important, we need new group norms and community values that say it is not okay for men to hit women and it is not okay to hit young people.

When we leave this classroom my head is still spinning with all the questions and comments, all the "what ifs?" You probably have some of your own at this point. It is crucial that each of us decide not to use violence. Regardless of our family circumstances, there are alternatives.

This is easier for co-parents to do than for single parents. It is easier if we have more family or economic resources than if we don't. The added demands and stresses of being a single parent or of being poor are significant. But there are ways to reduce violence in our families regardless of circumstances.

For example, children do endanger themselves occasionally, running into the street or playing with an electric socket. A quick removal of the object or the child from the object is usually all that's called for. An explanation or a distraction easily resolves the tension.

When children seem to be acting willfully or defiantly, it is important not to get angry at the defiance itself, but to look to its causes, to question one's own need for control, and to respect their need for power and participation.

Our three children are exuberant, assertive, excited, and curious. They reach out aggressively to contact the world. When my one-year-old plays with our dog, he pokes and hits and pulls and flails at him. We have to teach him to pat, not hit; to stroke, not pull. He needs help learning how to take his curious, exuberant energy and be gentle with it, soften it. When our four-year-old plays with her friends they are constantly bumping into each other, arguing, and getting into fights. They need help in learning how to communicate their needs and work things out together. Don't curb their energy, but give them skills to live with it and to use it in relation to others. When our eight-year-old walks by and bops the four-year-old on the head because he's happy and energized, he needs help realizing the effect that this has on his sister; he needs to learn to respect her space and her needs. She needs encouragement to tell him to lay off, to expect him to stop, and to ask for help from us when she needs it. That way, she doesn't end up defeated, discouraged, or angry.

Our children never intentionally hurt each other or try to destroy anything unless they're feeling angry and powerless and violence is the only way they think they can get back. Even then, as parents, we don't allow them to hurt others, although we may understand the frustration and pain that led to the anger.

In our home we start out with some simple, clear rules:

- No hitting, kicking, biting, or hurting others, including the animals and plants around us.
- No kissing, hugging, touching, or other contact with a person who does not want it.
- No teasing or name-calling.
- No throwing things in the house or at people; no threats or intimidation.

These rules apply even to the babies. There are explanations provided as the children grow old enough to talk, but the limits on violence come first. The rules apply to the adults. We are not allowed to do any of these things, even in retaliation for children breaking the rules.

Our children understand the importance of these rules because they can feel the danger from adults and adult anger. They don't always have the control to stop themselves, and sometimes they have no other way to express their anger, unless and until we teach them. So they do break the rules sometimes and hit, tease, or call each other names. They are given a time-out, a chance to sit quietly by themselves and think about what they did. If they do not voluntarily go into another room to take the time-out, my partner or I will pick them up, gently but firmly, and carry them to their room. Before the time-out is over we talk with them about whatever feelings remain from the event.

Our assumptions are that no one deserves to get hurt, and that there are always alternatives to violence. It is our role as adults to learn to model these alternatives for our children. The following are some of these alternatives:

- encouraging everyone to speak out and say what he or she wants and needs, without demanding to have it;
- encouraging everyone to talk about his or her feelings, to listen to each other, and to work out negotiated solutions;
- giving time-outs (a quiet time away from others to cool out, adults included) when they are too wrought up or involved to be able to continue nonviolently or cooperatively;
- instilling the expectation that they are important; that they can control when they are to be touched, hugged, and kissed; that they can meet their needs; that they deserve the respect and love of others;
- devising other ways to express conflict and painful emotions through writing, drawing, acting, playing, and sports.

We also try to help our children develop alternative, assertive responses to situations that are frustrating or difficult for them. We help them problem-solve when they are provoked, teased, or bullied. Some of the other kinds of situations in which they need help are when they are embarrassed or ignored, when they make mistakes or are challenged to fight, or when they need to stand up for their rights. They also need to know how to empathize with others, stand up for a friend, respond to peer pressure, and respond appropriately when winning or losing in sports. Any of these types of interaction can either be excuses for violence or opportunities for understanding and resolving differences. (Some useful resources for teaching young people alternatives to violence as well as negotiation and peacemaking skills are in the suggested reading list at the back of this book.)

Eliminating violence in our family has been a slow and difficult process. My partner and I were both raised to spank children, to tease and put them down, and to blame them when we lost control. It was a crucial first step for us when we decided to avoid using force and verbal abuse in raising our children and to involve them in creating a cooperative family environment in which everyone is fully respected.

We still struggle to develop alternatives to punishment and to set limits that show respect for and involve our children. Sometimes one of us will lose it and yell and scream or pick up one of the children for a time-out with more force than is necessary, although this occurs less often as we learn and practice alternative ways to setting limits. We have learned to step in for each other or suggest a time-out when one of us is out of control or simply too tired or stressed out to make good parenting decisions, which is another privilege of having two parents. We have had to learn to go back to our children later and apologize for our behavior when we have made mistakes or been unduly harsh.

Sometimes I have been discouraged that Micki and I are not the parents we would like to be. But then I think about how we were trained to pass on abuse to our children, and I appreciate how far we've come. We have been able to understand the training we received, and we've become allies with our children.

Understanding leads to change: seeing the broad patterns of domestic violence, seeing the assumptions that underlie men's attitudes toward women and their justification for the use of force. Thousands of years of male prerogative and power are put aside when we say that women are fully human and should be respected and not hit, and when we say that men are completely and totally responsible for male violence. We are now beginning to understand that we do not control women, we have mutual relations with them. We are beginning to understand that falling back on force to get our way is illegal, dangerous, and destructive.

We have been even slower and more reluctant to apply these understandings to our relationships with young people. When treated with respect, love, and dignity, children are capable of great intelligence, cooperation, caring, and understanding. We, in turn, are changing our age-old cultural tradition of adult domination and abuse of young people, as well as adult expectations and stereotyping of who young people should be.

Our families mirror our communities. Taking an active stand against abuse within our families is part of the effort to create communities without violence. An active stand against abuse would involve speaking up and challenging statements and values that demean young people, threaten them, or promote abuse against them. Such a stand also means intervening when young people are being hit and abused, instead of saying it is a family matter that doesn't involve us. It means challenging the assumptions about young people (and women and people of color, if we're white)—that they are too emotional, irrational, undisciplined; that they need us to be in charge; that we don't have to respect their feelings or their physical space.

Try saying to yourself, "I will never strike a child under any circumstances." How does it feel to say it? What feelings come up? What kinds of "But what if . . ." statements come up? For many of us just imagining this statement—"I will never strike a child under any circumstances"—is the next step in taking a stand against violence. For others, it is to challenge abuse when we see it. For still others, the next step is to examine our own lives to see where we have accepted self-blame, fear, and the inability to grow because we were abused as young people. If we each take the next step we will all move forward.

EXERCISE 22
Parenting Nonviolently

1. Was there hitting, molesting, slapping, spanking, or other physical discipline in your family when you were a child? What was the effect of this on you and other family members?
2. Were the children in your family put down, teased, told they were worthless, stupid, would never

amount to anything or other negative things? What
was the effect of this on you and other family
members?

3. Do you feel you got as much love and encouragement as you needed as a child?

4. Are there ways you want your children to grow
up with more love and encouragement than you
received? What can you do to give them that
attention?

5. Say to yourself, "It is never okay to hit a child."
What kind of "but what ifs" immediately come
to mind?

6. What keeps you from deciding not to hit, tease, call
young people names, or otherwise put them down?

7. What steps do you need to take to eliminate hitting
and verbal abuse in your family?

8. When you are tired, frustrated, or angry, what
specifically can you do to avoid taking out your
frustrations on your children? (e.g., taking a time-
out yourself, etc.)

9. Make a list of alternative, nonviolent ways to set
limits with young people. Which ones are you going to use?

10. What rules for respect and cooperative living
do you think your family needs to establish?

11. What are alternative ways for members of your
family to express anger, hurt, and frustration
nonviolently?

12. What phrases are used in your family to blame
people? What steps do you need to take to eliminate blaming in your family?

13. The abuse of alcohol and other drugs makes it difficult to parent effectively. If there is alcohol and
other drug abuse in your family, how does that in-
terfere with your ability to parent nonviolently?

14. How can you help your children feel strong about

their bodies, defend themselves, and ask for help when they need it? (Be specific and think of each of your children's needs individually.)

15. What do you need to do to give your children more control over their bodies and to prevent other adults or older children from kissing, hugging, teasing, bopping, spanking, or otherwise bothering them unless they consent?

16. What steps can you take to make your family praise and appreciate rather than criticize each other?

17. If you have daughters, how can you support them to be adventurous, independent, athletic, and confident of succeeding in whatever they do?

18. If you have sons, how can you help them resist the pressure to be tough, aggressive, and insensitive? How can you teach them to respect women?

19. One out of every ten children is gay or lesbian. How would you support your daughter or son if she or he were not heterosexual?

20. What are ways you can teach your children to be proud of their cultural, racial, and religious heritage and to know about and respect the heritages of others? How could you be a better model of tolerance of and respect for others?

21. Think of yourself *and* your children as peacemakers and conflict resolvers. Why is this hard to do? What specific steps can you take to give yourself and them the skills necessary to make these goals a reality?

22. Tell your children you love them.

Conclusion

We are all connected. The pursuit of world peace is sabotaged by the wars in our homes, in our neighborhoods, and in our relationships. At every level our lives are in danger.

Therefore, taking a personal stand against this cycle of pain and violence—taking a stand against racism, economic oppression, and the male role of enforcing this system—is taking a stand for ourselves. Taking a stand means taking care of ourselves and acknowledging our differences, our strengths, and our ability to care. It means supporting the efforts of women to gain power, safety, and respect in this society. It means challenging any man who says or implies that it is natural, inevitable, enjoyable, or otherwise human for men to be abusive. It means encouraging our children to be strong, gentle, and different, and respecting the differences of every one of us. It means not giving up on social change; it means expecting more from our government, our schools, the courts, and every institution in which we are presently encouraged to give in to and pass on violence.

Try this exercise now: Think for a minute of a time in your life when a man came through for you. Maybe it was a father, a brother, a partner, a son, a teacher—whoever. Think of a time when this person was there when you needed him.

(Pause)

We each know men who came through—men who didn't give up. When I say to you that we need to take a stand, I'm calling on those experiences, on that side of male strength and pride, caring and love.

Now is the time to take a stand. That stand is for an end to the violence. That stand is for our children. That stand is for the women in our lives. And most of all, that stand is for ourselves. Because truly, our lives are at stake.

Epilogue

Evaluating Men's Movements

I originally wrote this epilogue when the men's movement (as it was labeled) was strong and visible and before the Promise Keepers had been organized. I have decided to leave the original section because it identifies some important questions we need to ask about any group of men organizing without women. I have added a brief section on the Promise Keepers and then some final words on men's movements in general.

It is with great reservation and concern that I read flyers, ads, and announcements such as the following:

> Wingspan: Journal of the Male Spirit has emerged as the most comprehensive and widely circulated journal of male spirit and soul in the world. Inside this Issue . . . "A Walk with the King," "Initiation of Free Will," "Warrior Images" "Balls" and "Men from the Boys."*

> The Mythology of Gender, Conflicts, Truces and Harmonies Between Men and Women. Some themes for the workshop:
> - What are the wounds of men?
> - What are the feminine powers?
> - What rituals arise from the myths of gendered gods?
> - What does it mean to be rounded in one's own gender?†

---

* From an ad for *Wingspan* in *Creation Spirituality* July/August 1991.
† From a flyer for an event sponsored by the Dancing Ground.

The Male Journey: Workshops

A Day with Iron John. An experiential journey into the presence of the Wild Man. . . .

Phallos: The Sacred Essence of Masculinity. A re-introduction to the long-neglected archetype of masculinity. . . .

Mythology Group. A men's group using male myths and fairy tales to illuminate the journey from boyhood into manhood. . . .*

. . . This is the eighth year that a group of men will go deep into the Mendocino redwoods to drum, build masks, hear stories and speculate on the mythology and psychology of what it is to be a contemporary man. . . . Themes we will consider:
• Developing male beauty as a container for force, force without beauty being destructive.
• Joyful participation in the sorrows of the world.†

In the last few years there has been a movement among men to look at ways we have been hurt by gender roles, have lost our power, and have not been able to find strong male models with whom we can identify. Focusing on deep inner processes of individual growth in an all-male setting, movement leaders have been trying to help men shed some of the learning that has hurt us so that we can reclaim our male power. Leadership for this movement has come from Robert Bly and others through workshops, groups, articles, and gatherings.

Generally, the movement seems to attract middle-class white men who can afford to pay a fee for a workshop or gathering during which they can reclaim their maleness. These events use a variety of exercises, rituals, and group techniques to focus on images of masculinity, personal empowerment, unlearning gender-based training, and relearning the power of the male experience. The goal seems to be for men to achieve increased personal growth, self-awareness, and personal power.

---

* From a flyer advertising men's groups.
† From a flyer advertising the Mendocino Men's Gathering.

Is this movement part of the struggle to end gender roles, inequality, and violence, or is it part of the backlash against that struggle? It is important to reflect on this process among men and to evaluate its effects. When one is working with groups of people who already have a measure of social power, such as the power white middle-class men have at work and in their families, the potential for abuse is great.

The following seem to be some assumptions underlying this movement:

- Men have been hurt by the gender-based system we live in.
- Men have been disempowered by this system.
- Women have wielded power over men or have unwittingly contributed to teaching men disempowerment, particularly within the family.
- Individual men can regain their power.
- Men and women alike benefit from the men's movement.
- Men can do this work together because we share a common cultural training and our differences are not great.

Although these assumptions are not stated anywhere explicitly, or even acknowledged among the participants in men's movement events, they are implicit in the statements of the men who conduct these workshops. Since this movement is gaining media attention and public recognition, it is important that we look critically at its assumptions.

Men have been hurt by the gender-based system we live in.

I think few people would argue with this assumption. It seems crucial to acknowledge the hurt that happens to men in this society. We cannot deny the sexual assault, physical and emotional abuse, fights, and rigid, punitive gender-role training that boys as well as girls experience.

Men have been disempowered by this system.
More people would argue with this, citing male privilege as evidence of male power. Although there are frighteningly powerful men in our society, most of us do not qualify as powerful by the standard measures of power. Furthermore, is it a privilege to lead the dangerous, stunted lives that most men lead? Is it a privilege to be able to pass that pain and hurt on through violence to those we love?

Although most of us are not powerful, we do enjoy more privilege then women. We make more money than women, we are safer on the streets and especially in our homes. We have more respect, more importance, and more community standing than the women around us. We also have the courts, the media, the government, and history on our side when we are challenged by women. Women fear men's violence daily in the forms of rape, battery, sexual harassment, and verbal abuse. As men, our lives are not threatened by women in this way.

*Women have wielded power over men or have
unwittingly contributed to teaching men
disempowerment, particularly within the family.*
This assumption that women are complicit in this process is not clearly stated within the movement and is even denied at times. But the evidence for this belief is abundant. The two main targets for the complicity are mothers and feminists—that is, strong women.

"The male in the last twenty years has become more thoughtful, more gentle. But by this process he has not become more free. He's a nice boy who now not only pleases his mother, but also the young woman he is living with."*

Mothers are held accountable for raising us during our formative years, when fathers are not around, and providing us with female models for adulthood. They are seen as the primary force in our childhood. Our fathers are described as absent, missing, in-

---

* Robert Bly and Keith Thompson, "What Men Really Want" in *Challenge of the Heart,* 1985, ed. John Welwood (Boston: Shambhala Publications, 1985), 101.

visible, or unavailable. Our mothers, therefore, consciously or not, are said to disempower us and keep us from assuming powerful male roles.

This passage is excerpted from an interview with Robert Bly by Keith Thompson. Bly is relating the story of Iron John and the "wild man" energy.

> Bly: Iron John says, "The key is under your mother's pillow." Did you get that shot? . . . It's under his mother's pillow!
>
> Thompson: Would it suggest that the young male has to take back the power he has given to his mother?
>
> Bly: That's right. . . . There are very few mothers in the world who would release that key. . . . The possessiveness that some mothers exercise on sons . . . cannot be overestimated. . . . The issue is that the son has a difficult time breaking away from his parents' field of energy, especially the mother's field.*

Contrary to this assumption, my experience working with men has been that our father's presence is overwhelming in our childhood. Fathers and other adult men sexually assault us, hit us, emotionally abuse us, and train us to be "real" men. They may not be present physically in the way we demand of our mothers, but the power and influence they have on our lives is strong and relentless. Their lives, including their emotional absence, provide the role models by which we reach toward manhood.

Because our mothers are seen as not having real social power, we generally reject them as role models. We distance ourselves from them as quickly as we can. We are not disempowered by our mothers. We are empowered by our fathers, and male-dominated society in general, to be aggressively strong. This calls for us to be alone, uncommunicative, wary, and abusive toward others. I don't think this is a privilege, but it is one definition of power.

The other group of women seen as complicit in men's disempowerment is feminists. The women's movement demanded that male/female relationships be reestablished on the basis of equality

---

* Bly and Thompson, "What Men Really Want," in *Challenge of the Heart*, 106.

and mutual respect. It has been stated by some that because of the women's movement, many men gave up their power to women and became confused, passive, and unsure of their masculinity. A men's movement is therefore needed to counterbalance this trend and to help men reassert their power to match that of women.

> Thompson: Many young males step back from [masculine energy]. Perhaps it's because back in the sixties, when we looked to the women's movement for leads as to how we should be, the message we got was that the new strong woman wanted [emphasis in original] soft men.
>
> Bly: I agree. That's how it felt. The women did play a part in this.*

It is certainly true that the women's movement has forced many of us to examine our previous actions and to acknowledge how abusive those were. This would seem cause for celebration! It is clearly self-destructive and dangerous for men to continue acting from the gender-based system of power and violence. If the articulation of and challenge to this system of power and violence denotes the increasing strength of women, then it seems it can only be beneficial for all of us.

Strong women and a strong women's movement do not produce weak or passive men; they point out, with glaring painfulness, the weakness and emptiness of our male models of power and intimacy. We don't need to be stronger as men to compete with women or protect ourselves from their strength. We do need to take responsibility for our actions and change the models of male power that make us unable to appreciate and cherish the power in others.

Individual men can regain their power.
This seems true, in a limited sense. Through many forms of counseling, the men's movement, and various spiritual trainings, people can become healthier and happier. There are serious limits to

* Bly and Thompson, "What Men Really Want," in *Challenge of the Heart*, 106.

how far individual enhancement can go, however, in a society in which we are all vulnerable to various kinds of violence, exploitation, and inequality. Furthermore, this training is available only to those who can pay for it.

Men and women alike benefit from the men's movement.

It is not necessarily good for the rest of us when some people grow and obtain more personal power, especially if the imbalances of social power that make us all vulnerable to violence and abuse are left untouched. The men's movement has not evolved an articulated analysis of social power. With no political context, individual growth can as easily lead to abuse of power and more individual aggrandizement as it can to community development and change in power relationships. When men complete these trainings, they may or may not be more loving and sensitive to women or have better relationships with their families or be less self-serving or more community-oriented.

When the issues are defined as personal growth, personal power, and individual change, especially when issues surrounding men's personal change are juxtaposed with women's demands for social change, efforts to change the social structures that produce inequalities and institutionalize violence are seriously diminished.

Men can do this work together because we share a common cultural training and our differences are not great.

We do have similarities and common bonds as men. But we also share differences so deep that we have only begun to fathom how great they are. The men's movement has not yet even heard from most men because the differences between us are based on power and violence.

There is the threat of danger from other men. Women know this in the core of their being; so do men, even if we deny it. The threat of danger is different for each of us, depending on our place in society and the amount of power we have to protect ourselves. There is the threat of physical danger from men we meet on the street, and there is the threat of danger from men we work for and with. There is the threat of danger to our children, to the women we relate to as family, friends, or lovers. There is the threat of danger from men who hold administrative power over us, from those who hold racial power over us, from those who have more money than we do—from any man who has power to affect our lives if we don't "act right."

The threat of danger that we fear is not abstract. All of us were yelled at, intimidated, teased, and put down by older men in our lives. Many of us were sexually assaulted. Even more of us were physically hit by fathers or stepfathers. Almost every one of us was in a fight as a child to protect ourselves.

Any men's movement that does not directly address male violence, racism, class issues, and homophobia can only remain exclusive and superficial. We are not all the same, and our differences matter—sometimes in life-threatening ways—in this society.

We shouldn't write this movement off as just another personal growth industry with limited accessibility and less social value. It is part of a male backlash to the social gains and political insights of the women's movement. It would have us believe that women are powerful, that men are weak and vulnerable, and that male violence, racism, and economic exploitation are no longer significant problems. These are clearly lies that attempt to shift our focus from eliminating inequality and violence to helping individual men become more powerful.

We do need each other as men. We need to trust each other and to work together to build a caring community. We need to stop violence among ourselves and those around us. I want to see more men involved in that work. We don't need a men's movement to achieve those goals. We do need many more men working with women in the feminist, gay and lesbian liberation, antiracism, environmental, and peace movements to develop alternatives to violence.

The Promise Keepers

Much has been written already about the Promise Keepers so I will keep my comments brief.

I am always deeply fearful whenever I see male-only groups holding mass rallies or other large–scale events. In particular I am afraid of the Promise Keepers.

I fear their statements about men reclaiming their place at the head of the table because I believe in family and community structures which are democratic and in which everyone sits with authority at the table. There cannot be an equal partnership between men and women if the men are at the head of the table. Where does that leave women, to the side? At the foot? In the kitchen?

I fear the homophobic effects of statements by the leaders of the Promise Keepers, that homosexuality is a sin and an abomination to God. These comments exclude many men from the community and make not only gay and bisexual men but every man vulnerable to harassment, discrimination, and violence from others.

I fear statements by Promise Keepers that this is a Christian country, because I believe we are a multicultural and pluralistic country and have a separation of church and state. Unfortunately, we have a long history of Christians feeling superior to and then organizing to kill Jews, Moslems, infidels, pagans, Native Americans, witches, and other non-Christians.

I also fear the Promise Keepers' funding from right wing, conservative organizations like Focus on the Family, Campus Crusade for Christ, and the Christian coalition, and their funding from corporate sponsors. This funding has largely gone undisclosed. Why are large corporations, which have been cutting back jobs, moving factories overseas, and dumping toxic waste in our neighborhoods, funding the Promise Keepers?

I fear the Promise Keepers' lack of acknowledgment of the strength and leadership of the women's movement, and the gains in gender equality we have achieved in the last thirty years because I suspect it shows that they hope to undermine those gains.

We must also be wary of the language used by the Promise Keepers to describe the issues they address. One promise of a promise keeper is to not hit women. But, as we have seen in this book, the central issue for men is control, not violence. The Promise Keepers extols men not to hit their wives, but to remain in control under all circumstances. Yet the need to control is what leads men to abuse women. They may be telling men not to hit women, but they are not challenging the assumption of male control which leads men to justify all kinds of violence.

One of the promises talks about the need for racial reconciliation, but does not talk about racism. It is fine for men to come together across racial differences, but we need to address the systematic racism within our society, including the violence directed towards men of color. The Promise Keepers is notably silent on that.

In short, Promise Keepers' language addresses certain issues of power and violence in ways which obscure the social roots of these problems. There is a rhetoric of progressive change hiding a reality of traditional thinking on these issues.

No More Men-Only Movements

The Promise Keepers will probably come and go in much the same way as the Men's movement and other, earlier such efforts did. Why do they keep reappearing and what should our response be to them?

As this book has demonstrated there is something deeply damaging about men's roles in our society. Any organization which allows men an opportunity to come together in safety to acknowledge the hurt and pain of being men will have a ready audience. This doesn't have to be at the expense of women, or of men of color, or of gay men, or recent immigrants, or any other group, but it usually is. We cannot afford the advance of some at the expense of others. Unless men coming together deal with male power as well as male pain, with male privilege as well as male privation, there will always be the danger that these groups will turn into or be fronts for patriarchal political agendas fueling further violence against others.

These groups might be enormously therapeutic, educational or stimulating for the individual men who become involved. However, even the value such experiences have for individual men must be questioned when we live in a society which provides for such unequal distribution of these benefits. When those beneficial experiences are provided by exclusionary, discriminatory, or reactionary organizations we must focus primarily on the politics of the group itself to judge its worth and potential danger.

Below I have listed some of the questions I ask when evaluating such men's groups for possible endorsement or opposition. You might want to keep them in mind to help you evaluate the next round of male-only organizing.

1. Who are the leaders of the organization and what are their histories?
2. Who funds the organization?
3. Who is allowed in, who comes to events, and who is excluded from them?
4. What real needs are being appealed to by this organization or movement?
5. What can we learn from this movement?
6. Are there subtle or overt ways that women are blamed in the ideology of the organization?
7. Is male power and privilege acknowledged and dealt with explicitly?
8. Is the organization accountable to women, women's advocates or women's organizations?
9. Is the organization exploitative of the cultures of people of color in its stories, rituals, and other practices? Does it acknowledge and challenge racism?
10. Are gay, bisexual and transgender men welcome and safe? Does the organization challenge homophobia?

11. Do the experiences provided to men lead them to become advocates for social justice or to try and reclaim traditional forms of male power and control?
12. How large, powerful, and well connected is the organization? What might we have to fear from its success?
13. If the group is potentially dangerous, how might we be able to organize against it?

APPENDIX

Oakland Men's Project

Goals and Assumptions

Overall Goal One: Empower each individual present.

Assumptions:

- When a person makes choices—in areas of attitudes, actions, and values—they are made as the best perceived survival strategy at that time.
- Empowering individuals is *partly* a process of healing previous pain, hurt, and disempowerment.
- Attitudes held with emotional intensity need to be worked through emotionally to be changed. Information alone does not change attitudes.
- Individual growth and empowerment come from an individual's ability to put together information and past and present experiences into a conscious, emotional, and intellectual process of change.
- Empowerment happens best and is maintained most strongly with group support.
- People become empowered through active participation.
- Seeds of change can lie dormant for a long time.

Overall Goal Two: Encourage each person to be more active and involved.

Assumptions:

- An individual's personal empowerment comes through involvement in community activity.

- Individual growth without community activity is inherently limited and is of little value to our community.
- Powerlessness is reflected in inactivity, apathy, and cynicism.
- Community activity breaks down isolation, self-blame, guilt, misinformation, and extreme individualism—all of which are factors in powerlessness.
- Community activity helps people learn about the systems of power that personally disempower us.
- Community activity is not necessarily organized, formal, or traditional. Each person can and must define his or her own way to be active.

Overall Goal Three: Creating group solidarity, support networks, and an understanding of connection.

Assumptions:
- We are all connected.
- We are disempowered by believing we are separate individuals and by fearing others and not cooperating.
- Our greatest resources are in our own community.
- In any group of people, there is tremendous power to unleash, and each group already has the information and experience it needs to empower itself and its members.
- Individual empowerment happens most easily and effectively when it is supported and nurtured by group energy and action.
- Group energy snowballs to people outside the group.

The following are guidelines for Oakland Men's Project staff to use in facilitating workshops and trainings:
- Model, encourage, and support strength, openness, respect, growth, trust, love, and cooperation.
- Provide information.
- Respect the intelligence of everyone at all times.

- Help each person identify personal issues and solutions to problems.
- Provide a framework to aid in personal problem solving.
- Provide lots of options and encourage the creation of new options for problem solving.
- Do not try to force change on anyone.
- Prevent people from trashing one another.
- Being rude, lecturing others, having attitudes of disrespect, attitudes of "correct" information, or "correct" politics are each nonempowering.
- Taking small steps toward effectively dealing with issues, and participating in activities pertinent to those issues, are important and need to be encouraged.
- It needs to be acknowledged that people are already doing a lot of work to improve themselves and their communities.
- As outsiders to any particular group, we can focus attention on the issues, facilitate discussions of people's experiences of power, share infomation, and focus on group self-consciousness.
- Refer the group back to its own resources.
- Emphasize that the group obtain information and services through nonprofessional sources and networks that already exist.
- In most general situations, and in some specific aspects of all situations, emphasize there are some common issues.
- Help to break down the insularity of family and relationship concepts that prevent community intervention.
- Model and practice community intervention: friends and family reaching out to each other.
- Talk from the heart.

Suggested Reading

(Full references are in the bibliography on the following pages.)

Anger
Carol Tavris, *Anger: The Misunderstood Emotion.*

Class
Richard Sennett and Jonathan Cobb, *The Hidden Injuries of Class.*
William Ryan, *Blaming the Victim.*

Disability
Susan E. Browne et al., *With the Power of Each Breath: A Disabled Women's Anthology.*

Fathers
Samuel Osherson, *Finding Our Fathers: How a Man's Life Is Shaped by His Relationship with His Father.*

Helping others
Ram Dass and Paul Gorman, *How Can I Help? Stories and Reflections on Service.*

Jewish
Harry Brod, ed., *A Mensch Among Men: Explorations in Jewish Masculinity.*

Men
Marc Feigen Fasteau, *The Male Machine.*
Mark Gerzon, *A Choice of Heroes: The Changing Face of American Manhood.*

261

John Hough and Marshall Hardy, *Against the Wall: Men's Reality in a Codependent Culture.*

Sam Keen, *Fire in the Belly.*

Robert A. Lewis, ed., *Men in Difficult Times: Masculinity Today and Tomorrow.*

Michael S. Kimmel and Michael A. Messner, eds., *Men's Lives.*

Joseph Pleck and Jack Sawyer, eds., *Men and Masculinity.*

Doris Y. Wilkinson and Ronald L. Taylor, *The Black Male in America.*

Parenting

Kathleen McGinnis and Barbara Oehlberg, *Starting Out Right: Nurturing Young Children as Peacemakers.*

Letty Cottin Pogrebin, *Growing Up Free: Raising Your Child in the 80's.*

Power

Michael Lerner, *Surplus Powerlessness.*

Claude M. Steiner, *The Other Side of Power: How to Become Powerful without Being Power-Hungry.*

Practical

Edward W. Gondolf and David M. Russell, *Man to Man: A Guide for Men in Abusive Relationships.*

Daniel Sonkin and Michael Durphy, *Learning to Live without Violence.*

Race, culture, and history

Leonard Dinnerstein et al., *Native and Strangers: Blacks, Indians, and Immigrants in America.*

Philomena Essed, *Everyday Racism.*

Frederick E. Hoxie and Harlan Davidson, eds., *Indians in American History.*

Paul Kivel, *Uprooting Racism: How White People Can Work for Racial Justice.*

Matt Meier and Feliciano Rivera, *The Chicanos: A History of Mexican-Americans.*

Cherrie Moraga and Gloria Anzaldua, eds., *This Bridge Called My Back: Writings by Radical Women of Color.*

Gregory Orfalea, *Before the Flames: A Quest for the History of Arab-Americans.*

Al Santoli, *New Americans: An Oral History.*

David Schoem, ed., *Inside Separate Worlds: Life Stories of Young Blacks, Jews and Latinos.*

Ronald Takaki, *Strangers from a Different Shore: A History of Asian Americans.*

Sexuality and intimacy

Franklin Abbott, ed., *Men and Intimacy: Personal Accounts Exploring the Dilemmas of Modern Male Sexuality.*

Michael Castleman, *Sexual Solutions: An Informative Guide.*

James B. Nelson, *The Intimate Connection: Male Sexuality, Masculine Spirituality.*

Sexual identity

Loraine Hutchins and Lani Kaahumanu, eds., *Bi Any Other Name: Bisexual People Speak Out.*

Suzanne Pharr, *Homophobia: A Weapon of Sexism.*

Spirituality

Merle Fossum, *Catching Fire: Men's Renewal and Recovery Through Crisis.*

Teaching

Allan Creighton with Paul Kivel, *Helping Teens Stop Violence.*

Louise Dermon-Sparks and the A.B.C. Task Force, *Anti-Bias Curriculum: Tools for Empowering Young Children.*

Paul Kivel and Allan Creighton, *Making the Peace: A 15-Session Violence Prevention Curriculum for Young People.*

Veterans

Joel Brende and Erwin Parsons, *Vietnam Veterans: The Road to Recovery.*

Violence

General

Barrie Levy, ed., *Dating Violence: Young Women in Danger.*

Myriam Miedzian, *Boys Will Be Boys: Breaking the Link Between Masculinity and Violence.*

Elizabeth Stanko, *Everyday Violence: How Women and Men Experience Sexual and Physical Danger.*

Against Women

Susan Brownmiller, *Against Our Will: Men, Women and Rape.*

Mary Daly, *Gyn/Ecology: The Metaethics of Radical Feminism.*

Angela Davis, *Race, Sex and Class.*

Del Martin, *Battered Wives.*

D. E. H. Russell, *Rape in Marriage.*

Robin Warshaw, *I Never Called it Rape.*

Women

Anne Koedt et al., eds., *Radical Feminism.*

Robin Morgan, ed., *Sisterhood Is Powerful: An Anthology of Writings from the Women's Liberation Movement.*

Bibliography

Abbott, Franklin, ed. *New Men, New Minds: Breaking Male Tradition.* Freedom, Calif.: Crossing Press, 1987.

———. *Men and Intimacy: Personal Accounts Exploring the Dilemmas of Modern Male Sexuality.* Freedom, Calif.: Crossing Press, 1990.

Abrams, Grace Contrino. *Creative Conflict Solving for Kids.* Miami: Peace Education Foundation, 1986.

Acuna, Rodolfo. *Occupied America: A History of Chicanos* (2nd ed.). New York: Harper and Row, 1981.

Adair, Margo and Sharon Howell. *The Subjective Side of Politics, Breaking Old Patterns, Weaving New Ties: Alliance Building, and Democracy at Work.* San Francisco: Tools for Change, 1988, 1990, 1995. (Tools for Change, PO Box 14141, San Francisco, Calif., 94114.)

Adair, Margo. *Working Inside Out: Tools for Change.* Berkeley, Calif.: Wingbow Press, 1984.

Aguilar-San Juan, Karin, ed. *The State of Asian America: Activism and Resistance in the 1990s.* Boston: South End Press, 1994.

Albrecht, Lisa, and Rose M. Brewer. *Bridges of Power: Women's Multicultural Alliances.* Santa Cruz, Calif.: New Society Publications, 1990.

Allen, Paula Gunn. *The Sacred Hoop: Recovering the Feminine in American Indian Traditions.* Boston: Beacon Press, 1986.

Allen, Theodore W. *The Invention of the White Race.* London: Verso, 1994.

Allport, Gordon. *The Nature of Prejudice.* New York: Doubleday, 1954.

Amott, Teresa and Julie Matthaei. *Race, Gender, and Work: A Multicultural Economic History of Women in the United States.* Boston: South End Press, 1991.

Anthias, Floya, and Nira Yuval-Davis with Harriet Cain. *Racialized Boundaries: Race, Nation, Gender, Colour and Class and the Anti-Racist Struggle.* New York: Routledge, 1992.

Anzaldua, Gloria, ed. *Making Faces, Making Soul, Hacienda Caras: Creative and Critical Perspectives by Women of Color.* San Francisco: Aunt Lute Foundation, 1990.

Armstrong, Louise. *Rocking the Cradle of Sexual Politics: What Happened When Women Said Incest.*

Arnett, Ronald C. *Applying Nonviolence to Everyday Relationships.* Elgin, Ill.: Brethren Press, 1980.

Asian Women United of California, eds. *Making Waves: An Anthology of Writings by and About Asian American Women.* Boston: Beacon Press, 1989.

Augenbraum, Harold and Ilan Stavans, eds. *Growing Up Latino: Memoirs and Stories.* Boston: Houghton Mifflin, 1993.

Baker, Sally A. *Family Violence & the Chemical Connection.* Deerfield Beach, Fla.: Health Communications, 1991.

Barry, Kathleen. *Female Sexual Slavery.* Englewood Cliffs, N.J.: Prentice-Hall, 1979.

Barlett, Donald L. and James B. Steele. *America: Who Really Pays the Taxes?* New York: Simon & Schuster, 1994.

Barndt, Joseph. *Dismantling Racism: The Continuing Challenge to White America.* Minneapolis: Augsburg, 1991.

Beam, Joseph, ed. *In the Life: A Black Gay Anthology.* Boston: Alyson Publications, 1986.

Beck, Evelyn Torton, ed. *Nice Jewish Girls: A Lesbian Anthology.* Watertown, Mass.: Persephone Press, 1982.

Bell, Diane and Renate Klein, eds. *Radically Speaking: Feminism Reclaimed.* N. Melbourne, Victoria, Australia: Spinifex, 1996.

Beneke, Timothy. *Men on Rape: What They Have to Say About Sexual Violence.* New York: St. Martin's Press, 1982.

Berger, Maurice, et. al. eds. *Constructing Masculinity.* New York: Routledge, 1995.

Berry, Joy Wilt. *Let's Talk About Fighting.* Chicago: Children's Press, 1984.

Biale, David. *Power and Powerlessness in Jewish History.* New York: Schocken Books, 1987.

Blauner, Bob. *Black Lives, White Lives: Three Decades of Race Relations in America*. Berkeley, Calif.: University of California Press, 1989.

Bornstein, Kate. *Gender Outlaw: On Men, Women, and the Rest of Us*. New York: Vintage Books, 1994.

Brant, Beth, ed. *A Gathering of Spirit: Writing and Art by North American Indian Women*. Rockland, Maine: Sinister Wisdom Books, 1984.

Brende, Joel Osler, and Erwin Parsons. *Vietnam Veterans: The Road to Recovery*. New York: Signet, 1986.

Brod, Harry, ed. *A Mensch Among Men: Explorations in Jewish Masculinity*. Freedom, Calif.: The Crossing Press, 1988.

Brown, Dee. *Bury My Heart at Wounded Knee: An Indian History of the American West*. New York: Bantam Books, 1970.

Browne, Susan E., Debra Connors, and Nanci Stern, eds. *With the Power of Each Breath: A Disabled Women's Anthology*. San Francisco: Cleis Press, 1985.

Brownmiller, Susan. *Against Our Will: Men, Women and Rape*. New York: Bantam Books, 1975.

Bulkin, Elly, Minnie Bruce Pratt, and Barbara Smith. *Yours In Struggle: Three Feminist Perspectives on Anti-Semitism and Racism*. New York: Long Haul Press, 1984.

Butler, Judith. *Gender Trouble: Feminism and the Subversion of Identity*. New York: Routledge, 1990.

Butler, Sandra. *Conspiracy of Silence: The Trauma of Incest*. San Francisco: New Glide Publications, 1978.

Camper, Carol, ed. *Miscegenation Blues: Voices of Mixed Race Women*. Toronto: Sister Vision, 1994.

Carlsson-Paige, Nancy, and Diane E. Levin. *Helping Young Children Understand Peace, War, and the Nuclear Threat*. Washington, D.C.: National Association for the Education of Children, 1985.

———. *Who's Calling the Shots: How to Respond Effectively to Children's Fascination with War Play and War Toys*. Santa Cruz, Calif.: New Society Publishers, 1990.

Carmichael, Carrie. *Non-Sexist Childraising*. Boston: Beacon Press, 1977.

Castleman, Michael. *Sexual Solutions: An Informative Guide*. New York: Simon and Schuster, 1980.

Chesler, Phyllis. *Mothers On Trial: The Battle for Children and Custody.* Seattle: Seal Press, 1987.

Cloud, Kate, et al. *Watermelons Not War: A Support Book for Parenting in the Nuclear Age.* Philadelphia: New Society Publishers, 1983.

Colman, Arthur, and Libby Colman. *The Father: Mythology and Changing Roles.* Wilmette, Ill.: Chiron Publications, 1988.

Churchill, Ward. *Indians Are Us? Culture and Genocide in Native North America.* Monroe, Maine: Common Courage Press, 1994.

Collins, Patricia Hill. *Black Feminist Thought: Knowledge, Consciousness, and the Politics of Empowerment.* Boston: Unwin Hyman, 1990.

Comstock, Gary David. *Violence Against Lesbians and Gay Men.* New York: Columbia University Press, 1991.

Connell, R. W. *Gender and Power.* Stanford, Calif.: Stanford Univ. Press, 1987.

———. *Masculinities.* Berkeley, Calif.: University of California Press, 1995.

Cottle, Thomas J. *Black Children, White Dreams.* New York: Dell, 1974.

Council on Interracial Books for Children. *Guidelines for Selecting Bias Free Textbooks and Storybooks.* New York: Council on Interracial Books for Children.

Crary, Elizabeth. *I Can't Wait.* Seattle: Parenting Press, 1983.

———. *I Want It.* Seattle: Parenting Press, 1983.

———. *I Want to Play.* Seattle: Parenting Press, 1983.

———. *My Name Is Not Dummy.* Seattle: Parenting Press, 1983.

———. *Kids Can Cooperate: A Practical Guide to Teaching Problem Solving.* Seattle: Parenting Press, 1984.

Creighton, Allan, with Paul Kivel. *Helping Teens Stop Violence: A Practical Guide for Counselors, Educators, and Parents.* Alameda, Calif.: Hunter House, 1992.

Creighton, Allan and Paul Kivel. *Young Men's Work: Building Skills to Stop Violence.* Center City, Minn.: Hazelden, (Part 1) 1995, (Part 2) 1998.

D'Emilio, John and Estelle Freedman. *Intimate Matters: A History of Sexuality in America.* New York: Harper & Row, 1988.

Daly, Mary. *Gyn/Ecology: The Metaethics of Radical Feminism.* Boston: Beacon Press, 1990.

Dass, Ram, and Paul Gorman. *How Can I Help? Stories and Reflections on Service.* New York: Alfred A. Knopf, 1985.

Davis, Angela Y. *Women, Race & Class.* New York: Random House, 1981.

———. *Women, Culture, Politics.* New York: Random House, 1989.

Davis, Laurel R. *The Swimsuit Issue and Sport: Hegemonic Masculinity in Sports Illustrated.* Albany, NY: State University of New York Press, 1997.

Delacoste, Frederique, and Felice Newman, eds. *Fight Back: Feminist Resistance to Male Violence.* Minneapolis: Cleis Press, 1981.

Dennison, George. *The Lives of Children.* New York: Random House, 1969.

Derman-Sparks and Carol Brunson Phillips. *Teaching/Learning Anti-Racism: A Developmental Approach.* New York: Teachers College Press, 1997.

DiGiovanni, Kathe. *My House Is Different.* Center City, Minn.: Hazelden Educational Materials, 1989.

Dinnerstein, Leonard. *Natives and Strangers: Blacks, Indians, and Immigrants in America.* New York: Oxford University Press, 1979.

Dobash, R. Emerson and Russell Dobash. *Women, Violence and Social Change.* New York: Routledge, 1992.

Domhoff, G. William. *Who Rules America Now: How the "Power Elite" Dominates Business, Government, and Society.* New York: Touchstone Books, 1983.

Dorn, Lois. *Peace in the Family: A Workbook of Ideas and Actions.* New York: Pantheon Books, 1983.

Dreikurs, Rudolf. *Family Council: The Dreikurs Technique for Putting an End to War Between Parents and Children.* Chicago: Henry Regnery, 1974.

Drew, Naomi. *Learning the Skills of Peacemaking.* Rolling Hills Estates, Calif.: Jalmar Press, 1987.

Dumas, Lynne S. *Talking with Your Child about a Troubled World.* New York: Fawcett Columbine, 1992.

Durning, Alan Thein. *How Much Is Enough: The Consumer Society and the Future of the Earth.* New York: W.W. Norton, 1992.

Duvall, Lynn. *Respecting Our Differences: A Guide to Getting Along in a Changing* World. Minneapolis: Free Spirit Publishing, 1994.

Dworkin, Andrea. *Pornography: Men Possessing Women*. New York: Perigee Books, 1981.

———. *Life and Death: Unapologetic Writings on the Continuing War Against Women*. New York: The Free Press, 1997.

Ehrenreich, Barbara. *Fear of Falling: The Inner Life of the Middle Class*. New York: HarperCollins, 1990.

———. *The Hearts of Men: American Dreams and the Flight from Commitment*. New York: Doubleday, 1983.

Eisler, Riane. *The Chalice and the Blade: Our History, Our Future*. New York: HarperCollins, 1987.

———. *Sacred Pleasure: Sex, Myth and the Politics of the Body*. New York: HarperCollins, 1995.

Ellison, Ralph. *Invisible Man*. New York: Random House, 1952.

Englemann, Jeanne. *My Body Is My House*. Center City, Minn.: Hazelden Educational Materials, 1990.

Enloe, Cynthia. *Bananas, Beaches and Bases: Making Feminist Sense of International Politics*. Berkeley, Calif.: Univ. of California Press, 1990.

Essed, Philomena. *Everyday Racism*. Alameda, Calif.: Hunter House, 1991.

———. *Understanding Everyday Racism: An Interdisciplinary Theory*. Newbury Park, Calif.: Sage Publications, 1991.

Faludi, Susan. *Backlash: The Undeclared War Against American Women*. New York: Crown, 1991.

Farber, Adele, and Elaine Mazlich. *Liberated Parents/Liberated Children*. New York: Grosset and Dunlap, 1974.

Fasteau, Marc Feigen. *The Male Machine*. New York: Dell, 1975.

Fausto-Sterling, Augusta. *Myths of Gender: Biological Theories about Women and Men*. New York: Basic Books, 1985.

Featherston, Elena, ed. *Skin Deep: Women Writing on Color, Culture and Identity*. Freedom, Calif.: Crossing Press, 1994.

Fisher, Roger, and William Ury. *Getting to Yes*. Boston: Houghton Mifflin, 1981.

Fleugelman, Andrew, ed. *The New Games Book*. Garden City, N.J.: Doubleday, 1976.

———, ed. *More New Games and Playful Ideas.* Garden City, N.J.: Doubleday, 1981.

Folbre, Nancy. *The New Field Guide to the U.S. Economy: A Compact and Irreverent Guide to Economic Life in America.* New York: New Press, 1995.

Fossum, Merle. *Catching Fire: Men's Renewal and Recovery Through Crisis.* Center City, Minn.: Hazelden Educational Materials, 1989.

Fox, Mathew. *Creation Spirituality: Liberating Gifts for the People of the Earth.* San Francisco: HarperCollins, 1991.

Frankenberg, Ruth. *The Social Construction of Whiteness: White Women, Race Matters.* Minneapolis: Univ. of Minnesota, 1993.

Freeman, Lory. *It's My Body.* Seattle: Parenting Press

Freire, Paulo. *Pedagogy of the Oppressed.* New York: Harper & Row, 1971.

———. *Education for Critical Consciousness.* New York: Seabury Press, 1973.

Friedenberg, Edgar Z. *Coming of Age in America: Growth and Acquiescence.* New York: Alfred A. Knopf, 1963.

Frosch, Mary. *Coming of Age in America: A Multicultural Anthology.* New York: New Press, 1994.

Frye, Marilyn. *The Politics of Reality: Essays in Feminist Theory.* Trumansburg, N.Y.: Crossing Press, 1983.

———. *Willful Virgin: Essays in Feminism.* Freedom, Calif.: Crossing Press, 1992.

Fugitt, Eva D. *"He Hit Me Back First!"* Hills Estate, Calif.: Jalmar Press.

Fulani, Lenora, ed. *The Psychopathology of Everyday Racism and Sexism.* New York: Harrington Park Press, 1988.

Fussell, Paul. *Class: A Guide through the American Status System.* New York: Summit Books, 1983.

Gabelko, Nina Hersch, and John U. Michaelis. *Reducing Adolescent Prejudice: A Handbook.* New York: Teachers College Press, 1981.

Gandhi, Mohandas K. *Autobiography.* New York: Dover, 1983.

Gerzon, Mark. *A Choice of Heroes: The Changing Face of American Manhood.* Boston: Houghton Mifflin, 1982.

Gibbs, Jewelle Taylor, ed. *Young, Black and Male in America: An Endangered Species.* New York: Auburn House, 1988.

Giddings, Paula. *When and Where I Enter: The Impact of Black Women on Race and Sex in America*. New York: Bantam books, 1985.

Gilligan, James. *Violence: Reflections on a National Epidemic*. New York: Vintage, 1997.

Gilman, Sander. *Difference and Pathology: Stereotypes of Sexuality, Race, and Madness*. Ithaca, N.Y.: Cornell Univ. Press, 1985.

Gitlin, Todd, ed. *Watching Television*. New York: Pantheon, 1986.

Golderg, David Theo, and Michael Krausz, eds. *Jewish Identity*. Philadelphia, Temple University Press, 1993.

Goldstein, Arnold P., and Barry Glick. *Aggression Replacement Training: A Comprehensive Intervention for Aggressive Youth*. Champaign, Ill.: Research Press, 1987.

Gondolf, Edward W. *Men Who Batter: An Integrated Approach for Stopping Wife Abuse*. Holmes Beach, Fla.: Learning Publications, 1985.

Gondolf, Edward W., and David M. Russell. *Man to Man*. Bradenton, Fla.: Human Services Institute, 1987.

Gonzalez, Ray, ed. *Muy Macho: Latino Men Confront Their Manhood*. New York: Doubleday, 1996.

Goodman, Gerry, George Lakey, Judy Lashop, and Erika Thorne. *No Turning Back: Lesbian and Gay Liberation for the '80's*. Philadelphia: New Society Publishers, 1983.

Goodman, Mary Ellen. *Race Awareness in Young Children*. New York: Collier Books, 1964.

Gordon, Linda. *Heroes of Their Own Lives: The Politics and History of Family Violence*. New York: Penguin Books, 1988.

Gordon, M., and S. Riger. *The Female Fear*. New York: Free Press, 1988.

Gordon, Thomas. *P.E.T.: Parent Effectiveness Training*. New York: New American Library, 1970.

———. *P.E.T. in Action*. New York: Wyden Books, 1976.

Grahn, Judy. Another *Mother Tongue: Gay Words, Gay Worlds*. Boston: Beacon Press, 1984.

Greenberg, Selma. *Right From the Start: A Guide to Nonsexist Child Rearing*. Boston: Houghton Mifflin, 1979.

Greene, Laura. *Help: Getting to Know About Needing and Giving*. New York: Human Sciences Press, 1981.

Greenfield, P. M. *Mind and Media: The Effects of Television, Video Games and Computers*. Cambridge, Mass.: Harvard University Press, 1984.

Gross, Beatrice, and Ronald Gross, eds. *The Children's Rights Movement: Overcoming the Oppression of Young People*. Garden City, N.J.: Doubleday, 1977.

Grubman-Black, Stephen. *Broken Boys—Mending Men: Recovery from Childhood Sexual Abuse*. Blue Ridge Summit, Penn.: Tab Books, 1990.

Guberman, Connie, and Margie Wolfe, eds. *No Safe Place: Violence Against Women & Children*. Scranton, Pa.: The Women's Press, 1985.

Guidelines for Selecting Bias-Free Textbooks and Storybooks. New York: Council on Interracial Books for Children.

Haessly, Jacqueline. *Peacemaking: Family Activities for Justice and Peace*. New York: Paulist Press, 1980.

Haraway, Donna. Primate Visions: *Gender, Race and Nature in the World of Modern Science*. New York: Routledge, 1989.

Harding, Sandra, and Jean F. O'Barr. *Sex and Our Genes: Biology, Ideology and Human Nature*. New York: Pantheon, 1987.

Hernton, Calvin C. *Sex and Race in America*. New York: Grove Press, 1965.

Heron, Ann, ed. *One Teenager in 10: Writings by Gay and Lesbian Youth*. Boston: Alyson Publications, 1983.

Heyck, Denis Lynn Daly. *Barrios and Borderlands: Cultures of Latinos and Latinas in the United States*. New York: Routledge, 1994.

Holt, John. *How Children Learn*. New York: Pitman Publishers, 1967.

———. *Freedom & Beyond*. New York: Dell, 1972.

———. *Escape from Childhood: The Needs and Rights of Children*. New York: Ballantine Books, 1974.

———. *How Children Fail*. New York: Seymour Lawrence, 1982.

Hooks, Bell. *Ain't I a Woman: Black Women and Feminism*. Boston: South End Press, 1981.

———. *Talking Back: Thinking Feminism, Thinking Black*. Boston: South End Press, 1989.

Hough, John, and Marshall Hardy. *Against the Wall: Men's Reality in a Codependent Culture*. Center City, Minn.: Hazelden Educational Materials, 1991.

Hoxie, Frederick E., ed. *Indians in American History*. Arlington Heights, Ill.: Harlan Davidson, 1988.

Hull, Gloria, et al., eds. *All the Women Are White, All the Blacks Are Men, but Some of Us are Brave: Black Women's Studies*. New York: Feminist Press, 1982.

Hunter, Anne E., ed. *Genes and Gender Volumes I–VI* (particularly Volume VI: *On Peace, War, and Gender, A Challenge to Genetic Explanations*). New York: Feminist Press, 1991.

Hutchins, Loraine, and Lani Kaahumanu, eds. *Bi Any Other Name: Bisexual People Speak Out*. Boston: Alyson Publications, 1991.

Jaffe, Peter G. *Children of Battered Women*. Newbury Park, Calif.: Sage, 1990.

Jaimes, M. Annette, ed. *The State of Native America: Genocide, Colonization, and Resistance*. Boston: South End Press, 1992.

Jay, Karla, and Allen Young, eds. *Out of the Closets: Voices of Gay Liberation*. New York: Harcourt Brace Jovanovich, 1976.

Jewell, K. Sue. *From Mammy to Miss America and Beyond: Cultural Images and the Shaping of U.S. Social Policy*. New York: Routledge, 1993.

Jones, Ann. *Next Time She'll Be Dead: Battering & How to Stop It*. Boston: Beacon Press, 1994.

Judson, Stephanie, ed. *A Manual on Nonviolence and Children*. Santa Cruz, Calif.: New Society Publishers, 1977.

Kamin, Leon, et. al. *Not in Our Genes*. New York: Pantheon, 1984.

Katz, Jane B., ed. *I Am the Fire of Time: The Voices of Native American Women*. New York: Dutton, 1977.

Katz, Judy. *White Awareness: Handbook for Anti-Racist Training*. Norman, Okla.: University of Oklahoma Press, 1978.

Kaye-Kantrowitz, Melanie. *The Issue Is Power: Essays on Women, Jews, Violence and Resistance*. San Francisco: Aunt Lute Books, 1992.

Kaye-Kantrowitz, Melanie, and Irena Klepfisz, eds. *The Tribe of Dina: A Jewish Women's Anthology*. Montpelier, Vt.: Sinister Wisdom Books, 1986.

Keen, Sam. *Fire in the Belly: On Being a Man*. New York: Bantam Books, 1991.

Kelly, Liz. *Surviving Sexual Violence*. Minneapolis, Minn.: University of Minnesota Press, 1989.

Keniston, Kenneth, and the Carnegie Council of Children. *All Our Children: The American Family Under Pressure*. New York: Harcourt Brace Jovanovich, 1977.

Kimmel, Michael S., ed. *Men Confront Pornography*. New York: Crown, 1990.

———. *Manhood in America: A Cultural History*. New York: Free Press, 1996.

Kimmel, Michael S., and Michael A. Messner, eds. *Men's Lives*. New York: Macmillan, 1989.

Kimmel, Michael S., and Thomas E. Mosmiller, eds. *Against the Tide: Profeminist Men in the United States 1776–1990*. Boston: Beacon Press, 1992.

Kivel, Paul. *Uprooting Racism: How White People Can Work for Racial Justice*. Gabriola Island, B. C.: New Society, 1996.

Kivel, Paul, and Allan Creighton. *Making the Peace: A 15-Session Violence Prevention Curriculum for Young People*. Alameda, Calif.: Hunter House, 1997.

Klama, John. *Aggression: The Myth of the Beast Within*. New York: Wiley, 1988.

Knowles, Louis L., and Kenneth Prewitt, eds. *Institutionalized Racism in America*. Englewood Cliffs, New Jersey: Prentice-Hall, 1969.

Koedt, Anne, Ellen Levine, and Anita Rapone. *Radical Feminism*. New York: Times Books, 1973.

Kohl, Herbert. *36 Children*. New York: Plume, 1967.

———. *Growing with Your Children*. Boston: Little, Brown, 1978.

Kohn, Alfie. *No Contest: The Case Against Competition*. Boston: Houghton Mifflin, 1986.

———. *Punished by Rewards: The Trouble with Gold Stars, Incentive Plans, A's, Praise, and Other Bribes*. Boston: Houghton Mifflin, 1993.

Kozol, Jonathan. *Savage Inequalities: Children in America's Schools*. New York: HarperCollines, 1991.

Lapham, Lewis. *Money and Class in America*. New York: Weidenfeld and Nicolson, 1988.

Lerner, Michael. *Surplus Powerlessness: The Psychodynamics of Everyday Life*. Oakland, Calif.: Institute for Labor and Mental Health, 1986.

Levi, Primo. *If Not Now, When?* New York: Penguin Books, 1985.

Levy, Barrie, ed. *Dating Violence: Young Women in Danger*. Seattle: Seal Press, 1991.

Lew, Mike. *Victims No Longer: Men Recovering from Incest and Other Sexual Child Abuse*. San Francisco: Harper & Row, 1990.

Lewis, Robert A., ed. *Men in Difficult Times: Masculinity Today and Tomorrow*. Englewood Cliffs, N.J.: Prentice-Hall, 1981.

Lewontin, R. C., and L. J. Kamin. *Not in Our Genes: Biology, Ideology and Human Nature*. New York: Pantheon, 1984.

Lieberman, Mendel, and Marion Hardie. *Resolving Family and Other Conflicts: Everybody Wins*. Santa Cruz, Calif.: Unity Press, 1982.

Lobel, Kerry. *Naming the Violence: Speaking Out About Lesbian Battering*. Seattle: Seal Press, 1984.

Loescher, Elizabeth. *How to Avoid World War III at Home*. Denver: Cornerstone, 1986.

Lorde, Audre. *Sister Outsider: Essays and Speeches*. Trumanburg, New York: Crossing Press, 1984.

Lowe, Marian and Ruth Hubbard, eds. *Woman's Nature: Rationalizations of Inequality*. New York: Pergamon Press, 1983.

Madhubuti, Haki R. *Black Men: Obsolete, Single, Dangerous?* Chicago: Third World Press, 1990.

Majors, Richard and Janet Mancini Billson. *Cool Pose: The Dilemmas of Black Manhood in America*. New York: Touchstone, 1992.

Males, Mike A. *The Scapegoat Generation: America's War on Adolescents*. Monroe, ME: Common Courage Press, 1996.

Mallon, Gerald L., ed. *Resisting Racism: An Action Guide*. San Francisco: National Association of Black and White Men Together, 1991.

Mander, J. *Four Arguments for the Elimination of Television*. New York: Quill, 1978.

Manmer, Jalna and Mary Maynard, eds. *Women, Violence and Social Control*. Atlantic Highlands, N.J.: Humanities Press International, 1987.

Martin, Del. *Battered Wives*. Volcano, Calif.: Volcano Press, 1976.

McGinnis, Kathleen, and Barbara Oehlberg. *Starting Out Right: Nurturing Young Children as Peacemakers*. Santa Cruz, Calif: New Society Publishers, 1988.

McIntosh, Peggy. *White Privilege and Male Privilege: A Personal Account of Coming to See Correspondences Through Work in Women's Studies.* Wellesley, Mass: Center for Research on Women, 1988.

Meier, Matt, and Feliciano Rivera. *The Chicanos: A History of Mexican-Americans.* New York: Hill and Wang, 1972.

Memmi, Albert. *The Colonizer and the Colonized.* Boston: Beacon Press, 1965.

Messner, Michael A. *Power at Play: Sports and the Problem of Masculinity.* Boston, Beacon Press, 1992.

Messner, Michael A. and Donald F. Sabo. *Sex, Violence & Power in Sports: Rethinking Masculinity.* Freedom, CA: The Crossing Press, 1994.

Messerschmidt, James W. *Masculinities and Crime: Critique and Reconceptualization of Theory.* Lanham, MD: Rowman and Littlefield, 1993.

Miedzian, Myriam. *Boys Will Be Boys: Breaking the Link Between Masculinity and Violence.* New York: Doubleday, 1991.

Mies, Maria. *Patriarchy and Accumulation on a World Scale: Women in the International Division of Labour.* London: Zed Books, 1986.

Miller, Stuart. *Men and Friendship.* London: Gateway Books, 1983.

Mishel, Lawrence, et. al. *The State of Working American 1996–1997.* Armonk, NY: M. E. Sharpe, 1997.

Moraga, Cherrie, and Gloria Anzaldua, eds. *This Bridge Called My Back: Writings by Radical Women of Color.* New York: Women of Color Press, 1981.

Morgan, Robin, ed. *Sisterhood Is Powerful: An Anthology of Writings from the Women's Liberation Movement.* New York: Random House, 1970.

———. *Sisterhood Is Global: The International Women's Movement Anthology.* Garden City, N.J.: Doubleday, 1984.

Morrison, Toni, ed. *Race-ing Justice, En-gendering Power: Essays on Anita Hill, Clarence Thomas and the Construction of Social Reality.* New York: Pantheon, 1992.

Myhand, M. Nell and Paul Kivel. *Young Women's Lives: Building Self-Awareness for Life.* Center City, Minn.: Hazelden, 1998.

Nagler, Michael N. *America Without Violence: Why Violence Persists and How You Can Stop It.* Covelo, Calif.: Island Press, 1982.

Nelson, James B. *The Intimate Connection: Male Sexuality, Masculine Spirituality.* Westminster Press, 1988.

Nicarthy, Ginny. *Getting Free: You Can End Abuse and Take Back Your Life.* Seattle: Seal Press, 1982.

Nicarthy, Ginny, Karen Merriam, and Sandra Coffman. *Talking It Out: A Guide to Groups for Abused Women.* Seattle: Seal Press, 1984.

Niethammer, Carolyn, ed. *Daughters of the Earth: The Lives and Legends of American Indian Women.* New York: Collier Books, 1977.

Okihiro, Gary Y. *Margins and Mainstreams: Asians in American History and Culture.* Seattle: Univ. of Washington Press, 1994.

Orbach, Susie. *Fat Is a Feminist Issue: The Anti-diet Guide to Permanent Weight Loss.* New York: Paddington Press, 1978.

Orfalea, Gregory. *Before the Flames: A Quest for the History of Arab-Americans.* Austin, Texas: University of Texas Press, 1988.

Orlick, Terry. *The Cooperative Sports and Games Book: Challenge Without Competition.* New York: Pantheon Books, 1978.

———. *The Second Cooperative Sports and Games Book.* New York: Pantheon Books, 1982.

Osherson, Samuel. *Finding Our Fathers: How a Man's Life Is Shaped by His Relationship with His Father.* Columbine, New York: Fawcett, 1986.

Paley, V. *Bad Guys Don't Have Birthdays: Fantasy Play at Four.* Chicago: University of Chicago Press, 1984.

Patfoort, Pat. *An Introduction to Nonviolence: A Conceptual Framework.* Nyack, New York: Fellowship of Reconciliation, 1987.

Peachey, J. Lorne. *How to Teach Peace to Children.* Scottdale, Pa.: Herald Press, 1981.

Peck, M. Scott. *The Road Less Traveled: A New Psychology of Love, Traditional Values and Spiritual Growth.* New York: Touchstone, 1978.

Pfeil, Fred. *White Guys: Studies in Postmodern Domination & Difference.* London: Verson, 1995.

Pharr, Suzanne. *Homophobia: A Weapon of Sexism.* Little Rock, Ark.: Chardon Press, 1988.

———. *In the Time of the Right: Reflections on Liberation.* Berkeley, Calif.: Chardon Press, 1996.

Pinderhughes, Howard. *Race in the Hood: Conflict & Violence Among Urban Youth.* Minneapolis: University of Minnesota, 1997.

Piven, Frances Fox, and Richard A. Cloward. *Poor People's Movements: How They Succeed, Why They Fail.* New York: vintage, 1979.

———. *Regulating the Poor: The Functions of Public Welfare.* New York: Random House, 1971.

Pleck, Joseph, and Jack Sawyer, eds. *Men and Masculinity.* Englewood Cliffs, New Jersey: Prentice-Hall, 1974.

Pogrebin, Letty Cottin. *Growing Up Free: Raising Your Child in the 80's.* San Francisco: McGraw-Hill, 1980.

Pogrebin, Letty Cottin, ed. *Stories for Free Children.* New York: McGraw-Hill, 1982.

Potter-Efron, Ronald T., and Patricia S. Potter-Efron, eds. *Aggression, Family Violence and Chemical Dependency.* New York: Haworth Press, 1990.

Pratt, Minnie Bruce. *Rebellion: Essays 1980–1991.* Ithaca, N.Y.: Firebrand Books, 1991.

Prutzman, Priscilla, Lee Stern, Leonard M. Burger, and Gretchen Bodenhammer. *The Friendly Classroom for a Small Planet: A Handbook on Creative Approaches to Living and Problem Solving for Children.* Santa Cruz, Calif.: New Society Publishers, 1988.

Rainbow Activities: Fifty Multicultural/Human Relations Experiences. South El Monte, Calif.: Creative Teaching Press, 1977.

Report to the Nation on Crime and Justice. Washington D.C.: United States Printing Office, 1988.

Rich, Adrienne. *Blood, Bread and Poetry: Selected Prose 1979–1985.* New York: Norton, 1986.

———. *On Lies, Secrets, and Silence: Selected Prose 1966–1978.* New York: Norton, 1979.

Riley, Sue Spayth. *How to Generate Values in Young Children.* Washington D.C.: National Association for the Education of Young Children, 1984.

Roediger, David R. *The Wages of Whiteness: Race and the Making of the American Working Class.* London: Verso, 1991.

Root, Maria P., ed. *Racially Mixed People in America.* Newbury Park, Calif.: Sage Publications, 1992.

Rosenberg, Marshall B. *A Model for Nonviolent Communication.* Philadelphia: New Society Publishers, 1983.

Rossides, Daniel. *The American Class System*. Boston: Houghton Mifflin, 1976.

Rothenberg, Paula S. *Racism and Sexism: An Integrated Study*. New York: St. Martin's Press, 1988.

Rubin, Lilian B. *Families on the Fault Line*. New York: HarperCollings, 1994.

———. *Worlds of Pain: Life in the Working Class*. New York: Basic Books, 1976.

Russell, Diana E. H. *The Politics of Rape: The Victim's Perspective*. New York: Stein and Day, 1974.

———. *Rape in Marriage*. New York: Macmillan, 1982.

———. *The Secret Trauma: Incest in the Lives of Girls and Women*. New York: Basic Books, 1986.

Ryan, William. *Blaming the Victim*. New York: Pantheon Books, 1971.

Said, Edward. *Orientalism*. New York: Random House, 1978.

Santoli, Al. *New Americans: An Oral History*. New York: Ballantine Books, 1988.

Saracho, Olivia N., and Bernard Spodek, eds. *Understanding the Multicultural Experience in Early Childhood Education*. Washington, D.C.: National Association for the Education of Young Children, 1983.

Saxton, Marsha, and Florence Howe, eds. *With Wings: An Anthology of Literature by and About Women with Disabilities*. New York: The Feminist Press, 1987.

Schetcher, Susan. *Women and Male Violence: The Visions and Struggles of the Battered Women's Movement*. Boston: South End Press, 1982.

Schniedewind, Nancy, and Ellen Davidson. *Open Minds to Equality: A Sourcebook of Learning Activities to Promote Race, Sex, Class and Age Equity*. Englewood Cliffs, N.J.: Prentice-Hall, 1983, 1998.

Schoem, David, ed. *Inside Separate Worlds: Life Stories of Young Blacks, Jews and Latinos*. Ann Arbor, Mich.: University of Michigan, 1991.

Segal, Lynn. *Is the Future Female? Troubled Thoughts on Contemporary Feminism*. New York: Peter Bedrick Books, 1987.

———. *Slow Motion: Changing Masculinities, Changing Men*. New Brunswick, N.J.: Rutgers University Press, 1990.

Sennett, Richard, and Jonathan Cobb. *The Hidden Injuries of Class*. New York: Random House, 1972.

Shapiro, Joseph P. *No Pity: People with Disabilities Forging a New Civil Rights Movement*. New York: Random House, 1993.

Sharp, Gene. Exploring *Nonviolent Alternatives*. Boston: Porter Sargent Publishers, 1971.

Shor, Ira. *Critical Teaching and Everyday Life*. Boston: South End Press, 1980.

Silverstein, Olga & Beth Rashbaum. *The Courage to Raise Good Men*. New York: Penguin, 1994.

Sinberg, Janet, and Dennis Daley. *I Can Talk about What Hurts: A Book for Kids in Homes Where There's Chemical Dependency*. Center City, Minn.: Hazelden Educational Materials, 1989.

Singer, Bennett L. ed. *Growing Up Gay: A Literary Anthology*. New York: New Press, 1993.

Singer, Frieda, ed. *Daughters in High School: An Anthology of Their Work*. Plainfield, Vt: Daughters, 1974.

Sklar, Holly. *Chaos or Community? Seeking Solutions, Not Scapegoats for Bad Economics*. Boston: South End Press, 1995.

Smith, Barbara, ed. *Home Girls: A Black Feminist Anthology*. New York: Women of Color Press, 1983.

Snodgrass, Jon, ed. *For Men Against Sexism*. Albion, Calif.: Times Change Press, 1977.

Sonkin, Daniel, and Michael Durphy. *Learning to Live Without Violence*. Volcano, Calif.: Volcano Press, 1982.

Stalvey, Lois. *The Education of a Wasp*. New York: Bantam Books, 1971.

———. *Getting Ready*. New York: Bantam Books, 1974.

Stanko, Elizabeth A. *Intimate Intrusions: Women's Experience of Male Violence*. London: Unwin Hyman, 1985.

———. *Everyday Violence: How Women and Men Experience Sexual and Physical Danger*. London: Pandora Press, 1990.

Staples, Robert. *Black Masculinity: The Black Male's Role in American Society*. San Francisco: Black Scholar Press, 1982.

Starhawk. *Truth or Dare: Encounters with Power, Authority, and Mystery*. San Francisco: Harper & Row, 1987.

Statham, June. *Daughters and Sons: Experiences of Non-Sexist Childraising*. New York: Basil Blackwell, 1986.

Steiner, Claude M. *The Other Side of Power: How to Become Powerful without Being Power-Hungry.* New York: Grove Press, 1981.

Steiner, Stan. *The New Indians.* San Francisco: Harper Colophon, 1968.

Stoltenberg, John. *The End of Manhood: A Book for Men of Conscience.* New York: Dutton, 1993.

———. *Refusing to Be a Man: Essays on Sex and Justice.* Portland, Oregon: Breitenbush Books, 1989.

Stordeur, Richard A., and Richard Stille. *Ending Men's Violence Against Their Partners: One Road to Peace.* Newbury Park, Calif.: Sage Publications, 1989.

Suhl, Yuri, ed. *They Fought Back: The Story of the Jewish Resistance in Nazi Europe.* New York: Shocken Books, 1967.

Takaki, Ronald. *A Different Mirror: A History of Multicultural America.* Boston: Little, Brown and Company, 1993.

———. *Strangers from a Different Shore: A History of Asian Americans.* New York: Penguin Books, 1989.

Tavris, Carol. *Anger: The Misunderstood Emotion.* New York: Simon & Schuster, 1982.

Taylor, Dena, ed. *Feminist Parenting: Struggles, Triumphs & Comic Interludes.* Freedom, Calif.: Crossing Press, 1994.

Terkel, Studs. *Working: People Talk About What They Do All Day and How They Feel About What They Do.* New York: Avon Books, 1972.

Thompson, Cooper. *A Guide to Leading Introductory Workshops on Homophobia.* Cambridge, Mass.: Campaign to End Homophobia, 1990.

Tolley Jr., Howard. *Children and War: Political Socialization to International Conflict.* New York: Teachers College Press, 1973.

Valverde, Mariana. *Sex, Power and Pleasure.* Toronto, Ontario: The Women's Press, 1985.

Van Ornum, William, and Mary Wicker. *Talking to Children About Nuclear War.* New York: Continuum, 1984.

Vanneman, Reeve, and Lynn Weber Cannon. *The American Perception of Class.* Philadelphia: Temple University Press, 1987.

Vasquez, Hugh and Isoke Femi. *No Boundaries: A Manual for Unlearning Oppression and Building Multicultural Alliances.* Oakland, Calif.: TODOS Institute, 1993.

Walker, Alice. *Living by the Word: Selected Writings 1973–1987*. San Diego: Harcourt Brace Jovanovich, 1988.

Walker, Lenore E. *The Battered Woman*. San Francisco: Harper & Row Books, 1979.

Warshaw, Robin. *I Never Called It Rape*. San Francisco: Harper & Row, 1988.

Weiler, Kathleen. *Women Teaching for Change: Gender, Class & Power*. South Hadley, Mass.: Bergin and Garvey Publishers, 1988.

Wichert, Susanne. *Keeping the Peace: Practicing Cooperation and Conflict Resolution with Preschoolers*. Santa Cruz, Calif.: New Society Publishers, 1989.

Wilkinson, Doris Y., and Ronald L. Taylor, eds. *The Black Male in America*. Chicago: Nelson-Hall, 1977.

Williams, John Alfred. *The Man Who Cried I Am*. New York: Thunder's Mouth Press, 1967.

Winn, M. *Unplugging the Plug-in Drug*. New York: Penguin Books, 1987.

Young, *Gay and Proud*. Boston: Alyson Publications, 1980.

Woll, Pamela and Terence T. Gorski. *Worth Protecting: Women, Men, and Freedom From Sexual Aggression*. Independence, MO: Independence Press, 1995.

Women's Action Coalition. *Stats: The Facts About Women*. New York: New Press, 1993.

Zilbergeld, Bernie. *The New Male Sexuality*. New York: Bantam Books, 1992.

Zinn, Howard. *A People's History of the United States*. New York: Harper Colophon, 1980.

Reading List[*]

Stories can be powerful examples of other people dealing with the similar pressures and conflicts, resisting stereotypes and negatives expectations, and building new ways of being strong and caring adults. Act-Like-a-Man-box stereotypes are still glamorized in popular literature, there are also many books which show the realities: the pressures young and adult men face, the violence some men enact, and attempts at resistance or alternatives. The following books can provide background for thinking about men and can be useful reading for men trying to change their lives. While many of the books listed below include some stereotypes of masculinity, all address attempts at resistance.

This list contains popular recent fiction and autobiographies for adults and young men about men's and young men's lives in the context of growing up male in the United States. This list is by no means exhaustive. There is a scarcity of useful, recent and easily available writing about and for men with immigrant backgrounds, men from particular racial or ethnic groups, men and disabilities, as well as other important groupings. Nonetheless, the list includes wonderful, entertaining, and crucial works for thinking about the issues adult and young men face as we encounter the world today. Although not listed here, there is a burgeoning list of good books about the lives of young and adult women. They should also be included in any "men's" reading.

Adrian, C. Louis. *Skins*. New York: Crown, 1995.

Alexie, Sherman. *Indian Killer*. New York: Atlantic Monthly, 1996.

———. *Reservation Blues*. New York: Times-Warner, 1995.

Anaya, Rudolfo. *Bless Me, Ultima*. New York: Warner, 1972.

———. *Zia Summer*. New York: Warner, 1995.

---

[*] This list was compiled with Allan Creighton and the assistance of Daphne Muse.

Baca, Jimmy Santiago. *Martin and the Meditations of South Valley*. New York: New Directions, 1987.

Banks, Russell. *Affliction*. New York: HarperPerennial, 1988.

Bolden, Tonya, ed. *Rites of Passage: Stories About Growing Up by Black Writers From Around the World*. New York: Hyperion, 1994.

Boyd, Herb and Robert Allen, eds. *Brotherman: The Odyssey of Black Men in America*. New York: One World, 1995.

Berry, Wendell. *A Place On Earth*. San Francisco: Northpoint, 1986.

Bradley, David. *The Chaneysville Incident*. New York: Harper & Row, 1981.

Brodkey, Harold. *This Wild Darkness*. New York: Holt, 1996.

Brown, Claude. *Manchild in the Promised Land*. New York: Signet, 1965.

Chambers. Aidon. *Dance on My Grave*. New York: Harper Trophy, 1982.

Childress, Alice. *A Hero Ain't Nothing But a Sandwich*. New York: Avon, 1973.

Chin, Frank. *Gunga Din Highway*. Minneapolis Minn: Coffee House, 1994.

Cofer, Judith Ortiz. *An Island Like You: Stories of the Barrio*. New York: Puffin Books, 1995.

Davis, Ossie. *Just Like Martin*. New York: Simon & Schuster, 1992.

Ellison, Ralph. *Invisible Man*. New York: Vintage, 1989.

Ellroy, James. *My Dark Places*. New York: Vintage, 1996.

Ford, Richard. *The Sportswriter*. New York: Vintage, 1986.

Gaines, Ernest. *A Gathering of Old Men*. New York: Vintage, 1983.

Gaines, Ernest J. *In My Father's House*. New York: Vintage, 1972.

Gilb, Dagoberto. *Magic of Blood*. New York: Grove, 1993.

Hinton, S. E. *That Was Then, This Is Now*. New York: Laurel Leaf 1971.

———. *Rumble Fish*. New York: Delacorte, 1975.

Hirschfelder, Arlene B. and Beverly R. Singer. *Rising Voices: Writings of Young Native Americans*. New York: Ballantine, 1992.

Hong, Maria. *Growing Up Asian American*. New York: Avon, 1993.

Islas, Arturo. *Migrant Souls*. New York: Avon, 1990.

Kingston, Maxine Hong. *China Men.* New York: Vintage, 1980.

Kushner, Tony. *Angels in America* (Parts 1 and 2). New York: Theater Arts Communication, 1994.

Lee, Gus. *China Boy.* New York: Plume, 1994.

Levi, Primo. *If Not Now, When?* New York: Penguin, 1982.

Lopate, Philip. *Bachelorhood.* New York: Anchor/Doubleday, 1988.

Lopez, Tiffany Ana. *Growing Up Chicano.* New York: Avon, 1993.

Maclean, Norman. *A River Runs Through it and Other Stories.* Chicago: University of Chicago, 1976.

Mailer, Norman. *The Executioner's Song.* New York: Warner, 1979.

Martinez, Victor. *Parrot in the Oven: mi vida.* New York: Joanna Cotler Books, 1996.

Mason, Bobbie Ann. *In Country.* New York: Harper and Row, 1985.

Mastoon, Adam. *The Shared Heart: Portraits and Stories Celebrating Lesbian, Gay, and Bisexual Young People.* New York: William Morrow, 1997.

Mazer, Anne, ed. *Going Where I'm Coming From: Memoirs of American Youth: A Multicultural Anthology.* New York: Persea Books, 1995.

———, ed. *Working Days: Short Stories About Teenagers at Work.* New York: Persea, 1997.

Mazer, Harry, ed. *Twelve Shots: Outstanding Short Stories about Guns.* New York: Delacorte, 1997.

Monette, Paul. *Becoming a Man: Half a Life Story.* New York: Harper-Collins, 1991.

——— *Borrowed Time: An AIDS Memoir.* San Diego, Calif.: Harcourt Brace and Company, 1988.

Mosley, Walter. *Devil In a Blue Dress.* Thorndike, Maine: Thorndike Press, 1993.

Mowry, Jess. Way *Past Cool.* New York: Harper, 1995.

———. *Six Out Seven.* New York: Farrar Straus Giroux, 1993.

Mura, David. *Turning Japanese: Memoirs of a Sansei.* New York: Anchor/Doubleday, 1991.

———. *When the Body Meets Memory: An Odyssey of Race, Sexuality, and Identity.* New York: Anchor, 1995.

Muse, Daphne. *Prejudice: Stories About Hate, Ignorance, Revelation and Transformation*. New York: Hyperion, 1995.

Myers, Walter Dean. *Scorpions*. New York: Harper Trophy, 1988.

———. *Somewhere in the Darkness*. New York: Scholastic, 1992.

Napoli, Donna Jo. *Stones in Water*. New York: Dutton, 1997.

Neihardt, John. *Black Elk Speaks: Being the Life Story of a Holy Man of the Oglala Sioux/as Told Through John G. Neihardt*. Lincoln, Neb.: University of Nebraska Press, 1932.

O'Brien, Tim. *In the Lake of the Woods*. New York: Penguin, 1994.

Paulsen, Gary. *The Car*. New York: Laurel Leaf, 1994

———. *The Rifle*. San Diego: Harcourt Brace & Co., 1995.

Potok, Chaim. *The Chosen*. New York: Fawcett Crest, 1967.

Predes, Americo. *George Washington Gomez*. Houston: Arte Publico, 1990.

Price, Richard. *Clockers*. New York: Houghton-Mifflin, 1992.

Rawls, Wilson. *Summer of the Monkeys*. New York: Doubleday, 1976.

Rodriguez, Luis J. *Always Running: la vida loca, Gang Days in L.A.* East Haven, CT: Crubstone, 1993.

Silko, Leslie. *Ceremony*. New York: Viking/Penguin, 1977.

Singer, Bennett, ed. *Growing up Gay/ Growing Up Lesbian: A Literary Anthology*. New York: New Press, 1994.

Soto, Gary. *Jesse*. New York: Scholastic, 1994.

———. *Living Up the Street*. New York: Laurel-Leaf, 1985.

———. *Novio Boy: A Play*. San Diego, Calif.: Harcourt Brace and Company, 1997.

———. *Pacific Crossing*. San Diego, Calif.:

———. *Taking Sides*. San Diego, Calif.: Harcourt Brace and Company, 1991.

Spiegelman, Art. *Maus: A Survivor's Tale* (2 volumes). New York: Pantheon, 1986, 1991.

Stegner, Wallace. *Angle of Repose*. New York: Penguin, 1971.

Steptoe, Javaka. *In Daddy's Arms I AM TALL: African Americans Celebrating Fathers*. New York: Lee and Low, 1997.

Stolz, Mary. *Cezanne Pinto: A Memoir*. New York: Alfred A. Knopf, 1994.

Taylor, Mildred. *The Friendship*. New York: Dial Books, 1987.

———. *Roll of Thunder, Hear My Cry*. New York: Puffin, 1976.

Velasquez, Gloria. *Tommy Stands Alone*. Houston: Pinata Books, 1995.

Villarreal, Jose Antonio. *Pocho*. New York: Anchor, 1959.

Voight, Cynthia. *A Solitary Blue*. New York: Scholastic, 1983.

———. *David and Jonathan*. New York: Scholastic, 1992.

Watson, Larry. *Montana 1948*. Minneapolis, MN: Milkweed, 1993.

Welch, James. *Fool's Crow*. New York: Penguin, 1987.

Wideman, John Edgar. *Brothers and Keepers*. New York: Penguin, 1984.

———. *Fatheralong*. New York: Pantheon, 1994.

———. *Hiding Place*. New York: Vintage, 1987.

Wiesel, Elie. *Night*. New York: Bantam, 1960.

Wojnarowicz, David. *Close to the Knives: A Memoir of Disintegration*. New York: Vintage, 1991.

Wolff, Tobias. *This Boy's Life*. New York: Vintage, 1987.

Wright, Richard. *Black Boy*. New York: Harper Perennial, 1944.

———. *Lawd Today*. New York: Walker, 1963.

X, Malcolm. *The Autobiography of Malcolm X as Told to Alex Haley*. New York: Ballantine, 1964.

Ybarra, Ricardo Mean. *Brotherhood of Dolphins*. Houston: Arte Publico, 1997.

Yep, Lawrence. *Dragonwings*. New York: Harper Trophy, 1975.

———. *Mountain Light*. New York: Harper Trophy, 1985.

Yoshiko, Uchida. *Journey to Topaz*. Berkeley, Calif.: Creative Arts Book Company, 1985.

Videography*

Men are avid consumers of movies and videos. Many or most of the films we see present us with images of men in traditional and extremely limited male roles, using unrelenting control and violence to get what we want. Some movies, however, portray (or show a glimpse of) men with more depth and complexity. These films can raise questions for us about our roles and the choices we face. You can use such films or videos to talk with others and to look more deeply into the themes presented in this book.

We also need to see and think about women's roles in movies, beyond the narrow stereotypes to be found in most popular film. There are many films with powerful female characters; these can be used to start discussions of gender, sexuality, male/female relationships, family, race and economics. Ask the women you know for suggestions about movies which show the strength, dilemmas, complexities and diversity of real women's lives.

A Family Thing—1996—Two brothers, one black, one white, discover each other's existence late in life and try to find common ground.

American Me—1992—The realities of gang wars and drug life on the streets of East LA.

And the Band Played On—1993—Story of the AIDS epidemic as it affected the gay and scientific community.

Ballad of Gregorio Cortez—1983—Because of a misunderstanding of language a Mexican cowhand kills a white sheriff in self-defense and then tries to elude the law.

Blood In . . . Blood Out: Bound by Honor—1993—Violent portrayal of three youth in a LA gang and the choices they face.

Blue Collar—1978—The life of three auto workers trying to improve their lives by robbing the union.

* This list was compiled with Allan Creighton.

Bopha!—1993—A conservative police officer and his anti-apartheid activist son deal with moral values and family relationships in pre-liberation South Africa.

Born on the 4th of July—1989—A paraplegic veteran returns from Vietnam and becomes an antiwar protester.

Boyz N the Hood—1991—Four very different Black high school students try to survive LA gangs and bigotry.

Breaking Away—1979—Working class youth compete in bicycle racing against local college students while trying to figure out their futures.

The Chosen—1981—Friendship between the son of a Hassidic rabbi and the son of a Zionist professor in 1940's Brooklyn.

Coming Home—1978—A look at the life of a disabled Vietnam vet as he returns to civilian life.

Common Threads: Stories from the Quilt—1989—Documentary about the AIDS Quilt and some of the people infected with AIDS.

Crying Game—1992—Irish Republican fighter flees to London to deal with the aftereffects of killing a British soldier.

Dead Man Walking—1995—Anti-death penalty nun becomes spiritual advisor to a death-row murderer.

Five Heartbeats—1991—Relationships between five Black singers and their success and failures as individuals and as a group.

Follow Me Home—1997—Four men of color set out from California to paint a mural on the White House.

Get On the Bus—1997—A bus load of Black men drive from LA to Washington to be part of the Million Man March.

Hangin' with the Homeboys—1991—One night in the lives of four youth in the Bronx.

The Harder They Come—1972—Jamaican youth turns to crime before making a successful reggae recording.

Hoop Dreams—1994—Documentary about two inner city basketball star's lives through high school

Incident at Oglala: The Leonard Peltier Story—1992—A documentary about the murder of two FBI agents and the trial of Leonard Peltier in the context of recent US government/Oglala Nation history.

Jackie Robinson Story—1950—Jackie Robinson plays himself as he breaks the color bar in baseball.

Kids—1995—Docudrama follows a group of New York teenagers around for a day focusing on the consequences of the drug abuse, promiscuity, and violence they engage in.

King—1978—Docudrama about the life of Martin Luther King.

Kiss of the Spider Woman—1985—Cell mates in a South American prison, a revolutionary and a homosexual, struggle about issues of love, life, and freedom.

Lone Star—1995—Stories of fathers and sons in a border town dealing with race, class, immigration and family issues.

Longtime Companion—1990—A group of gay men and their friends dealing with the crisis of AIDS in their community in the 1980's.

Malcolm X—1992—The story of Malcolm X's growth from drug dealer to political leader.

Matewan—1987—Coal miners organize and strike during the 1920's.

Mi Vida Loca—1994—A look at the lives of Latina gang members in LA.

My Left Foot—1989—The life of a cerebral-palsy victim as he moves from an impoverished Irish community to success as a writer and painter using his left foot.

Once Were Warriors—1994—The story of a struggling Maori family who have left their rural roots to live in the city.

Philadelphia—1993—A successful corporate attorney is fired because he has AIDS and then fights a legal battle for justice.

Powwow Highway—1989—A look at life on the reservation as two Cheyenne young men travel to New Mexico.

A Raisin in the Sun—1989—The story of a Black family who face racism and greed when they move into a white neighborhood in the 1950's.

School Ties—1992—A story about what happens when private school classmates find out that the football star on campus is Jewish.

A Separate Peace—1973—Two young men deal with war and personal tragedy at a prep school during World War II.

Sounder—1972—the father of a Black sharecroping family is jailed for stealing to feed his family in rural Louisiana.

This Boy's Life—1993—A young man tries to choose between prep school and hanging with his friends when he and his mother move to a town near Seattle.

The Waterdance—1991—Autobiographical story of a man paralyzed in a hiking accident who has to deal with all facets of rehabilitation.

The Wedding Banquet—1993—Naturalized Chinese-American lives with his gay lover but agrees to marry a woman to appease his parents and get her a green card.

What's Love Got to Do With It?—1993—Drama of Tina Turner's rise from an abusive partnership to solo stardom.

Zoot Suit—1981—A Mexican-American is falsely accused of a murder in the 1940's during a time of intense racial conflict.

Index

About the Author

PAUL KIVEL cofounded the Oakland Men's Project in Oakland
California, in 1979. A violence prevention educator, Mr. Kivel is
an accomplished trainer and speaker on the issues of men and vio-
lence, racism, sexual assault, family violence, and homophobia.
He is the author of nearly a dozen publications, including *Young
Men's Work,* and *Uprooting Racism,* and he is the coauthor of
Young Women's Lives. He lives with his partner and three chil-
dren in Oakland.

Hazelden Foundation, a national nonprofit organization founded in 1949, helps people reclaim their lives from the disease of addiction. Built on decades of knowledge and experience, Hazelden's comprehensive approach to addiction addresses the full range of individual, family, and professional needs, including addiction treatment and continuing care services for youth and adults, publishing, research, higher learning, public education, and advocacy.

A life of recovery is lived "one day at a time." Hazelden publications, both educational and inspirational, support and strengthen lifelong recovery. In 1954, Hazelden published *Twenty-Four Hours a Day,* the first daily meditation book for recovering alcoholics, and Hazelden continues to publish works to inspire and guide individuals in treatment and recovery, and their loved ones. Professionals who work to prevent and treat addiction also turn to Hazelden for evidence-based curricula, informational materials, and videos for use in schools, treatment programs, and correctional programs.

Through published works, Hazelden extends the reach of hope, encouragement, help, and support to individuals, families, and communities affected by addiction and related issues.

For questions about Hazelden publications, please call **800-328-9000** or visit us online at **hazelden.org/bookstore.**